Economic Issues in Public Policies

Economic Issues in Public Policies

Richard B. McKenzie
Professor of Economics
Clemson University

McGraw-Hill Book Company

New York St. Louis San Francisco Auckland Bogotá Hamburg
Johannesburg London Madrid Mexico Montreal New Delhi
Panama Paris São Paulo Singapore Sydney Tokyo Toronto

This book was set in Times Roman by Automated Composition Service, Inc.
The editors were Bonnie E. Lieberman and Elisa Adams; the cover was designed by Mark Berghash; the production supervisor was Phil Galea.
The drawings were done by VIP Graphics.
Fairfield Graphics was printer and binder.

ECONOMIC ISSUES IN PUBLIC POLICIES

2 3 4 5 6 7 8 9 0 FGFG 8 3 2 1 0

Library of Congress Cataloging in Publication Data

McKenzie, Richard B
Economic issues in public policies.

Bibliography: p.
Includes index.
1. Economics. I. Title.
HB171.5.M148 330 79-21451
ISBN 0-07-045650-X

To
Robert and Frances Lewis

Contents

Preface

This book has one overriding message: Economics is a mode of analysis—a way of thinking—that can be applied to a wide variety of topics and can help us understand the world in which we live. The economic principles and concepts that are used most often in evaluating contemporary policy issues are relatively few in number. However, there are many subtle ways in which those few principles and concepts can be used in analysis.

This text was written with the beginning student in mind. Chapter 1 develops most of the basic principles and concepts that are employed throughout the book. Care has been taken to ensure that all tools of analysis are defined and introduced before they are applied to contemporary issues. Further, the analysis begins on an elementary level and becomes more difficult only after basic notions have been explained.

Principles and concepts in any science are important in their own right; however, they take on their full meaning only when they are used within the context of problems that have relevance to you. This book considers some of the most important issues of our time. In addition, it raises one central question: To what extent can or should people's behavior be controlled?

To aid you in your study for class and in your review for tests, each chapter begins with a preview that highlights the most important question addressed, the major objectives presented, the most important points developed, and the new terms and concepts used. Discussion questions and suggestions for additional reading follow each chapter. The questions that are posed help direct your attention to major lines of analysis used and suggest how the analysis can be extended to topics not covered directly in the chapter. Finally, quick self-tests are provided for each chapter. The questions and their answers follow Chapter 14.

When asked to write a research paper, many students borrow a number of books and magazine articles from the library and rely on what other people say. A primary purpose of this book is to show you how independent economic analysis can be used to unravel the complexities of many policy issues. A number of the chapters are directly related to legislation that has been recently passed or is pending in Congress. A major goal of what is written here is to encourage you to think for yourself, to evaluate policy issues with the "economic way of thinking." In that regard, the book challenges you to develop a point of view and to apply that point of view creatively to issues that are not covered.

I am greatly indebted to the many people who have commented on all or parts of this book: James Bennett, Yale Brozen, James Buchanan, Rex Cottle, Hugh Macaulay, Delores Martin, Mary Ann McKenzie, Thomas Schaap, Maureen Obrian, Robert Staaf, Howard Tuckman, Holley Ulbrich, Karen Vaughn, and Bruce Yandle. I am pleased that the editors of *Common Sense Economics*, *Library Trends*, *Ethics*, the American Enterprise Institute for Public Policy Research, *Social Science Quarterly*, Fiscal Policy Council, and *Public Choice* have given me permission to revise extensively and include here material previously published elsewhere.

I am also indebted to Gail Taylor for typing the first draft of the manuscript. As in past efforts, I am indebted to Dinah Lanning for editorial assistance and for expertly typing the final draft.

Richard B. McKenzie

Chapter 1

The Economist's Paradigm

"I don't rejoice in insects at all," Alice explained; "because I am rather afraid of them—at least the large kinds. But I can tell you the names of some of them."

"Of course they answer to their names?" the Gnat remarked carelessly.

"I never knew them to do it."

"What's the use of their having names," the Gnat said, "If they won't answer to them?"

"No use to them," said Alice; "but it's useful to people that name them, I suppose. If not why do things have names at all?"[1]

CHAPTER PREVIEW

Central Question

What are the basic principles in economic analysis?

Major Objectives

1 To develop basic concepts and principles most frequently used in economic analysis.

2 To show, in a limited way, how economic concepts and principles can be used to understand human behavior.

[1]Lewis Carroll, *Alice in Wonderland and Through the Looking Glass* (New York: A. L. Burt, Publishers, n.d.), p. 210.

Major Points

1 Economics is not defined by the topics that are discussed but by the concepts, principles, and tools of analysis that are used to analyze a variety of social issues.

2 A starting presumption of economic analysis is that people behave rationally, meaning that they can evaluate alternative courses of action and can take actions to achieve goals and objectives that they think are in their best interest.

3 Exchanges in a free market benefit both parties to the exchange.

4 There is a cost to every action.

5 The amount people will buy is inversely related to the price.

6 Marginal cost of production will rise beyond some point as output is expanded. The quality of a good that producers are willing to offer on the market tends to be directly related to the price.

7 A person will maximize satisfaction from production and consumption when the marginal benefit of the last unit consumed equals the marginal cost of producing the last unit.

8 Because there is a tendency for people to "free ride," voluntary collective action is frequently an ineffective means of achieving the common interests of people in large groups.

9 Competition tends to maximize market efficiency.

10 A firm with monopoly power tends to restrict output below the competitive output level and raise prices above the competitive price level.

11 External costs lead to overproduction in competitive markets; external benefits tend to lead to underproduction in competitive markets.

Important New Terms and Concepts

(Definitions are provided in text and at the end of the book.)

Utility
Property rights
Cost
Demand
Marginal cost
Law of diminishing returns
Supply
Marginal benefit
Pure monopoly
External cost
External benefit

People in different disciplines have different perspectives from which they evaluate social conditions and policy remedies for identified problems. Accordingly, as Alice had to do when she went through the looking glass, a student entering a new discipline frequently must shift to a new analytical framework and learn to "think differently" and often to draw conclusions about the "state of the world" that are at odds with analyses worked out in other disciplines. The contrast among the *modus operandi* of different disciplines is sometimes quite sharp; this may be the case regarding the disciplines of library science and the science of economics. At other times, however, the distinction between disciplinary boundaries is made pale by many similarities in approach that researchers in different fields take to social issues; this may be true of the distinction between social philosophy or mathematics, on the one hand, and economics on the other.

Disciplines are large amorphous conceptual superstructures. Nevertheless, they have names because of their widely recognized, distinctive characteristics, which largely prescribe the forms that analysis may take and the conclusions that are drawn. Since the reader of this book may have a conceptual framework that is at variance with that of economics, the purpose of this chapter is to present in brief, survey form the basic components of what may be called, for want of a better word, the "economist's paradigm." An important but subsidiary purpose is to show, in an elemental way, how economics has and is being used to explore social problems far removed from the workings of the markets for, say, toothpaste and hot dogs.

A discipline like economics cannot be bounded by traditional notions of what are its proper topics. Granted, economics has traditionally dealt with social issues that in one way or another relate to private markets, to money, to unemployment, and to prices. However, much research has been undertaken under the paradigm of economics in such diverse fields as crime, bureaucracy, politics, charity, and interpersonal relationships.[2] Following what I have written elsewhere, "the unifying factor [in economics] is the approach which economists take toward the study of human behavior. They have a distinguishing set of presuppositions about human behavior—a different image of behavior—leading to a different mode of analysis and to conclusions which complement and, at times, appear to conflict with those of other social scientists investigating the same problem."[3] Here, major elements of the economist's paradigm are developed. Basic propositions are stated succinctly, followed by elaborations on those propositions.

ELEMENTS OF THE ECONOMIST'S PARADIGM

Rational Behavior

Individuals are assumed to have a consciousness that allows them to do more than merely respond to environmental constraints. Their conscious-

[2]See, for example, Richard B. McKenzie and Gordon Tullock, *The New World of Economics: Explorations into the Human Experience* (Homewood, Ill.: Richard D. Irwin, Inc., 1978).

[3]Richard B. McKenzie and Gordon Tullock, *Modern Political Economy: An Introduction to Economics* (New York: McGraw-Hill Book Company, 1978), p. 8. See the first four chapters of this textbook for a more complete statement of basic elements in economic theory. See also any other textbook on principles of economics—for example, Campbell McConnell, *Economics: Principles, Problems, and Policies* (New York: McGraw-Hill Book Company, 1978), chaps. 1–4.

ness enables them to imagine alternative courses of action, to subjectively evaluate them, and to take those actions that they perceive to be in their best interest.

In contrast to the theoretical perspective of other disciplines, economics does not view individual behavior as passive reaction to the external forces of the immediate environment and the internal forces of genetic structures and physical conditions. Individuals are assumed to have "wants," "desires," or "preferences" that make their actions "inner directed," purposeful, and in part an influence on the environment. As opposed to *reacting* to the environment, individuals are perceived to operate within constraints on the environment, in such a way as to achieve to the greatest extent possible those goals that they, themselves, envision.

Freedom of individual behavior has a strategic place in the economist's paradigm because it not only provides the "elbow room" for actions to be organized effectively (or "efficiently," to use an economic term), but it also enables individuals to determine for themselves what they want and how they will go about satisfying their wants. Freedom is the substance of subjective evaluation. Subjective evaluation—the determination of individual wants—is of no consequence when freedom of action is denied. Similarly, in a conceptual framework in which all behavior is determined by environmental and genetic forces, freedom of action and responsibility for action have no role. B. F. Skinner, a psychologist who effectively denies that individuals have a "creative consciousness," makes this point with force: "Freedom and dignity illustrate the difficulty. They are the possessions of the autonomous man of traditional theory, and they are essential to practices in which a person is held responsible for his conduct and given credit for his achievements. A scientific analysis shifts both the responsibility and the achievement to the environment."[4]

The economist's perspective on human behavior leads inextricably to the question of how individual evaluations and actions are coordinated. The economist spends much of his or her intellectual efforts explaining the emergence of an "ordered anarchy" (which a free market is), describing the conditions under which individual efforts to achieve goals (or "to maximize individually conceived utility," which is satisfaction from consumption) will or will not be tolerably efficient, and assessing the consequences of governmental policies. At this level of discussion, the paradigm of the economist is notable for what Friedrich Hayek calls the "pattern of outcome," that is, the semblance of order that is expected. To say more about the types of specific actions that people will take, we must know more than just that people attempt "to maximize their preferences" or, what amounts to the same

[4]B. F. Skinner, *Beyond Freedom and Dignity* (New York: Bantam/Vintage Books, 1972), pp. 22–23.

thing, are rational.[5] We must know something about what they want. Even then, with that much additional information—which is a great deal of information—economists have been most successful in indicating only the *directional* movements of behavior, given changes, for example, in prices, and only modestly successful in specifying by how much consumer purchases will increase or decrease under any given set of market changes.

Mutually Beneficial Exchanges

Exchanges in a free market are mutually beneficial.

Property rights are socially defined and recognized limits to what people can do with things. Trade involves the exchange of property rights, which are socially defined and recognized, and people evaluate the rights they have to resources and goods and services differently. In the process of attempting to maximize their utility, people can be expected to trade on the basis of the differences in their evaluations of the resources, goods, and services that they possess. A person who evaluates oranges relatively very highly and apples very lowly can be expected to seek out and trade with someone who has an opposing assessment of the relative merits of apples and oranges. By giving up apples, which are evaluated lowly, and receiving oranges in return, the person can increase his or her welfare. If people are able to freely choose whether or not and to what extent they make trades, and if they are rational, then it follows that, in the absence of deception or fraud, the traders must gain by the trades. Otherwise, why do they make the exchanges? In this sense, all voluntary exchanges are profitable to both traders.[6]

Exchanges of goods are actually exchanges of rights—more specifically, property rights, and exchanges are predicated upon property rights' being commonly recognized and legally enforced. The initial distribution of property rights may or may not be just; and the social conditions necessary for bringing about justice in the initial distribution of rights have recently been a major issue in social philosophy.[7] However, regardless of the justice or injustice of the initial distribution, trades that may emerge in a free society improve the welfare of people *from what it would otherwise have been.* The resulting distribution of rights after trades may be construed as unjust; however, there is some value in the economic proof that people are better off because of the emergence of trades. The trades also tend to redistribute the rights to the relatively more efficient uses.

[5]For a more detailed discussion of rational behavior, see McKenzie and Tullock, *Modern Political Economy*, chap. 2. Succinctly stated, *rational behavior* assumes individuals (1) know what they want, (2) are capable of ordering their wants, and (3) are capable of acting consistently upon their ordering of wants.

[6]Ibid., chap. 5.

[7]See, for example, the major works of John Rawls, *A Theory of Justice* (Cambridge, Mass.: Harvard University Press, 1971); and Robert Nozick, *Anarchy, State, and Utopia* (New York: Basic Books, Inc., 1975).

Costs

When alternative courses of action are known and subjectively evaluated, every action is shown to have a cost.

Cost is the value placed on the most highly valued alternative foregone when a choice is made. While we presume that people have almost infinite capacity to envision new wants and new goals, everything that is wanted cannot be gained or done. To maximize welfare or self-interest (which can include giving aid to others), the individual must make choices: one cannot have all that one wants. By definition, when a choice is made, at least one alternative is not realized. The cost of the alternative that is taken is the value of the most highly valued alternative that is not taken.

Accordingly, there is a cost to buying a book, but there is also a cost to taking a walk or watching a sunset or making use of a free public library. Nothing can be "free" so long as there is an alternative way of using resources. A library can see the cost of its services rather vividly in its bills for new books, repair bills on old books, salaries, and lost and stolen books. Many of these costs are absorbed by the general public in the form of taxes, and taxes for library services force the public to forgo other goods and services that have value. Some of the cost of checking out a book at the library desk must, however, be borne by the user: the user is the one who must give up some other activity, which presumably has value, just to be at the library desk. To the user a library is rightfully "nonfree," and often one decides not to use the library simply because the value of one's alternative is greater than the perceived value of the library book.

The Law of Demand

The amount that people demand of any good is dependent upon the price they have to pay: The higher the price, everything else being equal, the lower the quantity purchased, and vice versa.

The stated relationship between price and quantity can be graphically represented by a downward-sloping curve, as can be seen in Figure 1.1. A reduction in the price, which is on the vertical axis, will cause the person to move downward along the curve, meaning that more will be purchased. Such a curve is referred to as the *demand curve*, because it describes the full relationship between what people are asked to pay for each unit of a good and what they demand (or will buy) at each price.

The inverse relationship between price and quantity can be explained in two ways. First, a decrease in the price of any one good increases real income of consumers of that good and *enables* them to buy more, which consumers will tend to do when they do not have all of a good they want. Second, a price reduction *induces* consumers to use more of the now lower-priced good in lieu of other goods that could have been and were purchased before the price reduction. The explanation for the "substitution effect" is

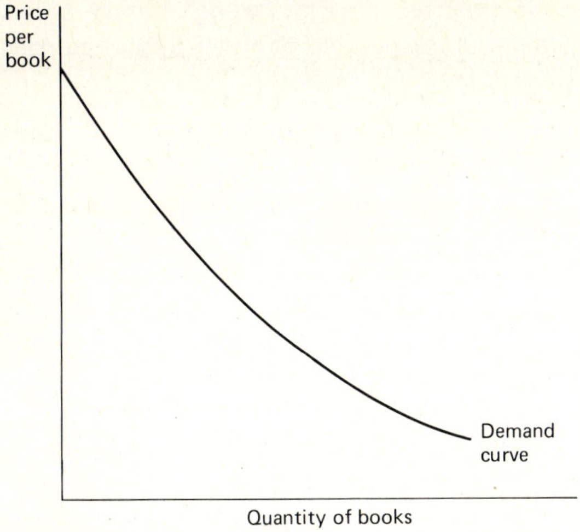

Figure 1.1

based on the assumption that people attempt to maximize their welfare. The rational, maximizing person will, given prices, allocate his or her income until the last dollar or penny spent on one good yields the same satisfaction as the last dollar or penny spent on other goods.[8] Given this condition, any price reduction will upset the balance that has been achieved. If the price of a book, for example, is reduced, consumers will initially get more satisfaction from a dollar spent on the book than they can get from a dollar spent on some other good whose price has not fallen. Consumers will then increase their purchases of books, reducing the money spent on and quantity purchased of other goods.

Regardless of how the concept is explained, *the inverse relationship between price and quantity* has been so firmly fixed in economic theory and repeatedly verified by empirical analysis that the relationship is known as a law—*the law of demand.*

Staying with our library example, the law of demand suggests (predicts) that an increase in the fee for using library books from zero (which is the price is most public libraries) to some positive level will cause a reduction in the number of books borrowed. Similarly, an increase in the fines levied against overdue books will cause a reduction in the number of times books are kept overdue; this is because the greater fines increase the "price" of keeping books out on a daily basis. Furthermore, the law of demand predicts that an increase in the penalty expected to be imposed on people caught stealing books will lead to a reduction in the number of books stolen; again,

[8]For greater specifications of what is called the "consumer equilibrium condition," see McKenzie and Tullock, *Modern Political Economy*, chap. 2.

the greater penalty increases the expected price of "using" library books and causes a downward adjustment in the number of books library patrons will want to use through theft.[9]

Marginal Cost and Output

Within the relevant range of most production processes, the additional (or marginal) cost of additional units of a good produced will expand as the output level expands.

An important observed technological law—called the *law of diminishing returns*—states that *as successive units of one resource*, such as labor, *are added to a fixed quantity of another resource*, such as a building, *there will be a point beyond which the additional units will result in progressively smaller increments in total output*—in other words, the returns to additional labor will diminish.[10] It stands to reason that if additional labor, which we presume is paid a constant wage, contributes progressively less to output, additional units of output must cost progressively more. *Marginal cost is the additional cost incurred in producing one more unit of a good.* The law of diminishing returns, therefore, means that the marginal cost must rise beyond some point in the production process.

The law of diminishing returns does not say that the additional cost of all units of output must rise from the very start, but it does say that the marginal cost of additional units will rise beyond some point and will continue to rise from that point onward as production expands. However, the general assumption of rising marginal cost is built on elaborate theory that concludes that, in competitive markets, firms will produce within the range of rising marginal cost.[11] If they are not within that range, then long-term reductions will be made in the quantity of the fixed factor of production, which is the building in our discussion. In order for (unsubsidized) private firms to be induced to expand production, the price of the good must rise in order that producers can cover the higher marginal cost of the greater output. Alternately, an increase in the price means that firms can more than cover the (marginal) cost of additional units and can, therefore, be expected to expand output. *Supply is the assumed direct relationship between the price and the quantity producers are willing to offer on the market.* It can be

[9]An implicit assumption in this analysis is that the probability of capture and punishment is not affected by the increase in the penalty levied against those caught in library thefts. An increase in the probability of capture can have the same impact on theft as an increase in the penalty. For an extended discussion of the economics of crime, on which the points of this section are based, see McKenzie and Tullock, *The New World of Economics*, chaps. 11–15.

[10]See McKenzie and Tullock, *Modern Political Economy*, chap. 5; or McConnell, *Economics*, chap. 25.

[11]For a more complete and complex discussion of why firms in competitive markets operate within the range of diminishing returns, see Richard H. Leftwich, *The Price System and Resource Allocation* (5th ed.; Hinsdale, Ill.: The Dryden Press, Inc., 1973), chap. 10.

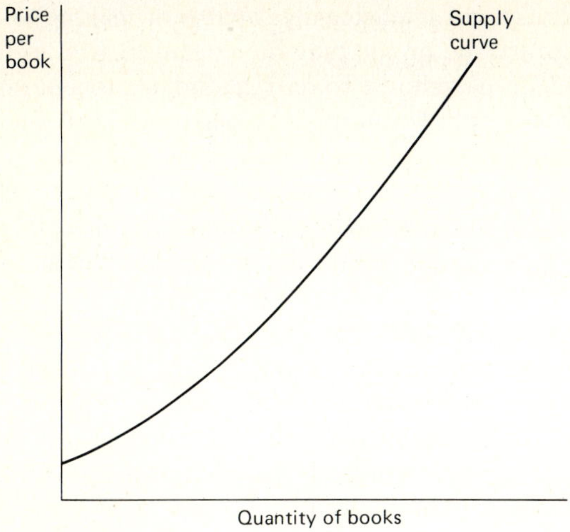

Figure 1.2

graphically described as an upward-sloping curve, appropriately called the *supply curve.* See Figure 1.2.

Maximization

Given individual subjective evaluation of alternatives, rational people will extend their consumption of a good, such as books read, until the marginal benefit of the last unit is equal to its marginal cost.

Marginal benefit is the value of an additional unit of a good consumed; marginal cost is the value of a rejected alternative when a choice is made. If the marginal benefit of the first unit of a good is greater than its marginal cost, then it stands to reason that a person gains by consuming the unit. Even though the marginal benefit of additional units declines and the marginal cost of those units increases, it still stands to reason that maximizing people will continue to raise their welfare so long as the marginal benefit is greater than the marginal cost. Rational people will not extend their consumption to the point that marginal cost is greater than marginal benefit, because that is the same as saying that people will choose to consume a unit on which they receive less value than they lose from forgoing some other more highly valued alternative. Consequently, people will extend their consumption of the good up to, but not beyond, the point at which the marginal benefit equals the marginal cost.[12]

We can conclude that so long as alternatives are subjectively evaluated, there is a self-imposed limit on behavior, which very often restricts behavior to some point below one's physical and technological capabilities. For

[12]McKenzie and Tullock, *Modern Political Economy*, chap. 4.

example, if a person is physically and intellectually capable of making extensive use of a university library, he or she may do extraordinarily well academically. However, a student may choose to restrict studying to a point well below physical limitations simply because of the perceived costs and benefits of the activity. Beyond some point, the additional cost (that is, value of forgone alternatives) may be greater than the additional benefits anticipated in terms of a higher grade, etc. In short, libraries may be empty on weekends because hours spent in the library are simply not worth, at that time, the costs, as individually and subjectively evaluated by students and faculty; they have better things to do!

Voluntary Collective Action

There is a tendency for individuals within very large groups to fail to pursue their common goals even when the goals are agreed upon by all group members. Therefore, voluntary collective action is not likely in very large groups.

In a very large group, the actions of any one individual are relatively insignificant. It is difficult for a person to perceive the impact of his or her own efforts and to realize benefits from the costs incurred. As a consequence, a person has little or no incentive to do anything toward the accomplishment of goals that are collectively acknowledged, and the individual tends to become a "free rider," one who waits on others to take action and to incur the necessary costs that are involved in achieving collective goals. If everyone attempts to become a free rider, then nothing will be done: voluntary action will fail to achieve what everyone wants.[13]

For example, an individual's tax payments are typically a minute part of the total tax collections of, say, the federal government. Consequently, an individual can correctly reason that his or her taxes, by themselves, will have no effect on the quantity or quality of public goods or services produced by government. One further understands that a total withdrawal of one's tax payments will not reduce the public goods and services produced and the subsequent benefits one receives. As a result, each individual in a large group, even when in total agreement with what the government aspires to do, has no incentive to make tax payments *voluntarily*. In order to get everyone to make tax payments, the government must threaten each potential taxpayer with a penalty for any failure to pay taxes. The penalty in this case provides the individual with the private incentive needed to pay the taxes that are prescribed by Internal Revenue Service (IRS) rules.

Furthermore, individual competitors, like farmers, collectively have an incentive to restrict their individual output levels. By voluntarily restricting output, they can materially reduce the market supply and increase the price received for the crops that are sent to the market. Collectively, farmers

[13]Ibid., chap. 6. See also Mancur Olson, *The Logic of Collective Action: Public Goods and the Theory of Groups* (Cambridge, Mass.: Harvard University Press, 1967), chaps. 1–4.

will then be better off. However, it may be reasoned that any restriction on the output of any one farmer will not affect the market price, given what the others do. The individual farmer, therefore, has no incentive to participate in a voluntary, collective action designed to improve the total income position of all farmers; indeed, there is a positive incentive to violate any collective agreement on voluntary crop restrictions.

Similarly, it may be in the interest of all students to read and learn more than they do while in college; if all students study harder, the reputation of the school for quality graduates can be enhanced and all students may improve their economic positions by receiving better job offers. However, the efforts of each student individually will have little impact on the overall reputation of the school; hence, the common interest of all students will have little or no effect on the behavior of individual students. All will tend to do what is in their private interest, narrowly defined.

Market Efficiency

To the extent that competition exists, a market will be efficient.

When placed on one graph as in Figure 1.3, supply and demand curves form a model of market behavior. Under competitive conditions, the market price and quantity sold will move toward P_1 and Q_1, the intersection of the two curves. The reason for convergence of price and quantity at the intersection is straightforward: if the price is above P_1, producers want to sell more than consumers want to buy. Producers will "compete the price down" as they attempt to find buyers for all that they want to sell. As the price falls, consumers expand their purchases and producers reduce their output

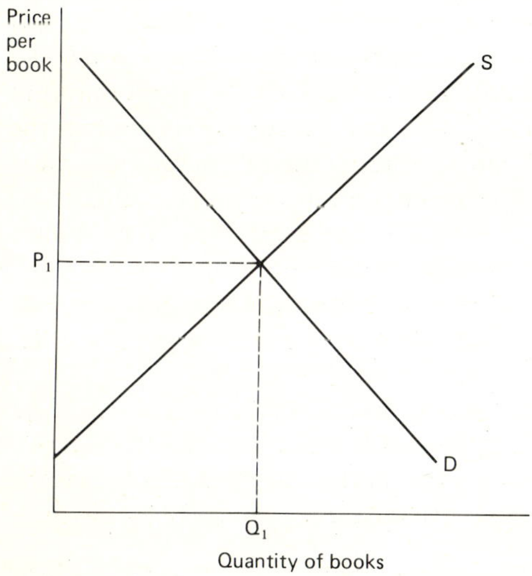

Figure 1.3

levels. At a price of P_1, the market clears and there is no reason for producers to cut the price further. If the price is below P_1, then consumers want to buy more than sellers want to produce. The consumers will compete the price up as they attempt to get what they want. As the price rises, the quantity consumers want contracts, and the quantity producers offer expands until the market clears.

Competitive markets are "efficient," in the sense economists use the term, in two respects.[14] First, given people's preference and the costs of production, competition *maximizes* output. This can be shown through Figure 1.4. The supply curve represents the *minimum* prices at which producers are willing to sell each quantity of books. Producers would gladly accept prices that are above these minimums. Consequently, the price-quantity combinations in Figure 1.4*a* that are acceptable to producers lie either on or above the supply curve, in the shaded area. Producers are not willing to go outside of that area into the nonshaded portion of the graph. The price would then not cover the cost of production.

On the consumers' side of the market, the demand curve indicates the *maximum* prices that consumers are willing to pay for each quantity of books. They are, of course, willing to pay less. (Someone who is willing to pay as much at $30 for a book will certainly be willing to pay $15 for it.) The price-quantity combinations that are, therefore, either on or below the demand curve are acceptable to consumers. These combinations are included in the shaded area of Figure 1.4*b*.

By combining Figure 1.4*a* and *b*, we are able to indicate the price-quantity combinations that are consistent with *both* the preferences of consumers and the willingness of producers to produce. This restricted set of combinations is indicated by the crosshatched area XYZ in Figure 1.4*c*. Combinations that are outside that limited area are inconsistent with either the preferences of consumers, the willingness of producers to produce, or both. Note that the quantity actually produced in the highly competitive market is Q_2. That combination is at the extreme right of the crosshatched area; there is no greater quantity within the restricted area. For this reason economists argue that the competitive market *maximizes* output. This does not mean that more of the good cannot be produced. More can, but consumers are unwilling to cover the full cost of producing the additional units. To be beyond Q_2, either producers have to be coerced into further production, or consumer purchases have to be subsidized.

Q_2 is also an *efficient* level of production for another reason. At any point before Q_2 the supply and demand curves indicate that consumers value an additional book at more than what it costs. The price, which is an indication of relative value, is greater than the marginal cost, which is an

[14] See McKenzie and Tullock, *Modern Political Economy*, chap. 7; or McConnell, *Economics*, chaps. 4 and 26.

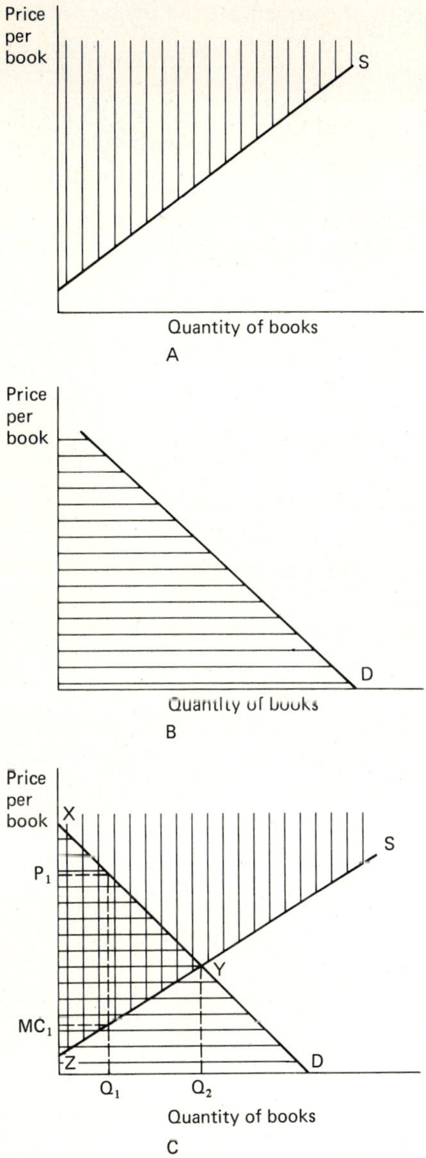

Figure 1.4

indication of the value of those things that are forgone. Take, for example, the Q_1st unit. Someone is willing to pay as much as P_1 for that unit; the marginal cost of it is MC_1. (P_1 is greater than MC_1.) By having the resources employed in the production of that book, the welfare of consumers is raised; consumers receive more pleasure out of the additional book than they could have received from some other good that could have been produced. Furthermore, the consumers of books can more than compensate the owners of the resources for any loss that may have suffered by not using the resources elsewhere. The producers can be paid a price in excess of MC_1.

The consumers are better off by having the Q_1st book, or else why would they have been willing to pay the price? The producers are also better off, or else why would they have been willing to employ their resources in the production of books? Both parties to the transaction are better off, which in view of economists is a desirable outcome. The same is true of all other units of books up to Q_2. Notice that we have argued all along that competition will tend to push the market toward the production level of Q_2.

Profit maximization is the motivational force that moves the competitive market toward the intersection of the supply and demand curves. Therefore, profit maximization is not generally seen by economists as undesirable. Indeed, to the extent that it makes firms produce efficiently, profit maximization has socially desirable consequences. Individual producers, interested in maximizing their own profit positions, are induced and pushed into revealing to consumers the lowest price they are willing to charge. If the price is too high, individual producers can reason that they can increase their market share and profits by reducing their price below the level charged by others. Also, they may reason that if they do not reduce their price, then other producers will; and they will have their customers attracted away by other profit-maximizing firms.

A competitive system of profit-maximizing firms also tends to provide consumers with the types of goods and services they want. A firm that wants to expand its profits can do so by providing those goods that consumers want relatively more than the goods available on the market. For those goods, the consumer should be willing to pay a higher price, which is the inducement profit-maximizing firms need to enter the market. If there are no barriers to entry into any market, then higher prices on goods that are newly introduced will entice other firms into the market; and the prices of the new products will tend to fall to competitive levels.

Profit maximization and competition provide consumers with a degree of protection from producers who are unconcerned about consumer welfare. A producer may reason that costs can be cut and profits raised by providing consumers with products that are shoddy or that quickly become obsolete. If consumers actually want higher quality or more enduring products than the ones provided and they are actually willing to pay for them, then new firms will emerge in the market, provide the products, and force the existing producer either to leave the market or to produce what consumers want and are willing to pay for. Granted, competitive markets will not fully protect consumers from an occasional faulty purchase in the market. That is impossible to do. In addition, consumers will not always buy perfectly reliable or safe products, simply because they cost too much. Consumers often prefer cheap, less-than-reliable, and unsafe products because they prefer to have other things and because they can't afford the alternatives.

Monopoly

Monopoly firms will tend to restrict output and increase the price of the products they sell.

A pure monopoly is a single seller of a product. Accordingly, the pure monopoly does not have to worry about being outmaneuvered or undersold by close competitors. It can, therefore, restrict its production and ask a higher price for the units of the good that it sells without fearing that some other firm will expand production and take over its market. There is no producer that can force or induce the monopolist to charge a competitive price.

Although the monopolistic firm is constrained in its behavior by the market demand for its product and the costs of production, the monopolist can choose any price-quantity combination along the demand curve; and, generally, the monopoly price will be higher and the quantity lower than these are under competitive market conditions.[15] The necessary condition for the long-term survival of a monopolist is the presence of barriers to entry into the market; without the barriers, firms interested in maximizing their profits will be attracted into the market by the monopoly profits that a higher price spells. The barriers to entry may be technological, which is the case when a production process cannot be duplicated; or the barriers can be legal, which is the case when the government gives exclusive franchises to bus companies or railroads to operate along certain routes.

Private firms can be expected to make full use of any monopoly position that is acquired. Similarly, government bureaus, interested in expanding their power, budgets, and employee perquisities, can be expected to make full use of their monopoly positions in the supply of public goods and services. The monopoly position of many bureaus is not fully recognized, but it can be felt nonetheless in terms of higher "tax-prices" and in terms of lower quantity and quality of goods and services provided for public use. Therefore, the elimination of duplication of services by government bureaus or governmental units will not necessarily be beneficial. Such eliminations can lead to the erection of a bureaucratic monopoly that can use its market position to reduce output and raise its tax-price.

Having several independent libraries in a metropolitan area, for example, may be desirable. In some strict technological sense, there may be duplication of services; however, the cost of library service to the public can be lower in such an environment if existing libraries are forced to compete with one another in offering their services to the funding agency, which is

[15]See McKenzie and Tullock, *Modern Political Economy*, chap. 10; or McConnell, *Economics*, chap. 27.

normally a local or state government. The library that offers any given quality service at the lowest price can be awarded the necessary funding for expansion and increases in employee salaries and fringe benefits. Without such competition among libraries, it may be impossible for funding agencies to know the true cost of libraries' services. Librarians, not politicians who are removed from the day-to-day operations of a library, are in the best position to know how best to provide services and the *minimum* prices that must be paid for labor, equipment, and supplies; however, the available technology may not be fully utilized and minimum prices for, say, labor may not be paid unless libraries are forced to compete, that is, to attempt to outdo one another in order to survive or to advance the welfare of librarians.

External Costs and Benefits

To the extent that costs are imposed on or benefits received by persons not directly involved in market transactions, the market will not be efficient.

External costs are costs that are imposed by a producer on someone who is not a buyer and who is not compensated for the harm done. When a producer can impose costs on others, the perceived costs of production to the producer will appear lower than they actually are. The producer will be willing to offer products at a lower price than otherwise and will be able to sell more than otherwise. There will be overproduction because of what we call "external costs"—for example, pollution.[16]

On the other hand, *external benefits are benefits received by people other than those involved in market transactions that are made.* External benefits are often generated in town beautification projects. When people do not have to pay for the benefits they receive, then producers will not be compensated for the full value of their products. As a result, they will be unable to charge as high a price as otherwise and, as a consequence, will produce less than they otherwise would. In the presence of external benefits, there will be underproduction of the product in a free market. In the case of town beautification, merchants who are unable to charge passersby for the improved appearance of their stores will be less inclined to improve the appearance of their storefronts than they would be if they were able to charge.

The market inefficiencies of external costs and benefits can be corrected by two forms of government action. First, standards of performance that consumers and producers must meet can be set. For instance, producers or business people may be forced to meet standards that relate to the amount of smoke a firm may emit or that relate to the size, shape, and color of storefronts. Second, inefficiencies can be corrected through taxes and subsidies. A tax on polluters can cause the price of the product to rise and the quantity

[16]See McKenzie and Tullock, *Modern Political Economy*, chaps. 13 and 19.

sold to fall, eliminating overproduction. Alternately, a subsidy can be given to store owners that lowers the net costs of beautification to the owners and, therefore, the price store owners must charge when they improve the appearance of their storefronts. This, in turn, can cause production to rise, eliminating underproduction.

ECONOMIC PRINCIPLES AND QUESTIONS IN POLITICAL ECONOMY

The elements of the economist's paradigm have been used and reused, with elaboration, to explore many diverse social issues. The answers to the following questions illustrate the range of issues that economic analysis can explore within one subject area, education.

How Should a Library Allocate its Limited Number of Book Lockers and Study Carrels?

If there are more lockers and carrels in a university library than there are students and faculty, then no allocation problem exists. However, if the reverse holds—if there are more students and faculty who want them than there are lockers and carrels available—then some method of distributing the supply must be instituted.

The limited supply of lockers and carrels can be distributed in a variety of ways: first-come–first-served, lottery, class status, or the personal preferences of the allocators. One allocation mechanism often overlooked by libraries is the pricing system. A price can be charged for the use of, say, a locker, and that price can be raised until the available number of lockers exactly matches the number of lockers demanded. We know that such a match will occur because of the law of demand. As the price is raised, the number of lockers demanded will fall for two reasons. First, the price increase will force some people out of the market because of lack of income. Second, the price increase will induce some people to substitute other goods and services (which they then consider relatively more valuable) for library lockers. Because of the downward-sloping demand for lockers, we know that there is some point at which the quantity of lockers demanded will be exactly equal to the number of lockers available.

Granted, the pricing system is not a perfect allocation mechanism; it discriminates against people with low income. On the other hand, the pricing mechanism has much to recommend it. First, it will allow people to give some expression to the relative intensity of their preferences for lockers: those who want the lockers most and are willing to pay for them can effectively bid for them. (Low-income people who want to raise their earning power through education can have a higher demand for lockers than higher-income people.) Second, the pricing system eliminates the need for what are often rather arbitrary rules for allocation of a good. Third, the charges that are collected for the use of lockers can induce the library to expand the number of lockers it has and can give it the financial resources it needs to expand. Alternatively, the revenue collected can be used to subsidize other functions of the library that the staff believes are more important.

In a similar way, economic analysis leads to the conclusion that market shortages for such diverse commodities as natural gas, water, and even "rights to pollute" can be effectively and efficiently eliminated by appropriate upward adjustments in their prices.

Should School Districts Be Consolidated?

An argument frequently heard in educational circles is that there are cost savings ("economies of scale") when the geographical area covered by a school system is expanded. Supposedly, the consolidation of school systems will eliminate duplication of administrative offices and enable school systems to offer a greater variety of programs. There may actually be economies of scale in education, but studies show that consolidation leads to a higher per student cost.[17] One possible explanation for the observed relationship between higher cost and larger school system size is that there actually are "diseconomies of scale" in school system expansion and that educators who propose the consolidation of school systems are unaware of this. Another explanation, drawn from economic analysis, is that the consolidation of school systems gives educational authorities monopoly power; the consequence is higher tax-prices and expenditures and lower quantities of educational services provided. With monopoly market power in hand, public employees cannot be presumed to act any differently than private employees.

CONCLUDING COMMENTS

The preceding discussion has necessarily been a terse description of the theoretical basics of economic analysis. Although much has been left unsaid, even a brief statement of the economist's paradigm suggests the course that much analysis within the discipline of economics tends to take: it suggests the likely dimensions and form of the analysis that will follow. I have related basic components of economic analysis to subjects in education, not so much because it may be a subject of interest to most readers, but because it emphasizes an important purpose of this volume: to demonstrate that

[17]Robert J. Staaf, "The Public School System and Transition: Consolidation and Parental Choice" and "The Growth of the Educational Bureaucracy: Do Teachers Make a Difference?" in Thomas E. Borcherding (ed.), *Budgets and Bureaucrats: The Sources of Government Growth* (Durham, N.C.: Duke University Press, 1977). The two papers by Staaf include citations to a variety of studies done by different people that make the central point: the more consolidated the school system, the greater the per student cost.

economics can be usefully applied to bureaucratic, as well as private, institutions.

In the chapters that follow, the basic principles that have been briefly developed here are applied to a variety of problems in both traditional and nontraditional subject areas. The expectation is that, through repeated application of these principles, you will not only learn the full dimensions of these basic principles but be able, in the end, to apply them to a variety of social problems not considered in this book.

QUESTIONS TO PONDER

1 "There are certain things, like heat in wintertime, that people need and will seek to get no matter what the cost is." Evaluate this statement with reference to concepts and principles developed in this chapter.

2 Given the following changes in market conditions, predict what will happen to the equilibrium price and quantity in a competitive market.
   - a The demand for the product rises.
   - b The supply of the product decreases.
   - c The cost of production falls.
   - d The number of buyers in the market increases.

3 During the winter of 1978 and 1979, imports of oil into the United States were reduced because of rioting and strikes in Iran. Given the reduction in imported oil, answer the following questions:
   - a What does economic theory predict will happen to the price of imported oil and the price of domestically produced oil?
   - b What does economic theory predict will happen to domestic consumption and production of oil products?
   - c What does economic theory predict will happen to domestic production, use, and price of coal?

4 Many areas of the country often experience dry spells during the summer months, resulting in water shortages. How are the shortages normally alleviated? What solution does economic theory provide for alleviating the water shortage?

ADDITIONAL READING

Alchain, Armen A., and William R. Allen. *Exchange and Production Theory in Use.* Belmont, Calif.: Wadsworth Publishing Company, Inc., 1977, chaps. 1–10.

Heyne, Paul. *The Economic Way of Thinking.* Chicago: Science Research Associates, Inc., 1976, chaps. 1–11.

McConnell, Campbell R. *Economics: Principles, Problems, and Policies.* New York: McGraw-Hill Book Company, 1978, chaps. 1–4.

McKenzie, Richard B., and Gordon Tullock. *Modern Political Economy: An Introduction to Economics.* New York: McGraw-Hill Book Company, 1978, chaps. 1–7 and 10.

Wonnacott, Paul, and Ronald Wonnacott. *Economics.* New York: McGraw-Hill Book Company, 1979, chaps. 1–6 and 17–21.

Chapter 2

The Common Sense of Economics: The Pricing of a Product

CHAPTER PREVIEW

Central Question

How can economic concepts and principles be used to explain the pricing arrangements in various markets?

Major Objectives

1 To demonstrate how economic concepts, specifically the laws of supply and demand, can be used to help one understand the pricing policies of journals and magazines, athletic departments in major universities, and state milk commissions.

2 To explore, in a preliminary way, the consequences of controls on market prices.

Major Points

1 Price discrimination, which involves setting different prices for various units of a good in a single market or in different markets, can increase the revenues and profits of firms.

2 Improvements in students' ability to learn in one subject can increase their achievement in other subjects.

3 By increasing their demand for their classes, professors can increase their course requirements and the stringency of their grading system.

4 The ticket price for all seats in a football stadium at a major university may be the same, but the effective price charged differs from one section to another, since contributions to the university's athletic fund are often necessary to obtain seats in some sections of the stadium. Tax laws encourage universities to use the pricing system that they do.

5 Prices set by state dairy commissions reduce the quantity of milk purchased by consumers. Although the contrary is claimed by dairy farmers, deregulation of milk prices will not bankrupt all dairy farmers and will not cause the price of milk to rise. Indeed, economic theory suggests that deregulation of milk prices will lead to a reduction in the price of milk.

6 Relative prices of goods and services reflect their relative marginal values, which are determined by their relative scarcities. Hence water, which is relatively scarce, sells in Saudi Arabia for a much higher price than gas, which is relatively abundant.

Important New Terms and Concepts

Price discrimination
Effective price

Many current issues to which basic principles of economics can be applied are not earth shattering; nonetheless, they can illustrate in an elementary way the usefulness of economics in understanding our individual circumstances. Such is the case with the first two topics of this chapter. There we draw out several elemental points of economic analysis by focusing attention on pricing schemes often used by scholarly journals and athletic departments in major universities. Later, the more complex topic of how the price of milk is controlled is analyzed. Finally, by directing attention to the prices of gas and water in Saudi Arabia, we show that prices in a free competitive market tend to reflect the relative scarcities of goods and services.

COMMON SENSE ECONOMICS

There is a small but interesting journal addressed to educated lay persons in economics appropriately called *Common Sense Economics*. The articles in the journal, which is published at the University of Waterloo in Canada, are short but frequently quite insightful. The fact may have gone unnoticed by many of the subscribers, but that journal is an economic good. It is produced, marketed, and in a certain sense "consumed" by the readership. There is, therefore, every reason to believe that the economic tools used elsewhere in those pages can be readily applied to this particular good, the journal. (Turn about is fair play!) Interestingly, we may increase our understanding of what the journal is all about with a little economic analysis. That is, we can assume that the economists who put the journal together are reasonably rational persons and that there should be "a madness to their method" (an interesting reversal of an old saying).

Price Discrimination

The board of editors have obviously recognized a demand for their good that has all the properties of the textbook concept of demand (see Chapter 1). They know very well that their pricing decisions will affect their subscriptions; they know that regardless of how good their readers think this journal is, there is some price that will cause many to substitute a great variety of other periodicals and goods for *Common Sense Economics*. (Why else would they be charging $3.00 for a year's subscription of two issues?) As is the case with many other periodicals, readers are offered an opportunity to purchase a 3-year subscription of six issues for $7.00. One might think that such a pricing scheme has something to do with journals' cost savings on renewing subscriptions, which it may very well have. Since there are economists behind the scheme, however, it is very probable that they are interested in moving many potential subscribers down their demand curves. By reducing the marginal price for the second and third years, they may be able to increase not only the number of years' subscriptions purchased, but also their revenues. Electric companies employ similar pricing schemes: the price per kilowatt of electricity decreases as total consumption of electricity increases. Similarly, "Ma Bell" reduces the price of additional minutes on long distance calls as the length of the conversation increases. These pricing arrangements are familiar cases of *price discrimination*, which involves *the setting of different prices for different markets* and which in the end can can increase profits and drain some of the subscriber's net benefits from consumption.

How, you ask? Consider the following example. Suppose that your demand curve for years of subscription to *Common Sense Economics* is downward-sloping, meaning that you are willing to pay $3.00 for the first year's subscription, $2.50 for the second year's subscription, and $1.50 for the third year's subscription. Suppose further that it only costs the journal $1.40 to produce each additional year of subscription, that is, the marginal cost of production is constant.

To get you to buy a 3-year subscription, the journal can use one of two basic pricing schemes. It can charge a constant price of $1.50 for each year's subscription, in which case it will receive $4.50 in revenue (3 years times $1.50) and will incur costs of $4.20 (3 years times $1.40) for a profit of $0.30 ($4.50 minus $4.20). Alternately, the journal can offer you the deal that it has, 1 year for $3.00 or 3 years for $7.00. By offering the 3 years for $7.00, it effectively charges you the prices for each year that you are willing to pay for each year: $3.00 for the first year, $2.50 for the second year, and $1.50 for the third year, all of which adds to $7.00. By using this second pricing scheme, the journal effectively walks you down your demand curve. In the process, it collects $7.00 in total revenues (as opposed to $4.50 when the subscription price is the same for each year). Since costs are basically unaffected by the pricing scheme that is employed, the firm experiences a profit of $2.80 ($7.00 minus $4.20). The use of this pricing scheme does not necessarily mean that the reader is not getting a bargain; we suspect that the journal is being subsidized by someone, a group, or an institution. The pricing scheme employed, however, reduces the amount of subsidy required. For other publications, like *Newsweek*, price discrimination allows for increases in profits.

Benefits

We must presume that the journal reader is also rational and that there is some reason for the reader to spend good money for the journal; there must be benefits to the reader that exceed the price of the journal plus the opportunity cost of time spent reading journal pages. These benefits may be very similar to those obtained from seeing a good movie or dining out; reading economics for some (perhaps the "crazies" of the world) may be a form of entertainment.

On quite a different level, if the reader is an instructor of economics or other subjects, he or she may consider the material contained in the pages to be an input into the learning process—a very complex production process, we might add. Some readers may be buying the journal because the material acquired can enliven their classes; in addition, there may be other private benefits that can come to them in the form of an increase in the efficiency with which their students can learn certain fundamental economic concepts. By doing this, these readers have effectively given their students an increase in their total real income. Students can *choose* to take all or part of the productivity gains in the form of greater achievement in the classes. One problem, however, which is constantly cropping up in educators' attempts to increase student achievement, is that very often students *choose* to take the productivity gains in the form of increased leisure. That is, if because of the material acquired from *Common Sense Economics*, a teacher is actually able, for example, to double the amount of economics the students learn in a given amount of time, this means they can choose to learn the same amount in half the time and to spend their extra time in other activities. It is hoped that the material will shift students' preferences toward economics; in this way, it will increase the effort that they will choose to expend in their classes.[1]

[1]For elaborations on this line of analysis, see Richard B. McKenzie and Gordon Tullock, *The New World of Economics* (Homewood, Ill.: Richard D. Irwin, Inc., 1978), chap. 20.

There are two other possible effects that may have benefits to the readers of the journal. By introducing new material into their classes, teachers may be making a sizable investment of time and energy. The return on that investment may come in the form of knowing that the job has been well done or in terms of seeing students learn more of what is thought important. However, teachers may recognize, implicitly or explicitly, that if the efficiency of the learning process is increased, not only can students learn more economics, but also teachers can reduce the effort necessary on their part to move their students to whatever achievement level the teachers may think desirable.

Further, instructors' standards are in part a function of the market condition in which they must operate; that is, the number and types of students that want to take their courses. This is particularly true of instructors whose livelihood is in some way dependent upon whether or not their classes fill. If we can accept this argument as being applicable to at least some instructors, we can conclude that by increasing the relevancy or quality of their courses instructors can experience an increase in the demand they face. Accordingly, they can raise their "price" in terms of what they demand of the students.

Consider Figure 2.1. We assume that there are only so many spaces available in a given instructor's class; this assumption is depicted by the vertical supply curve. (Even if the curve is upward-sloping, the analysis is not materially affected.) Assume that if the instructor uses conventional techniques and materials (that is, doesn't read *Common Sense Economics*), demand will be, say, D_1. If the instructor is going to fill the classes, the highest price he or she can charge students is P_1. If, on the other hand, the course is more attractive, the demand may shift to D_2, in which case there will be

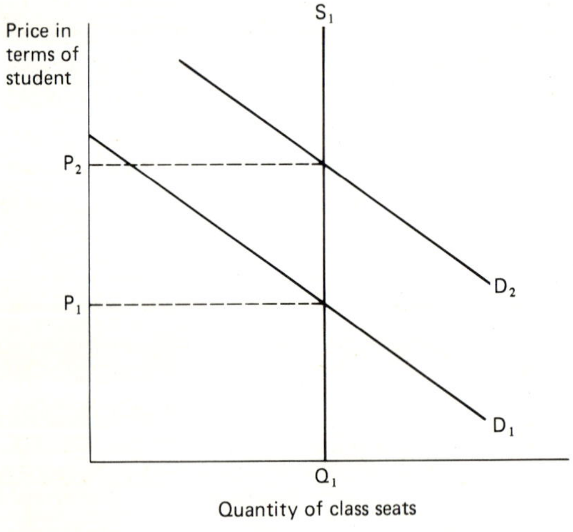

Figure 2.1

more students wanting to get in the classes at P_1 than can be admitted. Here, we have a classic problem of how to allocate the available resources (i.e., seats). The instructor can conceivably allow the computer to select the ones who get in; the spaces can be allocated in a first-come-first-served basis; or the instructor can raise his or her standards and make the students work harder. The ones who are not willing to do the work or pay the higher price can freely choose to take some other course or the same course under someone else. So long as the instructor does not go above P_2, the classes will be filled. This again should mean that the students' achievement should rise and the instructor can be benefited from knowing this. Additionally, as explained earlier, if the instructor can have the students work harder, it *may* be possible for the instructor to expend less effort. This is not to say that the instructor will then be loafing on the job; it may mean bringing the instructor's work week down to something that most people would consider reasonable or providing more time for research.

One interesting problem does emerge from this discussion: If instructors are able to raise their demand because of a quality change and if they raise their price to the new equilibrium level, how would their ratings by students be affected? Will the ratings go up, down, or remain the same? Tackling questions like this is what makes economics fascinating.

THE PRICING OF UNIVERSITY SPORTS EVENTS

Universities with major athletic programs often charge uniform prices for tickets to major sporting events like football and basketball games. The price of a ticket to a football game, for instance, is the same regardless of whether the seat is in the end zone or on the 50-yard line. From a strictly economic-marketing point of view, that may appear to be an odd way of pricing tickets. The demand for seats on the 50-yard line is typically far greater than the demand for seats in the end zones. With all tickets priced the same, there will usually be a shortage of tickets for seats on the 50-yard line and a surplus of tickets for seats in the end zones. Indeed, the only reason the end zone sections are often filled is that people who are unable to get seats on the 50-yard line are forced to accept seats in the end zone just to see the game.

Supply and demand curve analysis of the football-ticket market suggests that the university's athletic department should raise the price of tickets on the 50-yard line to eliminate the shortage there, and reduce the price of tickets in the end zones to eliminate the surplus there. Since the university will then allocate the seats to those who are willing to pay the market clearing price for them, the differential pricing of football seats throughout the stadium will increase gate receipts over and above that they would have been if all seats were sold at the same price.

Why do the universities usually charge the same price for seats? Of course, we should not overlook another question that is important in understanding the behavior of universities. Do the universities really charge the same price for all seats at football games? In terms of the explicit ticket price, which is normally written in the ticket, the price may very well be the same for all seats. However, the ticket price is not always the full price for preferred seats of major athletic events at many universities.

Effective Price

To fill the stadium with the same ticket price for all seats, universities know they will have to lower the price for all seats until there is a shortage of seats in the preferred sections. In preferred sections, universities have devised a variety of pricing systems that take advantage of the tax laws and that allow the universities to take in more funds for their athletic programs than they could otherwise. Almost all major universities have athletic funds that receive contributions from loyal alumni and friends of the universities; the contributions are used to pay the salaries of the teaching staff, the educational expenses of the schools' athletes, the expenses of the athletic office, and, at times, under-the-table bribes and payoffs to superstars. Schools normally have various classes of contributors, such as $1,000, $500, and $100 annual contributors. Regardless of their size, all contributions are tax deductions to contributors; they are funds that are considered by the Internal Revenue Service to be charitable donations to a worthy social cause. The donations that people make to university athletic programs, therefore, reduce the donors' taxable incomes and their tax obligations. Hence, when a person gives, say, $500 to the University of Michigan, he or she is giving away less than $500.

The rules used for allocating tickets at football and basketball games are rarely written down by athletic departments; nonetheless, sports fans of a university understand that preferred seats are to a large extent allocated on the basis of contributions to the athletic fund. The bigger the contribution, the closer will a person's seat be to the 50-yard line at football games or to the center court in basketball games. Indeed, the allocation system that is used is often so well understood by students that they can easily point to the sections of the university stadium or coliseum that are more or less reserved for $1,000, $500, and $100 contributors. Contributors also understand the system, and many make their contributions in order that they can secure preferential treatment in seating. In addition, they know that the size of their contribution will affect the parking space they are assigned for games and the number of tickets they will be permitted to purchase for any postseason bowl or tournament games the university teams are involved in. By making their contributions, these fans are effectively "buying" preferred seating and parking spaces, as well as other benefits. *The effective price of a product is the sticker price plus the implicit cost that must be incurred by the consumer to secure the product.* Because of the contribution that must be made to athletic funds, the effective prices of the seats bought by fans are far greater than the $8 or $10 ticket price. Obviously not all seats are sold for the same effective price.

Contributions and Tax Savings

Because the contributions are tax deductions to the sports fans, the effective, true price of each ticket is not the ticket price plus some pro rata share of the contribution. Allowance must be made for the tax savings of the contributors. Because of the tax savings, contributors should be willing to give more to the athletic fund than they would be willing to pay for the seats they are assigned. Hence, the university should be able to collect more in revenue from contributions and ticket sales than it would be able to collect from ticket sales alone if all seats were sold at their market clearing prices. If tickets were sold at their market clearing prices, then sports fans would not be able to even pretend that they were making a charitable contribution to a worthy cause. The price of the ticket would be no more tax deductible than the purchase price of a new automobile or fur coat. The allocation system, of course, benefits both the university and the sports fan: the university receives more contributions than it would otherwise and the sports fan pays a lower effective price for tickets than he or she would otherwise.

The tax-rate structure ensures that the benefits of the system are not equally distributed over taxpayers. The effective price of tickets, after allowing for tax savings, depends upon the tax bracket of the individual. For instance, if the donor is in a 30 percent tax bracket, meaning that his or her tax obligation falls by 30 percent of any reduction in taxable income, a $500 contribution to the athletic fund actually costs the individual, in terms of spendable income, $350 [$500 − (0.30 × $500)]. If the individual is earning a higher income and is, therefore, in a higher tax bracket, say, 40 percent, then the same $500 contribution will cost $300 [$500 − (0.40 × 1500)]. It follows that the effective price of tickets in any given section goes down as the individual's income goes up: the higher the income, the higher the tax bracket, the greater the tax savings from a contribution to the athletic fund. This explains why higher-income earners buy many of the preferred seats. To them, the effective price is lower than the effective price paid by lower-income earners.

Should this type of system be allowed to continue? Economics cannot answer that question for you. It can only explain why universities employ the pricing system that they do and the consequences of the system chosen. The university, its fans, and its students may benefit from the pricing system that is used. However, given government expenditures and the need for public goods and services, the contributions to athletic funds merely shift the tax burden to others. People who want preferred seating at football and basketball games get a tax break from their purchases. People who buy other goods not only have to pay higher prices for those goods, because resources are more extensively used in athletic programs, but also have to pay higher taxes to compensate for tax revenues lost due to athletic contributions. The trade-offs are apparent. Whether or not they are being made in the right direction or to the right extent is a decision that you will have to make for yourself.

SUPPORTING THE PRICE OF MILK

This sections seeks to illustrate how economic principles can be used to evaluate the arguments presented by a special-interest group, such as dairy farmers, before a regulatory agency. Like dairy commissions in many states, the South Carolina Dairy Commission controls the price of milk. It sets minimum prices at which dairies can pay farmers per hundredweight of milk and at which stores can sell milk in cartons to consumers.[2] In 1978, the South Carolina Dairy Commission ordered an increase in the price of milk. South Carolina consumer advocate Pete Parker objected, pointing out that the Dairy Commission must hold public hearings before any price increase can be mandated. At the hearings farmers and their representatives presented their case for a price increase.

Dairy farmers contended at the hearings (held in January 1979) that they were losing money and that, if the price of milk were not artificially raised by the Dairy Commission, many farmers would go out of business and, in the future, consumers would pay even higher prices for milk. The suggestion was that consumers would be worse off without a regulated milk price than with one.

Demand and Supply

This argument can be analyzed with reference to Figure 2.2. In the figure, the market demand for milk is represented by the curve that is downward-sloping to the right and labeled D_1; the market supply that would be realized in a *free* market (that is, a market without any control by the Dairy Commission) is represented by the curve that is upward-sloping to the right and labeled S_1. The price that will be established in a free, competitive milk market is P_1, and the quantity of milk sold in that market is Q_2.

In attempting to regulate the minimum price of milk, will the Dairy Commission set the official price at P_1 or below? The answer is clearly no. By its intervention in the market, the Dairy Commission is attempting to achieve a result that will be different from a free market result. The price will be set at P_1 in a free market, as already noted; therefore, a minimum price of P_1, set by the Commission, will do nothing to change market outcomes. If the regulated minimum price is set below P_1, the Dairy Commission

[2]For a detailed explanation of how the milk market is controlled, see William S. Rawson, *Public Regulation of Milk Prices: The South Carolina Experience* (Columbia: Bureau of Business and Economic Research, University of South Carolina, 1974).

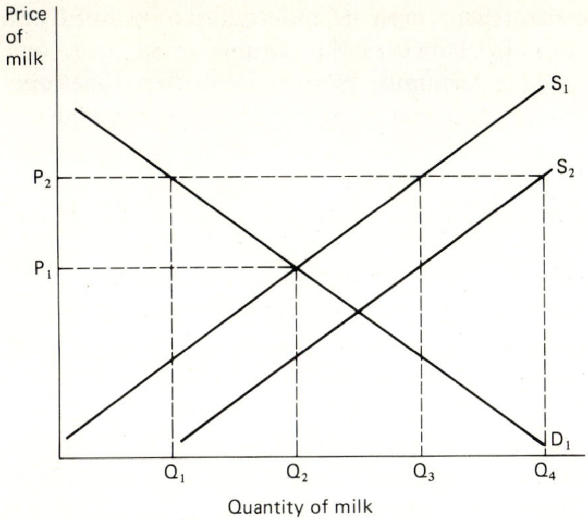

Figure 2.2

will still have no effect on the market: the market price, P_1, will then always be above the regulated minimum price. Therefore, if the price is controlled with the intent of having any effect at all, it must be set over time at any average level about P_1—for example, at P_2. However, notice that at that price the quantity of milk purchased by consumers will be Q_1, less than the quantity purchased under a free market; and the quantity offered on the market by farmers will be Q_3, more than will be offered under a free market. An expected result of the price control system will be a surplus, equal to the difference between Q_3 and Q_1.

Granted, by controlling the price, the Dairy Commission may stabilize—that is, eliminate fluctuations in—the price of milk; it may reduce a risk inherent in dairy farming; it may increase the number, productivity, and size of dairy farms and therefore increase the supply of milk to, say, S_2. Nonetheless, such a supply response does not alter the essential nature of the conclusion we have drawn, which is that a surplus will emerge at the regulated price; the supply response will only increase the surplus of milk in the market from $Q_3 - Q_1$ to $Q_4 - Q_1$.

Regardless of whether supply increases to S_2 or remains at S_1, something must be done about the surplus; otherwise, there will be farmers who will want to sell their milk (as indicated by the surplus) but who cannot. Historically, the problem of the surplus has been dealt with by government in three ways: (1) federal and state governments have bought up the surplus milk and stored it in dried form or converted it to cheese and butter, given it away to low-income people, or thrown it away; (2) governments have imposed production controls, telling farmers how much milk they can sell at the regulated price; and (3) governments have allowed farmers to join cooperatives that centrally control the supply of milk but are exempt from prosecution under antitrust laws. However the surplus is handled, our central conclusion is inescapable: Minimum price controls over time tend to raise the price of milk above what would be charged in a free market, reduce the consumption of milk, and create market surpluses that must be handled by additional government actions.[3]

What will happen if the price of milk is decontrolled? A little reflection on the above analysis suggests that the price of milk will fall, not rise. In Figure 2.2, the price will fall from P_2 to P_1. It is true that a number of farmers will, very likely, be pushed out of business or enticed into other lines of production. However, the farmers who drop out of the dairy business will help eliminate a part of the surplus of dairy products on the market. The rest of the surplus will be eliminated as the price of milk comes down and consumers buy more. The farmers who remain in business will be the ones who are relatively more efficient and can continue to operate profitably although receiving lower prices for the product they sell.

One might think that a move to deregulate the milk market will wipe out the entire dairy industry. That consequence, however, is illogical, the type of scare tactics frequently used by persons who have a vested interest in seeing the control system continued. If all farmers were to drop out of the market, the price of milk on a free market would rise substantially and profits on milk production would soar, meaning that there would be no reason for many farmers to stop production.

Indeed, economic analysis suggests that the price of milk will not rise at all. The mere existence of the price control system in the milk market indicates that there are farmers who would willingly continue production at a lower price. If that were not true, why then was the control system instituted in the first place? Why does the state have to prop up the price of milk artificially by way of the Dairy Commission?

Arguments for Price Regulation

There is definitely risk involved in the production of milk, but there is also a good deal of risk in just about every other line of production. The risk inherent in the milk industry is no necessary justification for government control of the price of milk. If it were, there would be a great deal of justification for the control of most other goods. To the extent that there is risk in the dairy market, the supply of milk and related products will be restricted, which will result in a higher (free) market price for the product, which, in turn, will tend to compensate farmers for the risk they incur.

[3]Government control of milk prices has tended to introduce an element of inflexibility into the pricing system, causing, at times, economic difficulties for farmers who find their costs rising faster than the regulated price. Still, over the long run, the regulated price has been above the equilibrium price.

As we indicated, government control of the price of milk may add stability to that market and reduce the risk of production. If the price of milk were deregulated, the risk of price fluctuations would be reintroduced in the market, the cost of production would rise, and the supply curve would be decreased. However, the market price would still not rise above the regulated price. The decontrol of milk prices would simply cause the supply curve to move from S_2 (which is where the curve would be under a control system) to S_1 (which is where the curve would be in a free market). Deregulation of the milk price would result in a drop in the price from P_2 to P_1. The quantity that producers would be willing to offer on the market would fall from Q_4 back to Q_2.

In short, the control system only keeps a number of farmers in business who could not compete successfully in a free market. These farmers would be the ones pushed out in the event the market were decontrolled.

Apart from purely market issues, there are other arguments for price regulation. Dairy farmers frequently contend that they operate in a "special" industry that deserves "special" treatment: they produce a highly perishable product, one that cannot be stored for very long in its natural state under the best of conditions. That characteristic of the market, however, is not special, by any stretch of the imagination, to the milk industry. A host of industries produce goods that are as perishable as milk or more so. The baking industry, for example, produces a variety of products, from doughnuts to Twinkies to hamburger buns, that are at least as perishable as milk. The list of highly perishable products can also include Big Macs, motel and hotel rooms, barber chairs, and airplane seats. And the list easily can be extended. If the price of milk is regulated because milk is perishable, should we, for the sake of consistency, have a state Twinkie Commission to regulate the price and control the production of Twinkies?

Granted, milk is more important in most people's diets than Twinkies. However, that fact indicates only that people should be willing to pay more for milk than Twinkies and that the dairy market should be more stable and predictable than the Twinkie market. Even then, it is debatable whether milk is more important to many people's diets than other products that are not controlled.

Finally, dairy farmers often and rightfully argue that they work hard. (I can sympathize with them, because I remember all too well having to get up during my teens at 3:30 in the morning to milk 60 cows. I didn't much appreciate the cleanup, either.) Hard work, however, does not necessarily justify higher incomes; producing something of value to consumers is what justifies higher incomes in a market economy. And producing something of value may be done in a variety of ways—for example, by substituting education and capital equipment for hourly toil. If income were distributed to groups on the basis of their claims of hard work, we can well imagine that most people would claim that they deserve higher incomes. The "politics of confrontation," which is periodically observed in the streets of Washington, would surely be encouraged.

In summary, elementary supply and demand curve analysis reveals that most of the claims of the dairy farmers are at best misguided. However, these are the types of arguments that fortify many groups who seek to have government protect them from the forces of competition.

THE GAS-WATER PARADOX

Early in the development of economic science, social philosophers contemplated what was to them an important question: "How can water, which is quite valuable to use, command such a low price in trade when diamonds, which are quite useless, command such a high price in trade?" This apparent inconsistency between the relative prices and values of water and diamonds became known as the "diamond-water paradox."

The paradox can be resolved with reference to supply and demand curves. The explanation is simply that the supply of water, relative to demand, is greater than the supply of diamonds. Although water may be much more valuable in use than diamonds, water still carries a lower price than diamonds. In terms of Figure 2.3*a* and *b*, the demand for water is assumed for purposes of illustration to be greater than the demand for diamonds. However, given the much greater supply of water in Figure 2.3*a* than the supply of diamonds in Figure 2.3*b*, the equilibrium price for water is much lower than the price of diamonds.

Relative Marginal Values

The diamond-water paradox serves the important purpose of stressing a basic economic principle: prices—more precisely, relative prices—reflect *relative marginal values* placed on goods and services. They do not reflect the total values received from goods, nor do they reflect, in some way, the "average" values of goods and services. Prices reflect relative marginal values and, in competitive markets, relative scarcities of goods and services.

To make this point with greater emphasis, we repeat a principle discussed in Chapter 1: A person interested in maximizing satisfaction, or utility, will allocate expenditures until the marginal benefit or utility of the last dollar spent on each good or service is equal. That is, for two goods, apples and books, a person will maximize utility when

$$MU_a/P_a = MU_b/P_b$$

where MU_a = marginal utility of the last apple purchased
MU_b = marginal utility of the last book purchased
P_a = price per apple
P_b = price per book

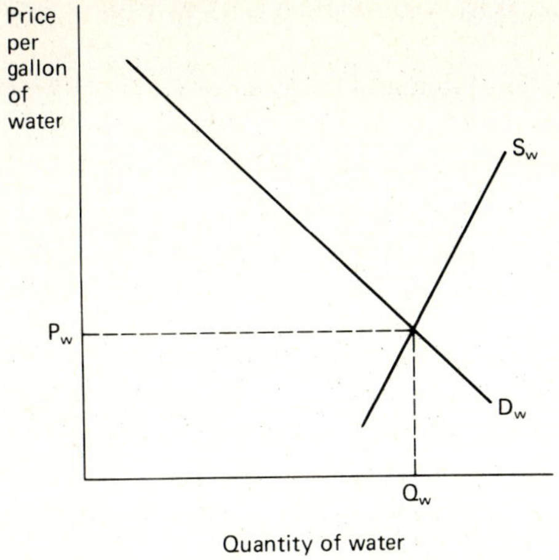

a
water

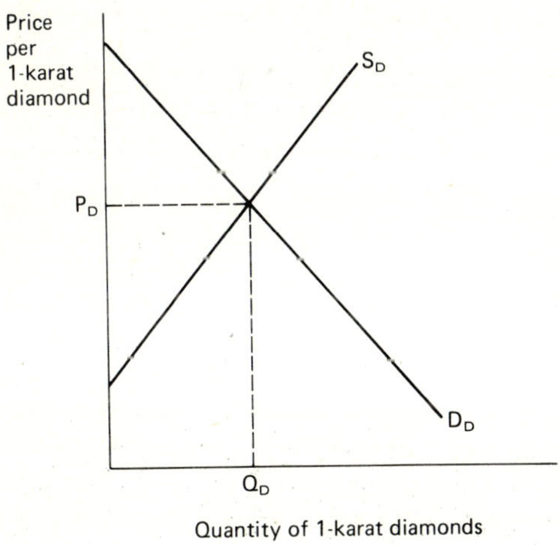

b
diamonds

Figure 2.3

If the ratios are not equal, then the individual can increase utility by reallocating expenditures between apples and books. For instance, if

$$MU_a/P_a > MU_b/P_b$$

the individual is getting more *additional* satisfaction from the *last* dollar spent on apples than from the *last* dollar spent on books. This means the individual can reallocate expenditures, buying more apples and fewer books, and can increase welfare. The rational individual will continue the reallocation process until there is no further reason to reallocate—until the ratios are equal.

As stated, a person has maximized satisfaction when

$$MU_a/P_a = MU_b/P_b$$

That equality can be rearranged to read

$$P_b/P_a = MU_b/MU_a$$

It indicates the relationship between relative prices and relative *marginal* values: in equilibrium, relative marginal values must, for maximizing individuals, stand in the same relationship as relative prices. If the price of books is twice the price of apples, then the marginal utility of the last book purchased must be twice the marginal utility of the last apple purchased. We know nothing about the *absolute* marginal values of books and apples. How could we? All we do know by observing prices is what the relative marginal values are. Again, if a 1-karat diamond sells for $785 and a gallon of water sells for $0.07, we can conclude that, for the person why buys both goods, the marginal utility of the last 1-karat diamond purchased must be over 11,214 times the marginal utility of the last gallon of water purchased. Still, the individual may get more *total* utility from all the water purchased than from all the diamonds purchased. Because the supplies of the goods, in relationship to their demands, determine prices in competitive markets, the marginal value of goods can be said to be determined by their "relative scarcities."

In the winter of 1979 in Saudi Arabia, gasoline sold for $0.24 a gallon, whereas water sold for nearly ten times the price of gasoline, $2.24 a gallon. Given the importance of transportation in modern line, these relative prices of gas and water may seem odd on first thought. How can this modern gas-water paradox be explained? Very simply. In Saudi Arabia water is relatively scarce; gas is not. The arid land sits on top of one of the world's largest known oil reservoirs. The demand for water in that country may or may not be greater than the demand for gas. We do know, however, that, relative to these demands, the supply of gasoline is greater than the supply of water. Consequently, the price of water is much higher than the price of gasoline. Given their relative prices, we also know something about the relative marginal values of the two goods: the marginal value of water is nearly ten times the marginal value of gasoline. This occurs because the Saudi's, having so much gasoline at their disposal and so little water, can afford to use gasoline for purposes that, relative to water, add little to their welfare. If the Saudi's oil reserves ever dry up, we can expect a change in the relative prices of gasoline and water and a change in the uses to which gasoline and water are put. These are the types of natural adjustments that are expected to arise in a market system and that continuously allocate *scarce* resources to their *relatively* more important uses.

QUESTIONS TO PONDER

1 Discos often charge, say, $5 for admission of a single person and $9 for admission of a couple. Explain the economic logic behind such a pricing scheme. What does the analysis suggest about the value of a date?
2 The demand for enrollment in colleges of business has expanded considerably during the 1970s. What should happen to academic standards in colleges of business relative to other colleges on campus? Explain with the use of supply and demand curves.
3 Give several economic explanations of why rich people may make more contributions to charitable organizations than people with much lower incomes. Does the United States tax code play a part in your explanation?
4 A dairy farmer has been quoted as saying, "Our costs of production have risen faster than the regulated minimum price of milk. Therefore, we need a higher price established by the dairy commission just in order to stay in business." Evaluate that argument. (Remember that a milk commission usually sets only a minimum price for milk.)

ADDITIONAL READING

Gwartney, James R. *Economics: Public and Private Choice*. New York: Academic Press, Inc., 1977, chaps. 2 and 3.
Heyne, Paul. *The Economic Way of Thinking*. Chicago: Science Research Associates, Inc., 1976, chaps. 8–11, 14, and 15.
McConnell, Campbell R. *Economics: Principles, Problems, and Policies*. New York: McGraw-Hill Book Company, 1978, chaps. 4 and 5.

Chapter 3

Regulation and Private Property Rights: The Case of the Gymnasium Locker Room

CHAPTER PREVIEW

Central Question

How and to what extent does government regulation change the distribution of property rights, and how and to what extent does government regulation affect incentives for self-protection?

Major Objectives

1 To clarify the meaning and importance of property rights.

2 To explain how government regulation of consumer purchases can affect people's incentives to protect themselves and the efficient use of resources.

3 To show how an understanding of economic concepts and principles in the context of theft in a gymnasium locker room can be used to

explain the impact of government health insurance and social security programs and government regulation of product safety on consumer behavior.

Major Points

1 Government regulation of production and consumer products is a means of redefining individual property rights.

2 In the absence of government regulation of consumer puchases, consumers can to some extent be expected to protect themselves. Furthermore, private firms can be expected to protect consumers from injury in the use of a product so long as the consumer is willing to pay more for the protection than the protection costs.

3 If universities are required to compensate locker-room users for the theft of property, a response on the part of locker-room users can be expected, leading to more locker-room thefts and an increase in the value of property lost in each incidence of theft.

4 Government-mandated health insurance will very likely lead to an increase in the number of illnesses, the frequency of doctor visits, and the cost of the health care delivery system. Due to the disparity between the cost of health care that is considered when people vote on public funding of a health care system and the cost they must incur when they individually make use of that system, a shortage of health care services will tend to result.

5 Required social security payments tend to reduce private saving for retirement and to reduce the growth in the capital stock of the country. However, these costs of the social security system must be weighed against the benefits of the system in determining the size and scope of publicly provided retirement benefits.

Issues surrounding government regulation of industry and consumer purchases are prominently discussed in daily newspapers and weekly magazines. Indeed, government regulation of the economy has become so pervasive that virtually no one remains untouched by "the long arm of government intervention." Rarely does a week go by without a government agency's announcing that it has uncovered an unsafe working condition, found a product that causes cancer, or discovered a deceptive advertising practice.

The current controversy over regulation is inextricably bound up in a controversy over "property rights" and "ownership." Essentially, as defined in Chapter 1, property rights are the limited actions people can take with regard to the things they possess. People "own" cars; this means they can do certain things with their cars. They can drive them on city streets and highways at certain speeds, they can wash them and paint them, and they can attach a variety of options to them. However, there are a number of things that people cannot do with their cars. They cannot drive them on city sidewalks, even though in some places such pathways may be wide enough; they cannot park them on other people's lawns; and they cannot drive them at speeds higher than the posted limits without running the risk of being fined. Whether the product is a radio or a lawn chair, we can itemize the things we can do and not do—the rights that we have and do not have by ownership.

Since, in the final analysis, property is a bundle of socially recognized and governmentally protected rights, the enactment of government regulation, if it actually is to affect what people do, will redefine and redistribute the rights people have. The enactment of regulatory rules for the pharmaceutical industry took from drug firms the right to distribute drugs without prior approval of the Food and Drug Administration. Similarly, the regulation of air quality in textile mills is perhaps designed to reduce the incidence of brown-lung disease among textile workers, but in legalistic terms the enactment of such rules takes from manufacturers the right to set the air-quality level within their factories. Furthermore, it takes from workers the right to work, at perhaps higher wage rates, in places in which the air quality does not meet governmentally approved standards. The minimum wage laws take from employers the right to legally employ workers at wages lower than those prescribed by the Congress.

The list of examples can be extended, but the central point is clear: whether or not regulation is well-intended and whether or not it achieves the desired results, regulation redefines individual rights. To the extent that it is democratically established, regulation reduces the importance of individual decisions in the economy because each individual no longer has as many rights to trade and use, and it increases the importance of collective decisions because the right to determine what people will be able to do is assumed by the legislative and administrative process. Accordingly, the debate over regulation is actually over how economic decisions will be made and by whom. It is also over the question of who should be held legally responsible for any harm that may result from these decisions.

The purpose of this short chapter on regulation and property rights is not to deny the legitimacy or social desirability of regulation. Rather, it is to show, with several concrete examples, the consequences of changing the structure of property rights by way of government regulation. Seeing the consequences of changes in the structure of property rights, the reader will be in a better position to evaluate various forms of regulation. At least, that is the hope and goal of economic analysis.

LEGAL RESPONSIBILITIES IN GYMNASIUM LOCKER ROOMS

Most colleges and universities have a gymnasium with extensive locker-room facilities. By paying a recreation fee (which is generally required), students are given access to the gym, including assigned lockers in the locker rooms. Faculty members are often assigned lockers with no explicit charge[1] or for a modest fee that covers the cost of laundry and some pro rata share of the equipment costs. Regardless of particular administrative procedures at different universities, students and faculty are given "property rights" to lockers: within bounds they effectively "own" the lockers. They can keep their gym clothes and shoes in them while they are not using the gymnasium or pool, and they can keep their street clothes in them while they have on their gym clothes. These are the rights they implicitly or explicitly "buy" when they decide to attend or work for the university. They do not, generally speaking, have the right to paint their assigned lockers or to beat the doors in when they forget the combinations to their locks. Generally speaking, they do not have the right to hold the college or university responsible for the value of any of their belongings that are stolen. In other words, the university does not usually have to reimburse students and faculty for articles that are stolen.

Granted, since renting is a form of selling property for a period of time, the university could give students and faculty the right to be reimbursed for stolen shoes, gym shorts, wallets, and the like; but this is not generally a part of the bargain. Typically, students and faculty are personally responsible for their own property in the lockers, which is another way of saying that students and faculty must protect themselves from potential theft. The system as described is one of full reliance on the legal principle of *caveat emptor* (Latin for "let the buyer beware").

Should the buyer beware? Should the government intervene in this market for gymnasium lockers and make the seller, the university, legally liable for stolen property in the locker rooms? To express it another way, should the university be required to sell as a part of its rental services the right of locker holders to compensation for stolen property? The relevant question in most consumer protection and regulation issues is not whether or not consumers will be protected at all but rather who is going to do the protecting and which form of protection makes the most economic and social sense.

To further illustrate the problem of government protection of consumers of locker-room services, consider a true-to-life example. A student

[1]Faculty members may not have to make an out-of-pocket payment for the use of the college's recreation facilities, but they may have to pay for the facilities implicitly by way of reduced salary or other fringe benefits. If the university offers its facilities to faculty "free of charge" and if faculty members want the use of the facilities, the number of faculty willing to work at the university will increase, reducing the wage rate the university pays. In graphical terms, the supply of labor curve shifts outward to the right, causing a competitive reduction in the wage. As a matter of fact, many universities (as well as private firms) make available fringe benefits, including gymnasiums, because it is less costly to them to provide those benefits than to pay their employees higher wages. Furthermore, these fringe benefits are not taxable; money income is.

paid $40 to the intramural department of his university for privileges in the university's athletic facilities: gymnasium, swimming pool, handball and tennis courts, and lakeside beach. In addition, the student got the use of a gym suit, socks, towel, and a small 3-foot-tall locker. The student had to supply his own lock and his own basketball shoes, which he kept in the locker while he was out of the gymnasium.

One day early in the semester he went to the gym to play basketball with his friends. He found his locker was open and his basketball shoes gone. Since he was a careful person about locks, he assumed that his combination lock has been picked by a crafty student or maintenance person. Consequently, he registered a complaint with the gymnasium office, suggesting to them that they had fallen down on their job of adequately patrolling the locker room. Although the people in the office were sympathetic to his loss, they did not offer to reimburse him for his shoes. Should they have been required to offer reimbursement?

The student grudgingly bought another pair of shoes and began playing ball again. Approximately 3 weeks later, however, the student found his locker open again and his shoes gone. He was incensed, especially since he had checked and double-checked his lock each time he left the locker room. He was convinced that he had been victimized by a common but apparently skillful thief and by a gymnasium staff that was not doing its job. He was supported in his views by the comments of his friends who had had shoes, watches, and wallets stolen from their lockers. His complaint to the gymnasium head office was far more vociferous than on the previous occasion; but still, he received no financial relief for the new $20 pair of shoes that he had lost.

Should the university be held legally responsible for the stolen property of its locker-room patrons? Should the consumer (the student, in this example) be protected by government from the loss of property that is kept in the lockers? Indeed, such a question raises a more interesting one: Would the student really want a governmentally imposed system under which the university was required (because of the rules of consumer protection) to compensate patrons for the loss of shoes and other articles? The answer to that last question is "probably not," at least if the student considered the consequences of the implied change in the property right structure. Let us explain.

Self-Protection

If in this example the university had been required to sell the right to reimbursement for stolen property, the student would have been paid about $35 (the depreciated value of the two pairs of shoes). He would have clearly gained *in that instance.* However, if he were to be compensated for the loss of articles from the locker, everyone else also would be compensated for such a loss. He and others would have less incentive to protect themselves by making sure that they bought strong and unpickable locks and kept their lockers locked when they were not in the room. Further, all locker-room users would have less reason to keep to a minimum the value of property left in the lockers while they were not in the building. In short, the avoidance of theft, which is a form of self-protection for consumers, is costly: it takes money to buy good locks and it takes time and effort to ensure that the locks are properly used. Under a system in which *caveat emptor* is legally dispelled, the locker-room users will have less incentive to incure the cost of self-protection. As a consequence, locker-room theft can be expected more frequently and the value of the property stolen in each incidence of theft can, on average, be expected to rise.

Required compensation to victims of theft will be translated into higher costs to operate the recreational facilities of the university. As a consequence, the university can be expected to raise the explicit or implicit fees to its students and faculty patrons. If the university does not initially charge students fees explicitly, it will have to introduce a recreation fee and/or raise the tuition payments. The higher costs of operating the athletic facilities will be reflected in either a higher fee for faculty members or lower salary payments.

For emphasis, a central point can be restated: When legal responsibility for losses due to theft is shifted from the locker-room users to the university, the overall cost of using the gymnasium increases. Granted, the student does not have to incur the cost of buying a good lock for keeping the locker locked and does not lose anything when the locker is raided. However, the student will have to pay higher fees for the use of the gymnasium. Since such a change in the property-right structure causes a behavioral response on the part of the students and professors (that is, they are more careless about their lockers), we can expect that on balance the cost of using the gymnasium will rise. Because of the higher costs, fewer people will use the recreational facilities in the short run; in the long run, fewer recreational facilities will be purchased.

Some may argue that the foregoing argument is defective because it assumes that the firms (universities) in the gymnasium market are competitive and, consequently, are operating at minimum costs and at minimum prices for their services before and after the change in the property right structure. Critics of the analysis may argue that universities have the powers of a monopoly; that is, they are able to raise the prices they charge above the costs of their services and are, consequently, reaping economic profits. That may or may not be the case, but it doesn't change the basic conclusions drawn thus far. *The change in the property rights structure implied in making universities responsible for stolen property does not in any way reduce the monopoly power of the universities.* If originally universities were able to extort monopoly profits from their market position, they should be able to do the same after a change in the property right structure. Their costs may be higher, but their prices can still be raised, given their monopoly position. Indeed, a law that requires universities to sell the "right" to reimbursement for stolen property in locker rooms is tantamount to a law that requires all competitors to raise the price of their product at once; there is no worry of competitors' underpricing their product because they do not sell the "right" of reimbursement.

Leaving the market free of direct government intervention, in the form of requiring one party or the other to assume the risk of loss or threat of damage, does not mean that market participants will be unprotected. First, as we have noted, people can protect themselves: locker room users can buy better locks and make extra efforts to ensure that the only articles left in their lockers are those of little value or that the locks are locked. Further, the seller of services like the use of lockers has a direct interest in the security of its facilities or the quality of its products. If people are frequently victimized by thefts in a locker room, the university can expect the demand for recreational facilities to drop. As a result, it will be unable to charge as high a price as it could if its locker room were relatively free of theft. The university, in short, has an interest in providing this kind of security; the security may be costly, but these costs can be more than covered by the added price that it can charge when the demand is increased because of the greater security. For this reason, most universities do keep a casual watch on their locker rooms. As least, they tend to become suspicious of anyone who enters the locker room with a crowbar! Keeping a watchful eye is not very costly and increases significantly the demand for the facilities and fees that can be charged.

The question, however, that any organization faces is, "How much protection is desired by our customers?" A market unobstructed by governmental intervention does provide a reasonable, albeit imperfect, means of answering that question. People are willing to pay for some protection. The firm can, therefore, provide protection so long as people are willing to pay more for the protection than the protection costs the firm (university). There will, of course, be some level of protection that will cost more to provide than the customers are willing to pay. Beyond some point, customers will not buy additional protection from the firm (university) simply because they can provide their own protection in a less costly manner through self-protection or self-insurance. That level of protection chosen in the free market may be considered an "optimum level of protection" in the sense that if the government requires more protection be provided, the additional protection will cost more than it is worth. Customers will be forced, through legally required protection laws, to pay for protection that they do not think is worth the cost and would not choose to buy.

HEALTH INSURANCE AND OTHER PRODUCTS

The general understandings uncovered by applying economics reasoning to the assignment of rights to locker rooms can be applied to a broad range of goods and services sold in the marketplace. Those principles are readily applicable to health insurance. Consumer advocates argue that the cost of health services is rising dramatically, which it is, and that the government ought to step into that market and protect consumers by providing a national insurance program. The expenses of the program can be paid for with taxes that are, like income taxes, deducted from paychecks. The program requires people to buy from hospitals and doctors health insurance and services that they would or could not otherwise purchase.

In other words, a national health insurance program requires people to buy the right to hospital and doctor services of particular kinds. Because there are costs involved in avoiding most illnesses, the publicly sponsored health insurance program is likely to increase the number of people who get sick and increase the number of times each person gets sick. People may reason that (similar to the student in the example of the gymnasium locker room) if they fail to follow good health habits, they stand a greater chance of coming down with the flu or becoming obese. However, under a government health program, their medical costs will be borne by the general population in the form of higher taxes. They may also have to pay higher taxes; however, the impact of their own illnesses and medical costs on their own tax payments is likely to be imperceptible. Effectively, although illnesses may be determined largely by noneconomic forces, the lower cost to the individual from his or her own illnesses will reduce the individual's incentive to avoid becoming ill.

Because many, if not most, people can be expected to react to national health insurance like our hypothetical individual, the cost of health care under a national health program can be expected to expand for two reasons. First, more people (including the needy and the not-so-needy) will seek health services. Second, there will be less prevention and more illnesses per person. Note also that under a national health insurance program that fully covers all medical costs, there is little incentive for people to go without health services for inconsequential problems like a cough or a scratchy throat; there is less reason for people to avoid poison ivy patches; and to the extent that dental work is covered, there is less reason for people to brush their teeth or go without the sweets that cause tooth decay. In fact, there is less incentive for people to learn what causes illnesses or tooth decay. Granted, the behavioral response of people to "free" national health insurance can mean that they all will pay more for health insurance than they would choose to buy in a private market. However, once the system exists, it makes no economic sense to avoid making use of it.

Furthermore, under a national health program, there will tend to be a shortage of medical services. Such a shortage exists in Great Britain. This is because when people go to the polls to vote for representatives (who will vote on appropriations), they will consider the *costs of the health delivery system* in determining how many medical facilities will be made available. However, the medical facilities and services that are provided through the political process are typically allocated (as they are in Great Britain) on a below-cost basis; often the services are provided free to the user. In determining how much in the way of medical services they will demand, users will individually base their decisions on the price that is charged, which is zero (meaning the services are free to the user), or below the cost of the service. As a result of the disparity between the price that is considered in the political process and the price that is considered by people individually, a shortage of services will tend to exist.[2]

The general economic principles we have studied are applicable to a host of other products. For example, if the government requires people to pay into a social security system on the grounds that they need to be protected from having inadequate retirement income, people can respond to the requirement by reducing their contributions to private retirement plans; they can be expected to reduce their own efforts to protect themselves. To the extent that people save less, the goals of the social security system are not achieved. Furthermore, there will be fewer funds available for investment in private business ventures, impeding the growth in the capital stock and worker productivity and impeding growth in the national income level. According to one important study by Martin Feldstein, all these effects have been observed.[3] Feldstein argues that forced social security contributions have cost the economy $3,500 per family in gross national product. In other words, if there had not been a social security system, private investment would have been greater than it has been over the last four decades; and, because capital stock would have been greater ($5 trillion instead of $3 trillion), the national production of goods and services and per capita national income would have been higher than it has been each year.

Safety requirements that protect the driver (as opposed to other passengers in cars) tend to reduce the cost of accidents to drivers and tend to increase the level of reckless driving.[4] Safety requirements on appliances can lead some people to treat their appliances more carelessly; such require-

[2]For a more in-depth analysis of the shortage of medical services in Great Britain, see James M. Buchanan, "The Inconsistencies of the National Health Services," in James M. Buchanan and Robert D. Tollison (eds.), *Theory of Public Choice: Political Applications of Economics* (Ann Arbor: University of Michigan Press, 1972), pp. 27–45.

[3]Martin Feldstein, "More Problems with Social Security," *Business in Brief*, Chase Manhattan Bank, (May 1978), p. 5.

[4]Sam Peltzman, "The Effects of Automobile Safety Regulation," *Journal of Political Economy* (August 1975), pp. 677–725.

ments may also increase the costs of applicances. As a result, people are forced by law to buy a form of accident insurance that they may not want and that they may be able to acquire at less cost by self-protection, which is a form of self-insurance.

Simply requiring producers to be liable for harm that is caused from the use of their products is no way to avoid these consequences. If firms have to pay damages for the harm that is caused in the use of the products they sell, they (like the university in the locker-room example) will incur higher costs and can be expected to raise their prices. If firms avoid the damage claims by producing a safer product, production costs will still go up. Consumers will then not be able to buy less safe products at lower prices and protect themselves through more careful use of the products. If firms continue to produce the same product, but protect themselves with insurance policies that cover the damage claims made against them, the insurance premiums will be an added cost that consumers can expect to pay in the form of higher prices for goods and services they buy.[5]

CONCLUDING COMMENTS

Economically justifiable arguments have been developed for many forms of government regulation.[6] Property rights per se presuppose some limited government control. A central point of this chapter has been to explain the meaning and importance of property rights in an economic system. However, we have tried to show, with reference to the problem of theft in a locker room, that efforts to protect people in the marketplaces are typically more complex than newspaper discussions suggest. Changes in the property-rights structure that are inherent in regulation do not always bring about the benefits that are commonly expected. In many instances, people prefer to protect themselves because that form of protection is less costly or more efficient.

QUESTIONS TO PONDER

1 Will a rational person try to prevent all accidents? Using supply and demand curves for accident prevention, graphically illustrate how many accidents a person will rationally choose to prevent.

2 Suppose people are frequently found to injure themselves from the use of a given

[5]James M. Buchanan, "In Defense of Caveat Emptor," *University of Chicago Law Review* (Fall 1970), pp. 64–73.

[6]For a thorough discussion of these arguments, see Armen A. Alchian and William R. Allen, *Exchange and Production Theory in Use* (Belmont, Calif.: Wadsworth Publishing Company, Inc., 1977), chaps. 1–5; see also Richard B. McKenzie and Gordon Tullock, *Modern Political Economy: An Introduction to Economics* (New York: McGraw-Hill Book Company, 1978, chaps. 12 and 13.

electrical appliance. Under what circumstances do and do not the injuries justify government intervention in private markets?

3 "Consumers do not always want to be protected by government, even when government protection is beneficial in terms of reductions in the number of injuries." How can the example of theft in the gymnasium locker room be used to explain that statement?

4 Why would producers of high-quality products in a given industry be interested in having the government set minimum quality standards for the production of goods in their industry?

ADDITIONAL READING

Alchian, Armen A., and William R. Allen. *Exchange and Production Theory in Use.* Belmont, Calif.: Wadsworth Publishing Company, Inc., 1977, chaps. 1–5.

______, and Harold Demsetz, "The Property Rights Paradigm," *Journal of Economic History*, vol. 33, March 1973, pp. 16–27.

McKenzie, Richard B., and Gordon Tullock. *Modern Political Economy: An Introduction to Economics.* New York: McGraw-Hill Book Company, 1978, chap. 5.

Chapter 4

The Economic Dimensions of Ethical Behavior

If we drop out all ethical-behavioral rules and altruistic concerns for others, . . . [then] only market exchanges, retaliations by those directly injured, or policing of formal laws would induce people to show any concern for others. . . . In this kind of world, the best time to hit anyone would be when he had his glasses on. . . . The best time for government or union officials to twist arms would be when the twistee was over a barrel for other reasons. Every interdependency would be exploited. . . . No holds would be barred by the enforcement of the law.[1]

CHAPTER PREVIEW

Central Question

How and to what extent can economics be used to explain the durability of ethical and behavioral rules?

[1]Roland N. McKean, "Economics of Ethical and Behavioral Codes," unpublished manuscript (Charlottesville: Department of Economics, University of Virginia, 1974), p. 14.

Major Objectives

1 To demonstrate how principles of individual behavior in large and small groups, developed in Chapter 1, can be used to explain the viability of ethical and behavioral rules in achieving what people want.

2 To explore economic reasons for the possible demise of many ethical standards of behavior.

3 To better explain the economic theory of group behavior.

Major Points

1 Individual actions tend to have little detectable effect in large groups, reducing the incentive that individuals have to pursue voluntarily what is in the common interest of all group members. In other words, individuals in large groups have an economic incentive to free ride in the production of what are called "public goods."

2 Ethical or behavioral rules of conduct are similar to laws, are public goods, and may be in the common interest of members of a community. However, there are strict limits to the economic incentives that people have to contribute to the development of ethical and behavioral rules.

3 In spite of the fact that ethical rules tend to be public goods, there are several possible economic explanations why people adhere, to a limited extent, to ethical precepts. (These reasons are explored in this chapter.)

4 There are several economic explanations, which range from technological changes to the importance of religion in society, for what many have called an "ethical crisis."

Important New Term and Concept

Public good

Economics as a distinct and modern discipline developed from moral philosophy 200 years ago. Adam Smith, the acknowledged founder of economic science, and his friend David Hume conversed and wrote in an intellectual climate in which questions of what is moral or immoral, just or unjust, obligatory or optional could not be ignored. In fact, one may claim with good justification that Smith's system of political economy emerged as a serendipity, so to speak, from his and others' more general concern with moral issues.

Although perceived as having his attention narrowly focused on the market as a social organizer, Smith argued forcefully that ethics undergird behavioral rules and that behavioral rules form constraints within which the market can function. Without these constraints, he wrote, "every passion would upon occasion, rush headlong, if I may say so, to its own gratification. Anger would follow the suggestion of its own fury; fear those of its own violent agitation. Regard to no time and place would induce vanity to refrain from the loudest and most impertinent ostentation. . . ."[2]

Adam Smith never argued that capitalism or the market system should or could operate efficiently and promote the general well-being without the system being predicated upon ethical considerations and implied standards of behavior. Aside from an ardent segment of the supporters of the market system, who may give the impression that the market can be all things to all people, most supporters of the market system have recognized the benefits of an ethical foundation for market behavior. In this chapter, by applying the analytical framework developed in the first chapter, we are able to consider the economic implications of what we call "behavioral rules." Because many people view modern society as being in the midst of an ethical crisis, our main concern is with factors that may lead to a change in standards of behavior or ethical rules.

THE PRECARIOUS NATURE OF BEHAVIORAL RULES

Voluntary acceptance of behavioral and ethical rules can make behavior among people within a group more predictable, and in this respect such rules are characteristically similar to laws. Knowing that others have agreed, implicitly or explicitly, to behave in certain ways, individuals can save on resources that would otherwise be used to predict how others will behave. The more generally accepted the rules are, the more efficiently an individual can move among and interact with others in spatial and time dimensions. Further, if people agree to refrain from such modes of behavior as lying, cheating, and stealing, each person can save additional resources by not having to protect his or her property.

Public Goods

When commonly observed, behavioral rules can lead to the development of trust, security, friendliness, and cooperation, all of which are, to one degree or another, public goods, like national defense or police protection. *Public goods are those which, if they are provided, benefit everyone within the relevant group; no one can be excluded from receiving the benefits.* The public goods of trust and security, for example, can pervade the total community and not only save time and energy, but also provide people with a sense of pride in being a part of the group. They can benefit everyone simultaneously.

Since behavioral rules are often in people's common interest, one might imagine that they would be adopted on a voluntary basis even in very *large*

[2]Adam Smith, *The Theory of Moral Sentiments*, in Herbert W. Schneider (ed.), *Adam Smith's Moral and Political Philosophy* (New York: Harper & Row, Publishers, 1970), p. 275.

groups. However, in the first chapter, we briefly presented an argument suggesting that the common interest does not serve as the basis on which large-group behavior can be organized. This is because the individual, when taken in the context of a large group, is such a small part of the total that his or her contributions to and influence on the group's attainment of whatever public good is at stake borders on being insignificant. There will be insufficient incentive for the typical individual to incur the private costs that must be borne in order to contribute to the common interest. In short, there will be underinvestment in the public good of public trust. People would like to have more public trust in large groups, but the nature of the incentive structure within large groups precludes its provision.

The argument just presented relating to public trust is in several respects analogous to the problem that an individual fisherman faces when he considers constructing a lighthouse. If an individual fisherman constructs a lighthouse, he may receive some benefits from his actions, but most of the benefits are external to him, that is, received by other fishermen in the area. The fisherman who builds the lighthouse cannot withhold the benefits of the lighthouse and, therefore, cannot charge for the benefits provided. Because the individual cannot charge others for the benefits received, construction of the lighthouse cannot be financially justified, even though all fishermen may want the lighthouse. The necessary funds for construction may not be collected on a voluntary basis because each fisherman may rationally try to hold back or free ride on what the others do. Hence, even though the lighthouse may be in the common interest, it is not constructed without the use of government (coersive) taxing powers.

The important difference between the lighthouse example and the public good of trust is that it is impossible for trust to be developed without the cooperation of a substantial portion of the people within the community or group. It is impossible for one person to construct a sense of trust in a community; one person can be trusted, but unless others within the community are also trustworthy, a presumption of trust will not carry to all members within the community. For example, a given used-car salesperson may be quite trustworthy; however, that individual may not be trusted by many within the community because of the general lack of trustworthiness of all used-car salespeople. In addition, the coersive powers of government cannot be used to produce the necessary sense of community trustworthiness that is independent of laws.

To illustrate further, Mancur Olson, on whose work this discussion is largely based,[3] shows how our central argument relates to the conventional

[3]Mancur Olson, *The Logic of Collective Action: Public Goods and the Theory of Groups* (Cambridge, Mass.: Harvard University Press, 1971). See also Richard B. McKenzie and Gordon Tullock, *Modern Political Economy: An Introduction to Economics* (New York: McGraw-Hill Book Company, 1978), chap. 6.

competitive market. In such a market all competitors can benefit in the same way that a monopolist can by restricting output: if an industry's output is restricted and the price is raised, total industry profits can be increased. The individual competitor, however, because of his or her relative insignificance in the total output, has no incentive to cut back production. Such a cutback will have no detectable effect and, therefore, no realizable benefits. The individual is just too small to matter. Clearly, the common interest can be served if *all* restrict their output and hold the line against market pressures (just as the common interest can be served if *all* fishermen contribute to the construction of the lighthouse), but that end is not served. The incentive structure is such that the individual is led to do what is contrary to the interest of the group. The intent is not malicious; on the contrary, the competitor, because of insignificant size, does not perceive that he or she is doing anything wrong or is not acting in the group's interest.

Similarly, the common interest cannot serve as the basis for an organizational structure, superimposed on the market, that can bring about the kinds of collective behavior necessary to generate the public good. If a structure is achieved, it is because private benefits, which are distinct from group benefits, are provided by the organization. A good example of what is implied here is membership in the American Economics Association (AEA). Olson would argue that economists do not belong to the AEA because of the public or external benefits that may be present or because membership is in their common interest. Rather, they belong because of the private benefits from the journals, the AEA's employment service, and the ability to tell others they belong. The private incentives are important because of the relative insignificance of the individual in the context of large groups.

Moral Law versus Private Maxim

James Buchanan has developed a similar line of argument, but his attention is squarely on the choice a person makes between two fundamental ethical positions.[4] The individual may choose to follow a moral law, something akin to Immanuel Kant's generalization principle,[5] or may choose the rule of private maxim. With regard to the former choice, the moral law, the individual's subsequent behavior will be constrained by the prior decision to adhere to the ethical precept. In this case of the generalization principle, the individual will do only those things which can be generalized to the rest of the relevant population. Doing what may be expedient in the narrow context of each situation is restricted, or made more costly from a psychic point

[4]James M. Buchanan, "Ethical Rules, Expected Values, and Large Numbers," *Ethics*, vol. 76 (October 1965), pp. 1–13.

[5]Kant argued that individuals are acting ethically if they act in such a way that they are willing to *generalize* their actions to the rest of the population. This rule of behavior is what is known as the "generalization principle" or, alternately, the "categorical imperative."

of view (this is because, having adopted a moral law, the individual would have to break his or her commitment to the ethical precept).

If one chooses, on the other hand, to abide by the rule of private maxim, subsequent choice of behavior is left unconstrained. Purely expedient behavior—meaning that only the cost and benefits of the particular situation are considered—can be expected. This does not mean that the individual will not, in a given situation, do what is morally right; the morally right course of action may very often be the expedient thing to do. A person may not steal, not because that action has been precluded by adherence to the ethical position that "thou shalt not steal," but because the cost and benefits of the particular situation make stealing an irrational act.

Buchanan's argument is involved and lengthy, but it is essentially the same as the one developed above: even though the individual may prefer that everyone adopt the moral law (because it is in the common interest), in large groups the individual will, probabilistically speaking, choose the rule of private maxim. Buchanan's argument is that, because of the insignificance of the individual and the absence of private benefits in a large group, the individual who adopts the moral law can expect little in terms of the expected benefits.

Additionally, individuals may not consciously perceive that they are, by choosing the route of expediency, doing anything that clearer insight would tell them was morally reprehensible. As mentioned, moral behavior is not necessarily precluded by the decision to follow the route of expediency. Further, one's behavior may have no *detectable* effect on others, and the effect one has on others may be the central concern of one's moral behavior.

In small groups, the probability of the individual having a significant impact on the rest of the group is raised and the adoption of the moral law is more likely, but, Buchanan writes, "there is some increase in group size that will cause him to modify his ethical rule and become a private maximizer."[6] In small groups we do tend to find individuals foregoing strictly expedient behavior and adopting ethical or other behavioral rules that serve the common good. Buchanan cites as examples:

> Volunteer fire departments arise in villages, not in metropolitan centers. Crime rates increase consistently with city size. Africans behave differently in tribal culture than in urban-industrialized settings. There is honor among thieves. The Mafia has its own standards. Time-tested honor systems in universities and colleges collapse when enrollments exceed critical size limits. Litter is more likely to be found on main traveled routes than on residential streets. Even the old addage, "Never trust a stranger," reflects recognition of this elemental truth, along with, of course, additional ethical predictions.[7]

[6]Buchanan, "Ethical Rules," p. 8.
[7]Ibid., p. 6.

This line of argument has an unsuspecting generality about it; it may be a major reason for highly decentralized organizational structures within business and government bureaucracies. The decentralized organizational structure puts people into departments—that is, small groups—and strengthens the viability of ethical rules. Indeed, the unethical behavior that so frequently catches newspaper headlines, both in government and business, can be a reflection of the sheer growth in size of these private and public bureaucracies. Watergate-type offenses can be a natural consequence of government and business growth.

FACTORS BOLSTERING BEHAVIORAL RULES IN LARGE GROUPS

Although one can point to a substantial number of instances in which behavioral rules acquire considerable potency in small-group settings, many instances also can be cited that demonstrate that behavior rules are prevalent, and, indeed, have potency in what may be considered very large groups. People litter, but, by the same token, many (but not all) refrain in cases in which to do so would be expedient. Knowing that they may go uncaught or, if caught, go unpunished, many people do not take available opportunities to steal. Cheating may be prevalent in universities, but many students refuse to cheat, having rationally decided to ignore the costs and benefits of the immediate situation, and go out of their way to avoid even the suggestion that they are behaving improperly, as judged by others. People do not take all opportunities they have to lie or divulge information about others even under circumstances in which no one else can possible learn what they have done and in which lying may be beneficial to themselves. Roland McKean has listed the following examples:

> Behavioral codes in certain cultures or during emergencies have caused individuals to sacrifice their lives. Numerous persons in Japan (e.g., the 47 Ronin), not just a few emotionally unbalanced individuals, have committed hara kira when the rules called for such action. In 1973, seventy-six passengers on a vehicle caught in a flood in India drowned rather than escape by means of a rescue rope that had just been used by passengers belonging to a different caste.[8]

We can reasonably assert that the incidence of such behavior is not trivial and that much of it is revealed in the context of a large group.

This is not to suggest that the arguments formulated are unsound. On the contrary, there is every reason to believe that group size has the perverse effect indicated by the public-goods theory of group behavior. However, as

[8]McKean, "Economics of Ethical Codes," p. 6.

Mancur Olson and James Buchanan both recognize, the problem at hand is a multidimensional one; variables other than number of people can have an influence and can work to offset the influence of size, at least to some degree. A complete theory must account for these instances in which behavioral rules are operational within large groups. Since this is not a book on just behavioral rules, no pretense of completing that theory is made here; however, within the space of a few pages, several factors that may bolster the viability of behavioral rules within groups can be cited. We will then be in a position to consider changes in the social and physical environment that may have led to what many perceive as an ethical crisis, a situation in which, as the phrase is interpreted here, the durability of previously accepted behavioral rules is called into question.

Costs and Benefits

There are several points of departure. First, although the benefits an individual may receive from contributing to a public good may be quite small, bordering on insignificant but not zero, the cost to the individual may be equally small, or smaller, making the act rational. If one does not lie, one may contribute to the public trust. The benefits from one's *own* act may be quite small, but because the lie may have been of trivial import to begin with, not telling the lie can still be quite rational, even though the only benefits considered are those which add to the public trust. The aggregate of all such individuals can add to what may develop into a certain level of public trust. The level of public trust developed may be below what everyone considers to be socially optimal, but still there will be some level of trust generated, as imperfect as it may be.

Obligations

Second, there is the possibility that people may act out of a sense of duty, a sense of obligation to the community as a whole that transcends the immediate circumstances of their own positions. This duty may be independent of rational behavior as narrowly defined by economists.[9] No pretense is in any way made here that economic factors can explain all behavior; that would be absurd. Exploration of the Christian or Kantian motives for individual action, which make the goodness of the act itself an end quite apart from the gain to the actor and the probability of reward, may yield useful predictions about behavior that can compliment the economist's insights founded on rationality.

[9]For a discussion of the various possible motives for charitable behavior, which is a part of what is at stake here, see Thomas R. Ireland and David Johnson, *The Economics of Charity* (Blacksburg, Va.: University Publications, Inc., 1970), pp. 17–25.

Values

Third, there is every reason to assume that behavioral rules, like other, more normal goods, are the product of a rather elaborate production process that begins at birth with parental labor as a main resource input and continues through formal education with a substantial quantity and variety of resources being applied. Values and rules are also developed and reinforced through an individual's everyday experiences and interaction with others. What constitutes acceptable or unacceptable behavior is learned or, using the terminology of the psychologist, "imprinted" in the mind. This does not mean that individuals are unable to exercise choice. The individual producing the values must make decisions on how many resources must be optimally applied to the "production" of the values. The choice behavior of the subjects is an obstacle that must be overcome in order that the value may be imprinted and in that way affect subsequent behavior.

The selection of behavioral rules is not a random process. A group, be it small or large, has limited resources with which to accomplish its objectives. There are a wide variety of rules that can be learned or adopted and obeyed, and it is reasonable to assume the group does not have the option of developing all possible rules. Because members of small groups know that their members will at times interact with members of other groups, they may concentrate their efforts on rules that can be generalized to a larger segment of the community. Families, for example, are small groups that are continuously involved in establishing and reinforcing family values and rules. Parents, however, have a serious optimizing problem in applying their resources toward the development of rules whose benefits are limited to the family and rules that reflect commonly held positions of the larger community. Because the individual or family has little influence on the total community values and rules, commonly accepted positions on behavioral rules have a built-in inertia that can make them resistant to change.

Interpersonal Relationships

Fourth, embedded in the economic theory of group behavior is one of two assumptions: either (1) the individual is assumed to be so small a part of the whole that his or her actions cannot materially affect anyone else if the total impact is directed at one particular person, or (2) the total effect of an individual's behavior is spread evenly over the entire group population with no noticeable effect on any one person. In this way an individual's unethical behavior or violation of group rules does not have adverse effects on anyone, and the interpersonal costs and benefits that have been discussed in preceding chapters do not come into play as a means of restraining behavior. Either of these two assumptions may describe with reasonable accuracy the relationship among competitors who must compete against the market, as opposed to against each other, or among voters who may cast their votes for different candidates through secret ballots in a political contest. These are situations in which personal relationships are incidental to behavior; the people involved may just as well be isolated from one another. However, such assumptions may have little relevance to many problems relating to behavioral rules, where behavior is revealed often in personal, one-to-one situations, the impact is direct, and the effects can be felt by someone. For example, someone who lies does so directly and may have to return to confront the person lied to. The consequences of this sort of behavior are not necessarily spread over the group evenly.

Interpersonal costs and benefits can cause behavioral rules to be adopted and, at least to some degree, obeyed, where the relationships are important. The interconnection of friendships can mean that the same rules are adopted by a large number of people. To illustrate: You behave according to certain rules of behavior with regard to a friend because of the cost you may suffer (for example, you may lose your friend's company) if you do not follow the rules. These costs may constrain your behavior and force you to adopt the behavioral rules. The same may be true of most of your friends. The friends, having the same relationship with others you may not know, adopt similar rules for their relationships with other persons. In this way, the size of the group within which a given set of behavioral rules applies can extend outward, possibly increasing the size of the group to where it might be considered "large." As in a decentralized bureaucracy, the common interest of the people may be achieved because the large groups are actually an interconnected web of small groups.

The viability of the behavioral rules will have its limitations. Persons who have strong and abiding friendships will incur considerable costs if those relationships are weakened by their own actions, such as violating a commonly adopted behavioral rule. On the other hand, casual acquaintances can be expected to exert little influence on the behavior of each other. We may also add that any technological change, such as mass transportation, that leads to a reduction in the reliance that people place on one another will tend to lessen the incentive to develop strong interpersonal relationships. Accordingly, the interpersonal cost-and-benefit structure necessary to maintain the behavioral rules in the small-group setting, and the larger community, will be weakened, and we may expect a deterioration of the force of behavioral rules in guiding the behavior of people.

Religion

Finally, religion lends support to standards of behavior in large groups. This factor is more complicated than others but may be more easily understood. Thus, more care needs to be taken in its development. A cornerstone of economic analysis is the a priori presumption that the private benefits must exceed the private costs before action can be expected. These costs may be real or imagined; the crucial point is that they must be viewed as relevant considerations. Once the individual weighs each cost and benefit, perhaps discounting it by the probability of its being relevant, the distinction between what is real or imagined becomes blurred.

An individual's conception of God as a universal force is a case in point. God may or may not exist; however, so long as a person believes that He does and perceives Him with certain attributes, the individual's behavior should be affected accordingly. The individual's subjective cost-and-benefit structure can be different from what it would otherwise be. For example, in most religious codes, God is conceived to be omniscient and omnipotent, pervading the total behavior of the individual, knowing the individual's every thought and move. Many believe that He is capable of imposing extremely heavy costs (external hell) for misdeeds and of granting infinite benefits (life in heaven) to those who hold certain values and behave according to certain rules. These values relate primarily to interpersonal, group relationships and to the individual's relationship with God. Possessing this conception, the individual who believes in God attributes a small, if not zero, probability to any of his or her actions escaping the knowledge of God.

In the absence of a conceptualized God, behavioral rules may be impotent in guiding the behavior of members of some critically large group. This is because of the free-rider problem that we have discussed. However, with a belief in God, the individual will expect private benefits if he or she behaves according to certain rules. In other words, the benefits of individual actions are internalized (made private).[10] If these perceived benefits are greater than the private costs the individual must bear, the rational person will choose to behave according to the rules and contribute his or her small part to the general welfare. The rationality of the act depends not only upon how the individual assesses the benefits that may be granted, but also upon the individual's assessment of the probability that the benefits will be granted. This in turn depends upon the individual's assessment of the probability of God's existence.[11]

[10]Another way of saying the same thing is that God can impose a cost on the individual who fails to obey certain rules.

[11]One interesting sidenote may be made at this juncture. If the external benefits from people behaving according to certain behavioral or ethical precepts, such as the Ten Commandments, are attributable to God's presence and they are realized as a result of belief in God's power to generate these benefits (that is, people take the necessary "leap of faith"), and if the relevant individuals obey the rules because of the perceived costs and benefits, then the benefits of collective behavior will be generated and belief in God will be immediately reinforced. God may not in fact exist, but because people believe that He does, public benefits are generated. The group may start small (as in the case of the Twelve Disciples) but may expand as others join to receive the benefits of the public good. Each individual may perceive his or her own behavior as having an insignificant effect on the public welfare, as discussed earlier. But the public good is present, and not being able to attribute its production directly to anyone else, the individual may conclude that it is the work of an external force—God. In this way "God's presence" may be felt; He takes on the quality of a "living force."

Regardless, the development of faith is not costless—resources are involved. But, on the other hand, the cost of generating collective behavior through belief in God can be lower than alternative ways—for example, through police and penal systems.

In other words, even if God does not exist, belief in God can perform a very useful function. It can encourage people to achieve socially beneficial goals that may not otherwise be realized. This is probably what Ovid meant when he wrote, "It is expedient that there be gods, and, as it's expedient, let us believe there are." Voltaire echoed the same theme two centuries ago: "If He [God] did not exist, it would be necessary to invent Him."

This discussion is not intended to imply that God does not exist. He may in fact exist; and there are, without question, benefits to belief in God that have not been mentioned here. It may be through the logic just outlined that He is "discovered," as He intended. Still, if He does not exist, there is economic reason to believe that He would be created in order that the benefits of collectively obeyed behavioral rules could be realized.

THE EROSION OF BEHAVIORAL RULES

Making generalizations about anything as hard to define and measure as standards of behavior is a difficult task at best. However, even the most casual review of the 1960s and 1970s suggests that it was a period in which commonly adopted behavioral rules came under considerable stress. Many changes occurred; without doubt, many of these were for the good of most people. Implicit dress codes among many groups have become more relaxed. Men no longer feel compelled to put on a tie in the mornings, and women have overcome the implied rule that only dresses are appropriate for work. Women are no longer required to plot the course of their lives solely on the basis of what their husbands do, and men no longer have to demonstrate their masculinity with the same vigor they once did. Such rules of behavior, which essentially defined the roles of sexes at work and in everyday sorts of relationships, dissipated when there was no longer an economic basis for them.

However, there have been changes in behavioral rules that in the view of many people have had and will continue to have far more serious consequences regarding the nature of social order than those types of changes just mentioned. As evidenced by the higher crime rate, the greater incidence of cheating in colleges and universities, the demise of the Puritan work ethic, and the general lack of trust among and between people, the strength of several very important rules of behavior has eroded, causing people to look for substitute means of guiding group behavior toward the social good. In general, this has meant that a greater amount of responsibility for directing social order has been handed over to government, and people have had to take measures to protect themselves against what amounts to the predatory practices of others.

Several reasons for the erosion of behavioral rules emerge from our prior discussion. First, there is the sheer growth in the population. Groups have become larger, and this has tended to aggravate the free-rider problem. Second, the last several decades have been years of rapid change. As Roland McKean has written, "rapidly changing values, technology and accumulation make it less clear what rules would in fact yield net social gains. In a relatively stable society, one in which technology changes slowly and people remain in one location for long periods of time, what people mean by fair play, reasonable noise levels, the Golden Rule, or civic-mindedness may become fairly clear. As the prople confront repetitions of the same events, unambiguous rules pertaining to specific situations can evolve."[12] Adam Smith, as we noted at the start of the chapter, stressed the importance of behavioral rules in guiding social conduct. However, we must note that Smith wrote from the vantage point of a small town in Scotland and in a relatively stable society. Perhaps he would have less hope for the effectiveness of such rules if he were writing today.

Third, over the years mobility has dramatically increased. People can now expect to move, on average, once every 5 years. Americans may be more hesitant today about making the necessary investment to establish the personal relationships so important to the maintenance of behavioral rules. When people change their social environment so frequently, they cannot expect to reap the *full* benefits of any contributions they may make to establishing relationships and contributing to the public good through their behavior. They can also avoid the full consequences of their failure to abide by commonly adopted rules.

Fourth, people have become more educated and sophisticated, and with this change has come greater understanding of their free-rider positions. Unfortunately, to the extent that this has happened, people have probably become more inclined to take advantage of their free-rider positions.

Fifth, there has been a decrease in the amount of emphasis that religious sects give to heaven and hell. This means that the apparent costs and benefits from ethical, group behavior have perhaps for some been reduced. There has also been a growing emphasis on personalized religion: "God is what you make Him" is not an uncommon attitude. All this has resulted in a reduced inclination to behave according to a commonly held set of rules founded upon ethical precepts.

[12]Roland N. McKean, "Collective Choice," in James W. McKie (ed.), *Social Responsibility and the Business Predicament* (Washington, D.C.: The Brookings Institutions, 1974), p. 124.

Sixth, perhaps in response to the weakening of behavioral rules, government has taken over more and more social responsibilities over the past decades. Though government action has contributed to the well-being of many, it has also probably contributed to a breakdown of a sense of personal responsibility that people may feel toward one another. One may take the attitude that one need not worry about the misfortunes of family members or neighbors because they can get relief from the government. Furthermore, if a person chisels on the government—for example, takes undeserved food stamps or claims higher deductions on tax returns than are legally permissible—the effects are spread over a very large mass of people. As the result, the cost of being dishonest becomes obscured. The attitude that one should try to "get away" with as much as possible may carry over into areas of social interaction that do not involve the government.

CONCLUDING COMMENTS

In many small but important ways, the world has been depersonalized. People complain more now than ever about their individual loneliness. The strong ties that bound people together and made them dependent on one another have eroded. Highly integrated small-group structures have been replaced with many nebulous large groups. Given the adverse effects that growth in group size and depersonalization can have on the willingness of people to contribute to the common interest, there should be no wonder that we have been witness to the demise of many ethical and behavioral rules.

The analysis helps us to understand a growing concern among many people regarding the morality of modern society and the growth in criminal activity and corruption in the public and private sectors of the economy. The analysis also suggests that, perhaps, in striving to achieve social goals, we ought to pay more attention to what the proposed change does to the group structure of society and, therefore, to the incentive individuals have to behave in ways that may be in everyone's interest.

QUESTIONS TO PONDER

1 Explain why students write curse words and draw nonsense pictures on the desk tops in University classrooms more than they do on the tops of their coffee tables at home.
2 Give an economic explanation for the importance of the family in social structure.
3 If there are more crimes committed these days than decades ago, does it necessarily follow that people are more immoral than they were? First, before you try to answer that question, define moral behavior.
4 Economics cannot possibly explain all ethical behavior. What other, noneconomic explanations can you give for ethical behavior?

ADDITIONAL READING

McKean, Roland N. "Collective Choice," in James W. McKie (ed.), *Social Responsibility and the Business Predicament*. Washington, D.C.: The Brookings Institution, 1974.

Olson, Mancur. *The Logic of Collective Action: Public Goods and the Theory of Groups*. Cambridge, Mass.: Harvard University Press, 1971, chaps. 1–4.

Chapter 5

Competition for Monopoly Profits: The Social Waste from Restrictions on Market Entry

CHAPTER PREVIEW

Central Question

How much "social waste" is created by the existence of monopoly?

Major Objectives

1 To demonstrate that a monopolist can, by restricting output, raise prices above the competitive market level and receive economic profits.

2 To explain how and to what extent firms will compete for a monopoly position in a market.

3 To explore the social waste that is created by a monopoly and by firms attempting to acquire monopoly positions in their markets.

Major Points

1 A monopoly will tend to restrict production in order to raise the price charged consumers and to maximize economic profits.

2 Monopoly power can enable firms to earn economic profits. Therefore, firms can be expected to compete for monopoly positions in markets. In the process, resources will be wasted, used to acquire monopoly power and not for the production of goods and services.

3 The waste resulting from monopoly in a market is greater than has been conventionally thought.

Important New Terms and Concepts

Economic profit	Consumer surplus
Average cost	Marginal revenue

A monopolist is a producer protected from competition by barriers to entry into the market. Consequently, the monopolist can choose to restrict output and raise the price above competitive levels. The monopolist is not all-powerful in the market, however, but is constrained by consumers' demand for the product and the cost of production. Nonetheless, the monopolist has some choice in the price to be charged, because of the monopolist's ability to restrict significantly the market supply of the product. The monopolist can, therefore, make economic profits. *Economic profit is that part of a firm's revenues in excess of all costs, including risk costs and costs that reflect the value of the owner's time used elsewhere.*

Unlike the individual competitor, the monopolist does not have to fear that other producers will undercut the price or expand their output when the monopolist's production is restricted. There are simply no close competitors in the market; furthermore, the barriers to entry into the market protect monopolists from would-be competitors.

The protective market barriers of the monopolist can be the result of economies of scale; that is, other producers simply may not have the credit standing to raise the needed financial resources to enter the market on a large enough scale to compete successfully.[1] The power of the monopolist also may arise because a single firm controls the entire known reserves of a strategic resource needed in the production of a good. More importantly for the purposes of this chapter, however, a monopolist may gain market

[1]This, it can be argued, is another way of saying that the existing monopolist is selling the product to consumers at a price lower than the product can be sold by others. To raise the needed capital, other potential producers would have to pay higher rates of interest and charge higher prices because of their higher costs of production.

power from government through a patent or copyright or through an exclusive franchise to operate, say, a given bus or truck route.

Economists have spent a great deal of their energies analyzing the economic consequences of monopoly power and measuring the actual economic harm done by monopolists. Many studies have found that monopolists, especially those whose market boundaries are protected by government, do not make the high economic profits and rates of return on their investment[2] that economic theory tends to suggest that they should make. Further, Gordon Tullock, on whose work the arguments in this chapter are largely based, has written, "in recent years a considerable number of studies have been published that purport to measure the welfare costs of monopolists and tariffs. The results have uniformly shown very small costs for practices that economists normally deplore. This has led [Robert] Mundell to comment in 1962 that 'Unless there is a thorough theoretical re-examination of the validity of the tools upon which these studies are founded . . . someone will inevitably draw the conclusion that economics has ceased to be important.'"[3]

Perhaps some of the monopolistic firms that have been studied do not have the market power to restrict output and raise price that has been attributed to them. Perhaps the markets for monopolistic producers have been too narrowly defined; that is, a firm may be protected from facing direct competition in a *given product line*, but it may face competition from distant substitutes. Therefore, the firm does not have the power to raise the price by seriously affecting the choice range of consumers. These are cogent explanations for the observed empirical findings of economists. The purpose of this chapter is not to discount their importance. Rather, our purpose here is to extend our understanding of monopoly behavior by an alternative, less-than-obvious explanation for the empirical findings on monopoly costs and profits. This explanation is that a monopolist often has to *compete* for monopoly position, meaning that, because of the benefits of monopoly power, if that power is obtained, the monopoly must have competed for that power before the power was acquired. The firm must have invested resources in trying to outwit or outmaneuver others who wanted the monopoly power, others who wanted the protection of barriers of entry but failed to acquire it. The resources that are used to acquire the monopoly position are part of the largely unrecognized social waste of having mo-

[2]The rate of return on investment is the ratio of the profit per year to the investment. If a firm earns $100,000 in profits per year on an investment of $500,000, the rate of return is 20 percent.

[3]Gordon Tullock, "The Welfare Costs of Tarrifs, Monopolies, and Theft," *Western Economic Journal* (June 1967), p. 224. Tullock quotes R. A. Mundell's review of L. H. Janssen, "Free Trade, Protection and Customs Union," *American Economic Review* (June 1962), p. 622. For additional contemporary discussion on this subject, see Anne O. Kruger, "The Political Economy of the Rent-seeking Society," *American Economic Review* (June 1974), pp. 291–303.

nopoly privileges in the economy. Furthermore, those invested resources expand the total financial commitment of the monopolist and reduce the rate of return on investment. To see these points more clearly, let us review for a few moments the standard economic analysis of monopoly.

THE MONOPOLY MODEL

The demand curve of the monopolist is downward-sloping to the right, like the curve labeled D in Figure 5.1. The downward slope of the curve reflects the fact that the monopolist has the capacity to restrict output and raise the price. The monopolist has the capacity to choose from a series of price-quantity combinations for the purpose of maximizing profits. (Individual competitors cannot choose because they have to worry about being undercut by other producers if they raise their price above the market price.) Assuming the marginal cost of production is constant, an assumption made only to simplify the discussion, the curve representing the marginal cost of the monopolist is horizontal like the curve labeled MC in Figure 5.1. This is because the marginal cost is the same for each unit. The marginal cost curve in this graphical illustration is also the average cost curve. *Average cost*

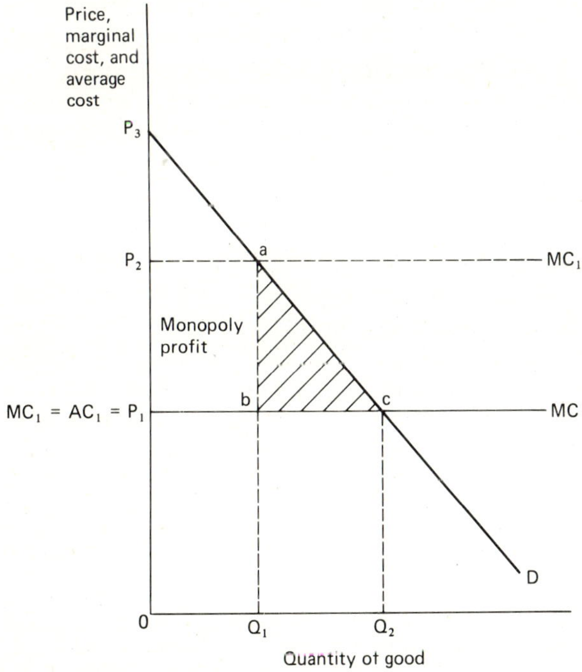

Figure 5.1

is the total cost of production divided by the quantity of output:

$$\text{Average cost} = \frac{\text{total cost}}{\text{quantity}}$$

If the marginal cost of production is constant at, say, \$5, the average cost of production at all output levels will also be \$5.

In a perfectly competitive market, the market will be at equilibrium—a state of balance—at the intersection of the marginal cost curve (which is the competitive supply curve) and the demand curve. The output level will be Q_2 and the price will be P_1. Given a choice, the monopolist will, for obvious reasons, not operate at that price-quantity combination. At the competitive equilibrium, the price P_1, which is equal to the marginal cost, is also equal to the average cost of production. Hence, profit is zero. Profit is equal to total revenue minus total cost. Total revenue at the competitive equilibrium is equal to $P_1 \times Q_2$; total cost is equal to $AC_1 \times Q_2$. Since the price and average cost of production are equal, $P_1 \times Q_2$ must equal $AC_1 \times Q_2$. Therefore, economic profit is zero.[4]

The monopolist can restrict output to a level below Q_2 and raise the price. Since the average cost of production in our graph remains constant, the price must rise above average cost as output is restricted. Profit must then emerge at an output of less than Q_2. The actual *profit-making* production level in our graph is Q_1, a quantity equal to one-half Q_2. At Q_1, total revenue of the firm is the quantity sold Q_1 times the price P_2. Total cost is equal to the average cost AC_1 times the output level Q_1. Profit is the difference between total revenue and total cost, or $(P_2 \times Q_1) - (AC_1 \times Q_1)$. Graphically, the profit is the area bounded by P_1P_2ab. (For a more complete discussion of how the profit-maximizing output level for a monopolist is obtained, see the appendix to this chapter.)

The economic inefficiency of monopoly power is represented by the shaded triangular area bounded by abc. *If* output had not been restricted and *if* output had been Q_2 instead of Q_1, consumers would have gotten additional benefits, as evident by the demand curve, equal to the area bounded by Q_1acQ_2. To acquire those benefits, on the other hand, additional costs, depicted by the area Q_1bcQ_2, would have been incurred. In summary, people would gain more by having the Q_1 to Q_2 additional units that those units would cost. By not getting those units of the good, there is, due to monopoly power, a welfare loss equal to the shaded area abc or $Q_1acQ_2 - Q_1bcQ_2$.

[4]The firm may be earning what is called "normal profit," which is minimum payment required to cover risk cost and opportunity cost and to keep the firm in the same line of business. Normal profit is, in effect, an implicit cost that revenues must cover.

THE SOCIAL WASTE OF MONOPOLY

The foregoing section graphically illustrates the way in which the welfare loss from monopoly is normally treated in economics. The rectangular area of monopoly profit is not normally viewed as social waste; the profit is considered to be a *transfer* of income from consumers to the monopolist. The total triangular area under the demand curve and above the marginal cost curve, P_1P_3c, is consumer surplus under a perfectly competitive market structure. *Consumer surplus is the total amount by which the benefits from consuming units of a good exceed their total cost of production.* If Q_2 units are produced, then the area under the demand curve up to Q_2 is the total benefits to consumers; the area under the cost curve up to Q_2 is the total cost of production. The triangular area P_1P_3c is the total amount by which total benefits exceed total costs of producing Q_2; it is, as stated, the consumer surplus.

Under a monopolistic market structure, the profit area, which is a part of the consumer surplus, does not evaporate; it is simply received by the monopolist. The only part of the consumer surplus that is truly lost from the presence of monopoly power is the shaded triangular area abc.

The traditional analysis, however, implicitly assumes that a monopoly is created and maintained in a costless manner; no resources are involved or, rather, wasted in creating or maintaining the market barriers to entry. The traditional analysis fails to see that firms will seek the monopoly market position and the profit, sometimes called "monopoly rents," that go with the market position. The new, emerging literature on what is appropriately called "rent seeking" attempts to deal with this deficiency in the theory of monopoly.

In an attempt to acquire monopoly profits, private firms will invest resources in trying to become the monopolist—the one firm in the market that is protected by barriers to entry. If, for example, a strategic resource used in the production of a good is needed to acquire monopoly position, then firms will compete for that resource. The ensuing competition among firms will drive the price of the resource up; and, even though the firm that wins the bidding war ends up as a monopolist, that firm may receive only what approximates a competitive rate of return on its investment. It may receive higher profit in terms of number of dollars, but it has a greater investment in the business. Indeed, the ratio of the dollars received to dollars invested, which is the rate of return on investment, should move toward, but not necessarily equal, the competitive rate of return.

Further, a firm may have to use resources to obtain and maintain its exclusive rights to a given market. Because of the monopoly profits and the higher price charged by the existing monopolist, other firms have an incentive to enter the market and compete. In order to continue to receive the monopoly profit, the existing monopolist may have to use resources to keep other sellers out. Therefore, the monopolist's profit will not likely equal the rectangular area in Figure 5.1.

For instance, the Mafia may have a monopoly position in heroin sales in a given city. It consequently restricts output and raises the price of its product and creates monopoly profits. Because of those profits, however, other sellers ("families") can be attracted to the market. To protect its market boundaries, the Mafia monopoly may have to keep constant surveillance of the existing market to see who is selling what to whom, and it may have to employ, on occasion, the servicies of "hit men." (That is what might really be called "unfair competitive practices"!) The sellers who want to enter the market may have to expend additional resources evading the protective efforts of the existing Mafia monopoly.

The total social waste of the monopoly is not just the shaded triangle: it is the shaded triangle *plus* the value of the resources (that are diverted from other uses) employed by potential competitors trying to enter the market and the resources used by the monopolist in trying to keep all the potential competitors out of the market. Hence, the social waste of the monopoly can be equal to, or even greater than, the area of the shaded triangle and the rectangle representing monopoly profits. The shaded triangular area may indeed be a minor portion of the total social waste of monopoly. As we mentioned at the start, statistical studies have revealed that the social waste of monopoly power is very small; one explanation for such findings may be that only a small portion of the waste is actually considered in the studies.

Another explanation is that, because of the added expenses of acquiring and maintaining barriers to entry on a continuing basis, the *measured* cost of production may shift upward until, at the limit, it is MC′. If MC′ is the cost curve used in statistical studies, then there may appear to be no welfare loss from monopoly. The *measured* marginal cost (which is above the *true* marginal cost) of production is equal to the marginal value of the last unit produced. There is, in this case, no *measured* welfare loss triangle; the welfare loss is hidden by the way costs are measured.

This analysis can apply fully to circumstances in which monopoly power is created and protected by, say, government regulation. To the extent that the social waste of monopoly is equal to the trapezoid P_1P_2ac (which includes the monopoly profits and the loss of consumer surplus), more direct—nonmonopoly—methods of helping those who seek monopoly profit can be socially attractive. For example, if the government, instead of granting monopoly privilege to a firm, simply gave the firm a cash grant, raised from tax collection, equal to the profit rectangle of Figure 5.1, then there would be less of a welfare loss. Certainly, profit-maximizing firms would seek, through resource use, the cash grant. Costs would be incurred. However, to the extent that the market remained competitive, consumers would not lose the welfare triangle abc. They would lose the equivalent of the monopoly profit area, but that is better for them than losing the entire trapezoid.[5]

APPLICATIONS

If the government, by way of exclusive franchises, creates a monopoly privilege that gives to the holder the ability to restrict output and sell output at higher prices, we can expect rational, profit-maximizing entrepreneurs to invest resources in securing the government franchises. Each entrepreneur should be willing to use resources trying to convince the appropriate government agency that he or she deserves a franchise. Each should be willing to invest resources in rent seeking up to the point that the expected marginal value of the last unit of the resource[6] is equal to its market cost.

In terms of Figure 5.2, the monopolist will, given the demand and supply of the resource, employ Q_1 units of the resource in seeking the monopoly rents. The total value of the resource (in terms of its alternative use) is equal to the area bounded by OP_1aQ_1, which is equal to the market price

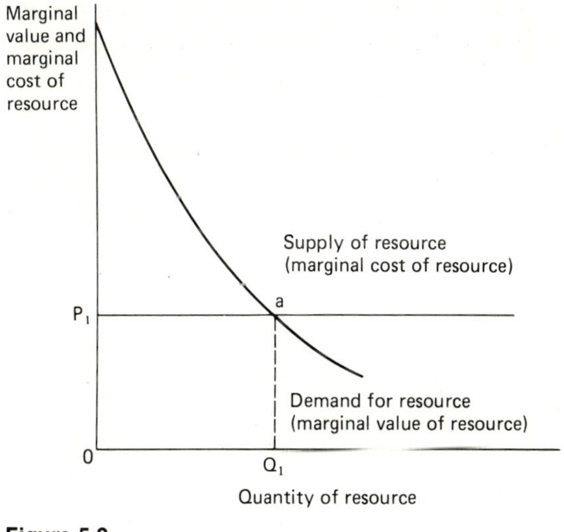

Figure 5.2

[5]Gordon Tullock, *The Backward Society: Static Inefficiency, Rent Seeking and the Rule of Law* (Blacksburg, Va.: Center for the Study of Public Choice, Virginia Polytechnic Institute and State University, 1978), p. 13. Tullock points out that the monopolist can be given more than the profit rectangle and consumers can still be better off with competitive markets and the cash grant.

[6]The expected marginal value of the resource is obtained by discounting the raw marginal value of the resource by the probability that the resource will be effective in securing the monopoly privilege.

of the resource times the number of units used. Other profit-maximizing firms will do the same thing, that is, invest resources until the marginal value of the resource is equal to its marginal cost. Again, the total social loss from the existence of the monopoly power is the lost benefits from the restrictions on production imposed by the monopolist plus the value of the resources that are used by *all* the firms in their efforts to become monopolists. If the government does not provide a producer with monopoly power, then firms should be willing to invest resources in lobbying Congress to provide, through appropriate legislation, the needed exclusive rights to operate. Resources will still be wasted.

To see better the relevance of the above line of analysis, consider the following two examples of the economic effects of rent seeking. Many cities restrict the number of taxicabs on their streets by issuing licenses or what are called "medallions." In order to operate legally within the city, a cab must have a medallion, which can be traded among cab operators. Since the supply of cabs is restricted via the limited number of medallions, people compete for the medallions. And although the cabs are able to charge higher-than-competitive prices, they do not necessarily receive higher-than-competitive rates of return. The competition for the monopoly profits forces up the market price of the medallions and the required investment to enter the cab business. The cab company must pay not only for the cab itself but also for the medallion, which can be several times the price of the cab. The existing cab companies also may have to use their resources to ensure that the city governing body does not decide to increase the number of cabs that are allowed on the streets. A greater number of cabs would, if the demand for cab service remained constant, mean a reduction in the value of the medallions that are outstanding and, accordingly, a reduction in the wealth of the existing cab companies.

A tariff on textiles increases directly the price of an imported textile. It therefore enables domestic producers to raise their prices and expand their share of the domestic market for textiles. Tariffs increase the profits of domestic producers. Because total domestic consumption of any good that is subjected to tariff protection is reduced, there is a net welfare loss from the protection. However, the total welfare loss of the existing protection of the textile industry is greater than just the loss to consumers; it is that loss plus the resources that are expended by all domestic firms in getting the tariff protection.[7]

Demonstrating the waste that can be created from rent seeking is not always easy in a classroom setting. However, Jeffrey Brennen, an economist at Virginia Polytechnic Institute, has devised a classroom game that has

[7]To be perfectly correct, the total welfare loss due to government-provided tariff protection must include the value of resources expended by all industries that tried to get tariff protection from foreign competition but failed in their efforts.

been used in several universities and has proved to be instructive. The Brennen game requires that the instructor offer a prize of, say, $2 for bids among students in the class. The students are told to write the amount of money they are willing to pay on a signed piece of paper and hand it in to the instructor. They are also told that the highest bidder will take the prize and that they must pay in to the instructor the amount of their bid regardless of whether they are the highest bidder. If there is more than one high bidder, the prize is appropriately divided. There is no requirement that the students bid anything or in any way play the game. The instructor can, of course, lose money if the total of the bids is less than the value of the prize. On the other hand, the instructor can gain when the total of the bids exceeds the value of the prize.

The prize can be viewed as the classroom equivalent of the (present discounted value of) monopoly profit that is offered by, say, government and is sought by rent seekers. The bids the students make for the prize can be viewed as the value of the resources they are willing to expend in their efforts to acquire the monopoly position. Will the value of the resources employed in rent seeking be greater than the monopoly profits? The Brennen game does not, of course, provide us with the real world data that we would like to have; however, it is suggestive of the types of results that can be expected. The total of the bids submitted does tend to rise as the size of the class (number of competitors) increases. In large classes of more than 40 students, the experience of instructors has been that the high bid will be close to the $2 prize and the total of the bids will almost always be greater than the $2 prize, often several times the value of the prize. In the 1977–1978 academic year, several instructors played the game in their classes, and the totals of the bids submitted for a $2 prize were all above $6. In two classes, the bids were $11.45 and $24.37. In those two instances, the instructor, as you can imagine, was taken aback by the profit he had made by the demonstration.

CONCLUDING COMMENTS

Anne Kruger has written that "in many market-oriented economies [like the United States], government restrictions upon economic activity are pervasive facts of life. These restrictions give rise to rents of a variety of forms, and people often compete for the rents. Sometimes, such competition is perfectly legal. In other instances, rent seeking takes other forms, such as bribery, corruption, smuggling, and black markets."[8] Government restrictions that produce economic rents for market participants include minimum wage laws; licensing requirements for a variety of skilled trades, like barbering, and professions, like law and medicine; tariffs on many different com-

[8]Kruger, "The Political Economy of the Rent-Seeking Society," p. 291.

modities; and restrictions on entry to such industries as trucking, electric power production, insurance, communication, drug, railroad, banking, telephone, hospital, taxicab, funeral, and public accommodation. The list could easily be extended. The deadweight loss from monopoly power, created artificially by government intervention, is greater than has been traditionally thought in economics. The deadweight loss of monopoly power must include not only the loss in consumer benefits due to the underproduction of monopolies, but also the resources that are used by firms in their attempts to obtain monopoly rents.

This has been the central lesson of this chapter. However, one additional point needs to be stressed. If, for any reason, the government decides to redistribute the national income to one group at the expense of another through market (monopoly-creating) restrictions, it should understand that many of the rents that are to be redistributed can be "wasted away" as rational entrepreneurs try to maximize their profits. The group the government wants to help, in short, may gain little or nothing from the market restrictions. (Consider the analysis of natural gas regulation in Chapter 6.) The restrictions may only serve the purpose of misallocating resources and reducing the national income. It is this line of thinking that in part has caused many social philosophers and economists to recommend that constitutional restrictions be placed on government's ability to control market activities of people.

George Stigler, concerned about the ability of government to be exploited by special-interest groups, has developed a provocative new theory of regulation based on the assumption that rational entrepreneurs will seek rents that are created by government.[9] As opposed to assuming that much government regulation has been imposed upon industry in pursuit of the public interest, Stigler argues that industries have procured the regulation in their pursuit of monopoly power in their markets and the economic rents that power can create. He contends that firms that have to compete with one another in an industry have an economic interest in and a demand for securing governmentally established barriers to entry into their industry. Politicians, on the other hand, can "produce" the protection and, according to Stigler, will do so if the right price is paid. In the Stiglerian theory of regulation, the regulation that is observed is a consequence of the interaction of the supply of and demand for regulatory services produced by government. The effective price that is paid—in terms of votes, campaign contributions, and/or cash payments—determines how many regulatory, rent-producing services will be provided and the number of those services demanded. The price will also determine who gets the benefits of government regulation. Stigler suggests that politicians are major recipients of

[9]George T. Stigler, "An Economic Theory of Regulation," *Bell Journal of Economics and Management Science*, vol. 2 (Spring 1971), pp. 3–21.

the benefits of monopoly power that they create; that is, they are the ultimate rent seekers who should be watched closely.

QUESTIONS TO PONDER

1 In competing for monopoly profits, is it possible that all firms will incur costs that add to more than the monopoly profit that is sought?
2 The author writes that if the government just gives away cash grants, the social waste will be lower than if the government gives away a monopoly position in a market. Do you agree? Explain the logic behind your position.
3 List several examples of how people compete for monopoly market positions.
4 From an economic perspective, explain and evaluate the statement, "Monopolies earn competitive rates of return."

ADDITIONAL READING

Alchian, Armen A. "Competition, Monopoly and the Pursuit of Money," *Economic Forces at Work*. Indianapolis, Ind.: Liberty Fund, Inc., 1977, chap. 6.
Friedman, Milton. *An Economist's Protest*. Glen Ridge, N.J.: Thomas Horton and Daughters, Inc., 1972, chap. 11.
McConnell, Campbell R. *Economics: Principles, Problems, and Policies*. New York: McGraw-Hill Book Company, 1978, chaps. 27 and 34.
McKenzie, Richard B., and Gordon Tullock. *Modern Political Economy: An Introduction to Economics*. New York: McGraw-Hill Book Company, 1978, chaps. 6 and 10.

APPENDIX TO CHAPTER 5: A Primer on Monopoly

The profit-maximizing production level for a monopolist can be developed with more precision than we have in the chapter. The profit-maximizing monopolist will actually seek to produce at the level at which the *marginal revenue* of the last unit produced is equal to the marginal cost of its production. That is a basic rule of production for any firm. To see the importance of the rule, we must define and derive marginal revenue. First, the definition: *Marginal revenue is the additional revenue gained by a firm from selling one additional unit.*

Because additional revenues are affected by the price and quantity sold, marginal revenue must be related mathematically to the demand for a product. Table 5.1 contains the necessary data for a downward-sloping demand curve of a monopolist. As the price falls in column 1, the quantity sold in column 2 increases. Total revenues, computed by simply multiplying the price by the quantity, are recorded in column 3 of the table. Throughout column 3 total revenue rises; but the *additional* or *marginal revenue* gained from each unit falls as the quantity sold increases. The

Table 5.1 Demand and Marginal Revenue Schedule for a Monopolist

Price charged by monopolist (1)	Quantity sold by monopolist (2)	Total revenues received (3) (1) × (2)	Marginal revenue of each unit (4)
$15	0	0	
14	1	$14	$14
13	2	26	12
12	3	36	10
11	4	44	8
10	5	50	6

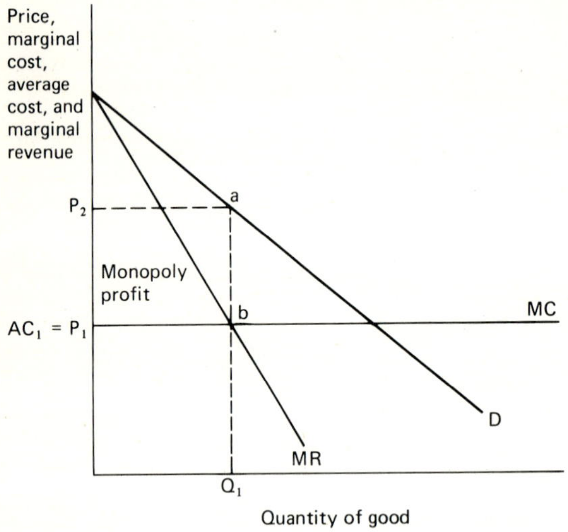

Figure 5.3

marginal revenue for the first unit sold is $14; for the second, $12; and, at the end of the table, the marginal revenue for the fifth unit is only $6. The important point to notice, however, is that, like price and quantity, marginal revenue and quantity are inversely related. Therefore, a marginal revenue curve, constructed from the table, will be downward-sloping to the right, just like the demand curve, but the marginal revenue curve will lie under the demand curve. The relationship between the marginal revenue and demand curves is depicted in Figure 5.3. The demand curve is labeled D and the marginal revenue curve is labeled MR.

A firm will increase its profits by producing additional units so long as they add more to revenue than they add to cost. A firm should, therefore, produce every unit for which the marginal revenue is greater than the marginal cost. In terms of Figure 5.3, the firms should produce as many as Q_1 units. The marginal revenue of each of those units, indicated by the marginal revenue curve MR, is greater than the marginal cost, indicated by the marginal cost curve MC. Granted, as output is expanded toward Q_1, marginal revenue falls; still, for every one of those units marginal revenue is above marginal cost. More is being added to total revenue by producing each of those units than is being added to cost. Beyond Q_1, marginal cost is greater than marginal revenue. Hence, if output is raised above Q_1, profits will fall from the maximum achieved at Q_1.

The area in Figure 5.3 that represents profit is obtained the same way it was obtained in the main body of the chapter. At an output level of Q_1, the total revenue of the firm is price P_2 times the quantity sold Q_1. The total cost is the average cost AC_1 times the quantity produced Q_1. Profit, which is total revenue minus total cost, is the area bounded by P_1P_2ab.

Chapter 6

The Efficiency-Equity Dilemma of Deregulation: The Case of Natural Gas

CHAPTER PREVIEW

Central Question

How can government move to deregulate an industry, like natural gas, in a way that improves economic efficiency and promotes equity?

Major Objectives

1 To explain how the benefits of regulation can be capitalized in an asset that is connected with a regulated product but is not subject to control.

2 To demonstrate how the government, once it decides to control an industry, can get into a "regulatory trap," a trap from which it is difficult for the government to extricate itself without causing inequities.

3 To reveal the trade-offs between efficiency and equity in movements to deregulate an industry.

4 To consider economic proposals for bringing about both efficient and equitable results from deregulation.

Major Points

1 The price of natural gas has been held down below the market clearing price. As a result, a shortage of natural gas has emerged, giving rise to government restrictions on natural gas connections. The benefits of natural gas regulation have been capitalized in the value of homes and businesses with natural gas connections.

2 The meter price of natural gas has been controlled by government, but the effective price, which includes the meter price and hidden charges stemming from higher mortgage payments, has not been controlled. The result: The effective price of heating homes with natural gas has been on par with the price of heating homes with other energy sources.

4 A move to deregulate natural gas will take away benefits of controlled natural gas prices and will cause the market price of homes with natural gas connections to fall. The consequence will be a reduction in the wealth of natural gas homeowners.

5 A move to deregulate the natural gas industry will cause the effective price of natural gas to fall, not rise.

6 A move to deregulate the price of gas can be made efficient and equitable in two ways: (a) by a tax-compensation scheme, and (b) by deregulating several industries at once.

Important New Term and Concept

Capitalization

Elemental but strategic points of economic and legal analysis are commonly obscured by the rhetoric of political debate. And the full complexity of policy issues often lies just beneath the surface of public pronouncements of more or less "obvious" solutions to critical social issues. Such was certainly the case in the historic debate over the deregulation of natural gas that occurred in 1977 and 1978. Very likely, political rhetoric will shroud any future debate over the deregulation of any other industry, such as trucking, airlines, and electric utilities.

At one time, not too many years ago, all the government seemed to be interested in was the regulation (as opposed to deregulation) of various industries. Now, with much experience with government regulation and with a number of studies showing that many regulatory efforts of government have not benefited the general public or accomplished the stated objectives, a number of proposals for deregulation have been made by the Nixon, Ford, and Carter administrations. In Chapter 2, we considered several problems associated with the regulation of industry. In this chapter, we consider the problems the government faces when the deregulation of an industry is contemplated. Specifically, we are concerned here with the regulatory trap, which involves questions of equity as well as efficiency, the government often gets itself into; we are concerned with the political opposition to deregulation. We focus our attention on the deregulation of the natural gas industry simply because it is a reasonably clear example of the regulatory trap of government, and it enables us to draw out points of analysis that are applicable to a wide range of deregulation proposals.

THE ECONOMIC CASE FOR DEREGULATION

Economists are quick to support almost any deregulation movement on "efficiency grounds," as that term is understood in the economic profession. Their argument for deregulation is straightforward: If prices are allowed to move freely in response to the forces of supply and demand, scarce commodities like natural gas can be allocated in the least costly manner to those uses which are most highly valued in a relative sense. Problems of shortages, restricted entry of consumers into the market, and forced production and allocation schemes will be eliminated in deregulated markets. As Robert Helms, a student of natural gas regulation, has written: "The main conclusion of the study on regulation of natural gas is that thirteen years of experience with market regulation in the United States provides an example of an unsuccessful attempt to improve social welfare through price controls. Shortages of natural gas are a direct consequence of these price controls. Deregulation of the field market would reduce this country's future energy costs."[1]

The economic argument of deregulation proponents is decidedly one-sided, so much so that the resistance of the political system to the advocated reforms may not be fully understood or appreciated. Some assume that opposition to deregulation of gas stems almost exclusively from natural gas users who do not wish to see their heating bills raised and from others who mistakenly perceive natural gas supplies as unresponsive to price changes, in which case deregulation means a movement of (unearned) economic profits from consumers to producers.[2]

The public debate over deregulation has failed to grasp important points that reveal the true complexity of deregulation efforts. It has failed to recognize that while gas prices have been regulated, the prices of houses and businesses that have gas connections have not been. Through secondary market adjustments, the perceived benefits of regulation have been capitalized into the market values of these freely salable assets. Since these adjustments have occurred, deregulation reduces to a problem of achieving not only *efficient* results but also *equitable* results.[3]

[1]Robert B. Helms, *Natural Gas Regulation: An Evaluation of FPC Price Controls* (Washington, D.C.: American Enterprise Institute for Public Policy Research, 1974), p. 4.

[2]See ibid., chap. 5, for an example of the way in which the argument is typically developed.

[3]Gordon Tullock has referred to this problem as the "transitionary gains trap" ["The Transitionary Gains Trap," *Bell Journal of Economics* (Autumn 1975), pp. 671–678]. Actually,

The immediate purpose of this chapter is to clarify the conflict between efficiency and equity in deregulating the natural gas industry. However, the case of natural gas should be viewed as a convenient means of broaching a much broader objective: How can social reforms be made that are not only efficient but equitable? If complete equity cannot be achieved, how can we make the consequences of change largely equitable or sufficiently equitable so that efficient changes will be readily accepted and implemented through political process? These questions force us to consider alternatives for social change, their merits and demerits, for a sequence of conceived changes across industries and through time. Hence, this chapter is concerned with presumed need for social change and the problems associated with particular changes, but it is also concerned with the "constitution of social policy change."

In pursuit of these goals, we must be concerned with *capitalization, which is the process by which anticipated future benefits are captured in the price of an asset that is owned and can be traded.* Further, we must explain how and under what circumstances the benefits of regulation can be captured or capitalized in freely traded assets, like houses, that are not subject to control. We can then consider two alternative means of obtaining collective agreement for deregulation; (1) tax-compensation schemes and (2) across-the-board deregulation of a number of industries. (We assume for purposes of argument that the empirical studies that show inefficiency in many regulated industries are essentially correct.[4])

REGULATION OF NATURAL GAS AND CAPITALIZED ENTITLEMENT

Regulation of natural gas prices has the commonly acknowledged effects of eventually restricting current supplies of natural gas and providing homeowners and businesses using natural gas with a subsidy on each unit of gas consumed. The per unit subsidy can be approximated by the difference between the regulated price and the price at which the restricted supply would have cleared the market. These standard conclusions can be illustrated in terms of Figure 6.1. The supply and demand curves in the figure are assumed

---

Tullock and I, quite independently of each other, devised the central thesis of the wealth effects of any regulatory program. Tullock's argument focuses on taxicab regulation and Sunday blue laws, while my original concern was with the wealth effect of many farm subsidy programs. Tullock's presentation, however, is more general in approach and more rigorously developed. As we will see in the discussion that follows, the problem of capitalized entitlements has also been recognized by Vic Goldberg, who is concerned with the general problem of redistribution as articulated by Tullock and George Stigler. See Victor P. Goldberg, "On Positive Theories of Redistribution," *Journal of Economic Issues* (March 1977), pp. 119–132.

[4]For studies that show the growing recognition of the inefficiencies government regulation has engendered, see Paul W. McAvoy (ed.), *The Crisis of the Regulatory Commissions: Introduction to a Current Issue of Public Policy* (New York: W. W. Norton and Company, Inc., 1970); and Almarin Phillips (ed.), *Promoting Competition in Regulated Markets* (Washington, D.C.: The Brookings Institution, 1975).

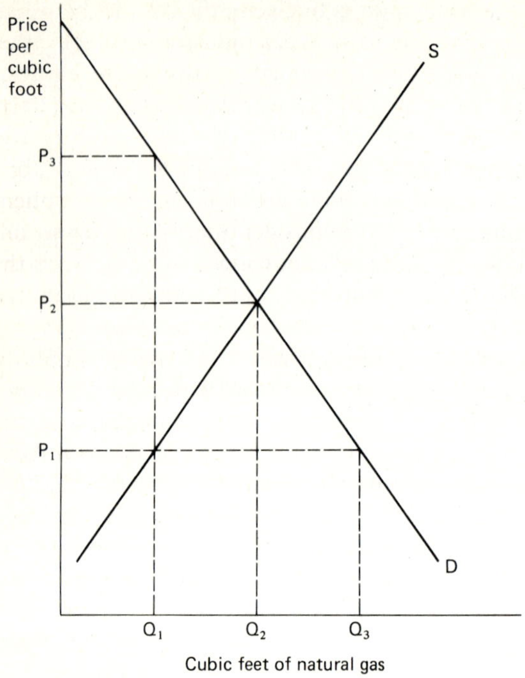

Figure 6.1

to take on their normal shapes; that is, the demand curve is downward-sloping and the supply curve is upward-sloping. In a completely free, unregulated, competitive market, the price of natural gas will be P_2 and the quantity of gas consumed during each time period will be Q_2. However, if the government believes the free market price is too high or exploits consumers and decides to regulate the price at a lower level at P_1, a shortage will (eventually) emerge in the market equal to the distance between Q_1 and Q_3; there will not be enough gas to go around. Eventually, the economic effect of natural gas regulation will be that not all potential gas consumers can be served and/or there will be instances in which homeowners will not get all the gas they need to heat and cool their homes and businesses will not get all the gas they need to continue full operations.

The subsidy to gas users is equal to the difference between the regulated price P_1 and the market clearing price for Q_1 gas, P_3. This subsidy effectively reduces the cost of operating homes and businesses with gas connections. Because of benefits of regulation, the capitalized value of gas-supplied homes and businesses increases. This happens because the operating cost of natural gas facilities will be relatively lower and the market demand for them will be greater. However, the distribution of the capitalized benefits of regulation over time depends upon (1) the state of people's expectations through time, which in turn depends on how much people know about the prospects of regulation, and (2) the extent to which the number of natural gas connections can increase with price (technically referred to as "elasticity of supply").

This latter condition has been considered at length by Buchanan and Tideman in terms of the wealth effects of price controls on gasoline.[5] Their argument is fully transferable (and perhaps more appropriately applied) to our discussion of natural gas controls. Buchanan and Tideman demonstrate that wealth transfers of price controls increase with a decrease in the responsiveness of supply to price. If the supply is totally unresponsive, the benefits of controls will be fully capitalized into some asset that is salable and whose price is not subject to control. Such assets in the case of natural gas are homes and businesses with natural gas connections.

Although it has not always been the case, the supply of natural gas *connections*, as opposed to the gas itself, has, for several years, been fixed in many parts of the country. New connections have simply been prohibited by government regulators. The prohibition of new gas hookups was instituted because the regulated price has been held below the market clearing price. The current supply of natural gas to many areas has been restricted by the lack of incentive that firms have had to explore for new reserves, and because gas producers, anticipating deregulation, have in recent years withheld a portion of their known reserves from the market and have been enticed to sell in nonregulated intrastate markets such as Texas. The prohibition on new hookups has been a means of disguising the shortage of natural gas at the ceiling price and of attempting to ensure that those homes and businesses with connections will have adequate supplies.

Admittedly, the Federal Power Commission (FPC) has not fully succeeded in keeping homes and businesses with gas connections adequately supplied. During the unusually cold winters of 1976, 1977, and 1978, there were major interruptions in supplies to gas users, and many businesses and schools had to close down for a short time. These shortages were a consequence of the unexpected severe weather and the long-term growth in demand for gas by those with connections. However, regardless of the imperfect results of regulation, the important point for our purposes is that the FPC tried to eliminate or reduce the revealed shortages among gas users and was dedicated to that end. The result was a fixed supply of gas connections, which provided the basis for full capitalization of benefits of the regulated price in homes and businesses.[6]

[5]James M. Buchanan and T. Nicolaus Tideman, "Gasoline Rationing and Market Pricing: Public Choice in Political Economy," *Atlantic Economic Journal* (November 1974), pp. 15–26.

[6]The benefits of the regulated prices may have been partially capitalized prior to the prohibition on new connections. The complete prohibition just made the capitalization process complete.

THE MARKET FOR RIGHTS AND EXPECTATIONS

Rights (or entitlements) are fundamentally bundles of expectations as to what can be done with "things." These expectations will depend in part upon the information people have concerning the course of future events, including such events as the regulation or deregulation of commodity prices. If regulation has been anticipated in previous time periods, the capitalized value of regulation may not be received by the owners of gas connections at the time of effective regulation. To the extent that regulation is anticipated, the prices of facilities with gas connections will be bid up prior to the act of effective regulation, not at the time of regulation. It may therefore be said that persons with gas connections at the time of regulation are not the sole beneficiaries of regulation: they have already "paid out" a portion of the benefits to prior owners of gas connections. (Indeed, under conditions in which regulation is anticipated but never enacted, owners of gas connections will suffer a capital loss due to market adjustment to change in expectations.[7])

Victor Goldberg has made the interesting observation that in a world of perfect information and fully rational people there can never be redistribution of wealth (from that which was originally established in some prior millennium) due to change in, for example, government policy.[8] The value of change will always be fully and accurately anticipated and capitalized into the value of the entitlements that were the subject of the initial distribution. In a world of perfect ignorance, where there is, in effect, no basis for evaluating change before the fact, the opposite is true: all changes have redistributional effects; no change can be anticipated and incorporated into the capitalized value of entitlements.

There are two reasons for highlighting the extreme conditions of perfect information and ignorance. First, in real world markets in which there is always partial ignorance, the wealth effect of change is partially capitalized prior to change and partially capitalized (that portion which is unanticipated) at the time of change; there are, in other words, partial redistributional effects from changes in government policy. The focus of this chapter is on the wealth effect at time of change; we may discuss this dimension as if capitalization is fully completed at the time of change, to simplify the discussion, but we must recognize that capitalization is not always completed at the time of change.

Second, much regulatory power is intended to help one group at the expense of another because of the dictates of perceived social values or goals. If this kind of regulation is to have the intended redistribution effect,

[7] I do not mean to suggest here that people whose property value depreciates because of changes in expectations are necessarily worse off. They may feel that buying property in anticipation of regulation was worth a gamble, even though the gamble did not actually pay off. A series of such gambles can, in net, make buyers better off, even if it can be shown that they are poorer for taking losses on individual gambles.

[8] Goldberg, "On Positive Theories of Redistribution."

it must be predicated upon some user's ignorance or other market imperfections or upon the capability of the reform proponents to foster the necessary ignorance, misinformation, or misconception that makes real redistribution possible. Assuming that law is intended to increase the accuracy of expectations, this requirement means that proponents of redistribution must have the capacity to either work outside established laws, whether formal or informal, or create new laws that cannot be fully anticipated from the established procedures (which have the characteristics of law or are themselves laws) for making new law.

Three points, although they are somewhat aside from the main argument, are worth noting for purposes of rounding out the discussion. First, regulation does not necessarily begin at the same time that the regulatory agency is given the power to regulate. In the case of natural gas, the FPC effectively used its newly acquired regulatory powers only after it was forced to do so by the courts. Second, shortages do not necessarily emerge immediately after the price is restricted by regulation. When producers are convinced that the price is fixed and there is no reasonable possibility that it will rise in the near or intermediate future, they have less incentive to hold to their known reserves. When there is no price restriction, producers will hold onto a larger portion of their reserves in anticipation of future price rises; and they are consequently compensated for the interest forgone on any sales revenue that could have been earned. So, we should expect regulated prices to lead at first to greater, not lower, supplies of a product like natural gas. This response on the part of producers will mislead the public as to the ultimate consequences of regulation.[9] The effect of government policy change, that is, regulation, is to increase the level of ignorance.

Third, there is the common presumption in discussions of regulation of this or that industry that regulation keeps the price down below what it would otherwise be. Therefore, *de*regulation will mean a price increase. This may be true for the meter price of gas; however, it does not follow that the *effective* price—that is, the meter price plus the price paid in hidden charges—of the product is held down. In the case of the freeze on gasoline prices during the Arab oil boycott several years ago, the effective price of gasoline went up, although the pump price per gallon was held down. Because people had to waste time in line waiting for their allotted number of gallons, there was a hidden charge on each gallon purchased. Similarly, the increase in the price of gas-heated and gas-cooled homes has imposed a

[9]Increased supplies of natural gas at the start of effective regulation will make the shortage worse at some future date. However, one can argue that regulation is, through its effect on the intertemporal flow of gas supplies, a means of redistributing wealth in the form of the natural gas stock from future generations to present generations. Dwight Lee has developed empirical evidence that shows that effective regulations do immediately increase the supplies of the regulated product. Dwight R. Lee, "Price Controls, Binding Constraints, and Intertemporal Economic Decision Making," *Journal of Political Economy*, 86 (April 1978) pp. 293–301.

hidden addition to the effective price of natural gas. The person who buys a home at a price inflated by the advantage of regulated gas prices realizes the hidden charge in the form of larger mortgage and interest costs on his or her home. The original homeowner, who may not have purchased the home at the inflated price, may not feel the hidden charge, but his or her equity in the home rises nonetheless. By holding onto the home, this individual forgoes the opportunity to invest his or her greater home equity in interest-bearing assets.

Fourth, it should be noted that the effective price of natural gas, which includes both the meter and hidden charges, will tend to be greater than the market price of natural gas in the absence of regulation. Without regulation, the current supply of natural gas will be greater because producers have the incentive to explore and make available the reserves. The selling price in the absence of regulation will be higher than the regulated meter price; on the other hand, the greater supply will mean that consumers will be further down their demand curve for natural gas. The new *meter price* of natural gas will be lower than the old *effective price*. Seen this way, the attention given to the impact of deregulation on the meter price, as opposed to the effective price, has caused both opponents and proponents to miss altogether the reason for users' opposition to deregulation. The effective price paid by gas users will, because of deregulation, go down, not up. This is just another way of bringing to light a point to which we can now turn: the capitalization problem associated with regulation and the wealth transfer that will inevitably result from deregulation.

THE DEREGULATION OF NATURAL GAS AND CAPITALIZED ENTITLEMENTS

On average, Americans move once every 5 years. We will assume for purposes of discussion that these moves are evenly distributed among homeowners who have gas connections and those who use other energy sources. In this case, about 20 percent of the homes utilizing natural gas turn over each year. In short, a substantial percentage of natural gas homes and businesses have been sold and resold over the past several years. A significant portion of the people who now own natural gas homes and businesses did not own them when effective regulation began. These people paid inflated prices for their homes on the assumption that the below-market meter price would continue. Because of their greater home investment, they have been, perhaps, only marginally better off than they would have been if they had bought, for example, oil-heated homes. Indeed, many who at one time owned homes with gas connections were no doubt induced to sell their homes in part because they expected they could sell their gas homes at inflated prices, use their greater equity to reduce the mortgage payment of, say, oil-heated homes, and use that differential to pay for higher-priced oil.

Much of the political and ethical opposition to deregulation of natural gas is now apparent. When natural gas prices are deregulated, the meter price will rise. The effective subsidy given gas homes and businesses will evaporate or be substantially reduced, and the demand for natural gas homes will fall, along with their resale values. The *effective* price of natural gas will fall. By way of these market forces, natural gas companies will receive a wealth transfer from the present owners of homes using natural gas, many of whom bought their homes at prices distorted by past government policies. The wealth increase of gas companies will be reflected in the present value of their higher income stream and in the higher value of gas company stock.

Those who lose wealth because of deregulation will include more than just gas users. An increase in gas supplies due to deregulation and the opening up of the gas market to new connections will lead to an increase in the number of gas homes and businesses that can be purchased. The demand for oil and electric homes and businesses will fall, along with their resale values. These owners will also experience a wealth loss and should join the forces opposing deregulation. On the basis of size alone, the group of people who are harmed directly or indirectly from deregulation can present formidable political opposition to the best efforts of the Federal Power Commission and the gas companies that seek deregulation. Furthermore, this group can be expected to oppose deregulation with the moral fervor of anyone who has been harmed—as this group has been—by deliberate government action. Theft may be defined as the act of taking "without right or permission, generally in a surreptitious way" or the act of getting or effecting "secretly or artfully."[10] Deregulation has many of the same characteristics as theft. If prospects of deregulation were to be fully disclosed, the market would be able to adjust to those prospects and there would not be a wealth transfer problem: there would not be such opposition to deregulation. The prices that people have paid for gas homes and businesses will be reflected only in the present discounted benefits of the period during which regulation was expected to be effective.

As in the case of regulation, the distribution of the wealth loss from deregulation over time depends upon the state of expectation and the availability of information on which those expectations are formed. All that is really required for wealth transfers to occur is that the market perceives that deregulation will occur. The prospects of deregulation will cause buyers and businesses to temper the demands for facilities with gas connections. Furthermore, gas suppliers, anticipating deregulation, will withhold a portion of their reserves for the purpose of receiving relatively higher profits in the future. These actions will aggravate any existing shortage of fuel and tend to make deregulation all the more certain. Such actions will also make

[10] *American Heritage Dictionary of the English Language* (Boston: Houghton Mifflin Company, 1972).

deregulation more palatable to gas users. The gas shortages will decrease the market value of gas homes and businesses and, along with that, the effective price of natural gas.

Many gas users will have already incurred the capital loss by the time the political decision on natural gas is made; others will have bought their homes and businesses in anticipation of deregulation. Still others will have to weigh the benefits of continued regulation against the threat of continual supply interruptions, which may then be seen as a real possibility. After supply interruptions like those which occurred in the winters of 1977 and 1978, it is understandable why the main opposition to deregulation is likely to come from those who want to reacquire the benefits of regulation by encouraging Congress to shy away from the deregulation movement. However, it is also understandable why this group wants to couple a revitalized regulatory authority with mandatory allocation schemes that will ensure that the homes and businesses with gas connections will have adequate supplies.

THE EFFICIENCY-EQUITY DILEMMA

Deregulation of the natural gas industry or, for that matter, almost any other industry, poses a real dilemma for government policy makers. On the one hand, continued *regulation* of natural gas means higher effective prices for gas customers, a continued misallocation of resources, a prohibition against new gas connections, and a continuation of a national income level that is lower than it otherwise would be. On the other hand, *deregulation* can mean a capital loss for many gas users. As we have stressed, many of these owners bought their gas homes and businesses at inflated market values on the presumption, which was deliberately fostered by government policy, that the price of natural gas will be held down below market clearing levels. Perhaps these owners should know better. Perhaps the government should not mislead them into believing that regulation of natural gas is a fixed, long-term policy course. Indeed, if the government were a private company, it seems likely that in the event that it deregulated gas, it could be sued for violating its own laws against misleading advertising. However, in spite of the "perhaps's" and "if's," the dilemma remains a fact of social politics that cannot be summarily set aside by politicians who are concerned with equity as well as efficiency and who wish to be elected or reelected.

What can be done to get out of the dilemma? Unfortunately, economists do not have a store of practical solutions. There are, however, two possible policy courses that we can discuss here: (1) compensatory payments to those harmed by deregulation, and (2) a broad-based deregulation program that will subject several industries at once to the forces of competitive markets.

Compensatory Payments

The policy remedy most often advocated by economists is tax-compensation arrangements. Clearly, a movement away from a regulated gas industry to a deregulated one will generate benefits that will be reflected in a larger real national income. The problem of deregulation concerns the distributional effects, not the aggregate effects. The government can counter the adverse distributional effects by taxing those who gain from deregulation—for instance, the natural gas producers—and using the revenue collected to compensate the owners of homes and businesses who are harmed. Those who are taxed, so the argument goes, may not like their greater tax payments; however, they may recognize that deregulation has little chance of passage without higher taxes. So long as the increase in their taxes is less than the higher profits they may make because of deregulation, they gain by agreeing to higher taxes. So long as the affected homeowners and business owners are compensated for their wealth loss, they are no worse off from a move to a deregulated gas industry. So long as no one is made worse off but someone is made better off, the tax-compensation scheme can lead to an unequivocal welfare improvement.

This solution, however, is not as practical as it first appears. There is in it the inherent difficulty of determining who is harmed and who is benefited and how much each must be compensated or taxed. The difficulty of determining the distribution will be enormously complicated by the sheer number of people involved, since owners of electric as well as gas homes will suffer a wealth loss from deregulation. Further complicating the distribution is the fact that present owners of natural gas (and electric) homes made their investments under various degrees of uncertainty over whether or not gas would be deregulated.

In summary, questions that are raised by any tax-compensation proposal are numerous, perhaps too numerous to make tax compensation an even approximately equitable or efficient solution. How much do we compensate current homeowners who made their purchases in different locations of the country, under different expectations about government and nongovernment changes in market forces, and under different estimations of the probability that gas will be deregulated? How much do we compensate people who, for example, bought their homes in 1968 when continued long-term regulation was a reasonable expectation and sold their homes in 1976 when deregulation was at least contemplated?

Moreover, if the compensation is restricted to those people who bought their homes and businesses at inflated prices after regulation and before deregulation, the homeowners who had their homes when effective regulation began will have an incentive to sell their homes to capture the wealth effects of the announced intentions of government to compensate homeowners for the damages of deregulation. Similar problems exist in trying to determine the distribution of the tax burden. Do we tax just the gas companies or the stockholders? If we tax the incomes of companies, then problems of equity are not entirely avoided. Many current stockholders in gas companies bought their shares expecting that gas would soon be deregulated and the prices they paid were inflated for that reason. If the incomes of companies are taxed, then the after-tax income of gas companies will fall and stockholders will suffer a wealth loss similar to the wealth loss of the homeowners. Do we then tax previous stockholders who have sold their shares at inflated prices? Do we tax the incomes of future generations who will gain from the deregulation of natural gas? If we agree that we should, then how do we do it?

Needless to say, a tax-compensation scheme in any form will be extremely complex, so much so that complete equity is not likely to be even closely achieved. Tax-compensation schemes devised for a series of deregulation proposals taken over time are likely to require a significant quantity of government resources just to administer the schemes. If such schemes are considered seriously at all, politicians may proffer a tax-compensation scheme that will only be sufficiently broad for its proponents to secure the needed votes to pass a deregulation proposal. Political influence is, thereby, likely to influence the structure of the taxes levied and the compensation payments made.

Broad-Based Regulatory Reform

If the government does not find the tax-compensation schemes very attractive, it may consider deregulating several industries, including natural gas, at once, or at approximately the same time. There are a number of industries that economists have identified as securing the benefits of protective regulation; that is, these industries are being protected from competitive forces by government regulators who set monopoly prices, divide the market, and restrict entry into their markets. Trucking, agriculture, insurance, aviation, banking, and broadcasting are notable examples. In all these markets, regulation has created market inefficiencies. With respect to all these industries, the government has been caught in a transitional gains trap in much the same way that it has with regard to natural gas. If each is deregulated independent of deregulation of all other protected industries, problems of wealth transfers and of solving the efficiency-equity dilemma will emerge, and political opposition to isolated deregulation can be expected.

What can be done to make deregulation of industries workable? If all regulated industries, including natural gas, are deregulated at one time, there will be wealth transfers, but some will be offsetting. The losers from the deregulation of natural gas will be compensated in part for their losses by the gains generated from the deregulation of, say, the trucking and agriculture industries. Similarly, the losers from the deregulation of trucking can be partially compensated for their losses by the deregulation of natural gas and aviation. In short, this proposal, in order to make deregulation palatable and politically acceptable, should be viewed as a move to reconstitute social and economic policy: it is a proposal to move to a constitutional setting in which the give-and-take of political bargains can guide social and economic policy across otherwise isolated events. Taken independently, each instance of deregulation can be viewed as efficient but largely inequitable; taken collectively, they can be not only efficient but, perhaps, quasi-equitable and politically acceptable.

The proposal for across-the-board deregulation is, of course, not without its deficiencies. It will not produce complete equity; few policies can hope to do so. Many will question whether social welfare after broad-based deregulation is higher or lower than before. There will be people who, on balance, will be caught up in political bargaining. Representatives of various interest groups will attempt to acquire special favors for their consent to deregulation, increasing the cost of developing reform. By the same token, the political bargaining that is likely to emerge makes across-the-board deregulation a plausible proposal. Explicit vote trading can occur and a package of reforms that may all fail if considered independently of one another may pass. The participants in this reform movement do not have to incur the risk or fear that the political climate will change during the time that isolated reform proposals are considered. Furthermore, the total effects of a broad-based institutional change can then be evaluated, and this would be hard to do if the parts of the total reform movement were taken up at different points in time.[11]

CONCLUDING COMMENTS

The capitalization approach to the study of deregulation is instructive mainly because it reveals the true complexity of bringing about reform in government policy. Furthermore, the approach illustrates the distributional effects that changes in policy can have and, therefore, forces the reform's proponents and opponents alike to consider the questions of equity and to devise ways of bringing about change that is equitable as well as efficient. This chapter has dealt with two alternative means of achieving equitable social reform: tax-compensation schemes and broad-based regulatory reform.

As has been suggested, the analysis we have developed in this chapter is applicable to a wide range of regulated industries that many economists would like to see deregulated, returned to private-market status. These industries include trucking, airlines, agriculture, insurance, banking, and drugs, among others. The benefits of regulation of the trucking industry

[11]Still, if politicians meet to devise a broad-based deregulation proposal, we cannot be sure that the participants will agree on a deregulation proposal. As I have argued elsewhere, the participants, although ostensibly interested in deregulation, may agree on more regulation in a constitutional setting. The outcome of such a meeting depends on, among other factors, the makeup of the meeting (i.e., what industries and interest groups are represented) and the pervasiveness of the regulation at the time of the meeting. See Richard B. McKenzie, *A Contractarian Perspective on the Deregulation Movement*, Working Paper Series (Clemson, S.C.: Department of Economics, Clemson University, 1978).

have, to one extent or another, been capitalized in the value of the trucks and truck terminals that have been erected over the decades. The benefits of government regulation of the agriculture industry have been capitalized in the value of land and equipment farmers have purchased assuming that the regulation (which has come in the form of price support systems and acreage allotment programs) will continue into the future. The benefits of regulation of the banking industry have been capitalized in the many branches that banks have constructed in order to attract deposits.

If trucking, for example, is deregulated, many truck terminals that were erected to accommodate the regulated route patterns will lose much of their economic value. The government will be caught in a regulatory trap, having to cope with the problem of making the trucking industry more efficient through the introduction of competition and at the same time having to deal with the political problems of equity that deregulation creates.

One overriding conclusion should be drawn from all that has been said: It may be far easier for the government to start something, like the regulation of an industry, than to stop it. The government should, therefore, be very careful in choosing any course of action to bring about social improvements. It may actually find that it does not really help the intended persons, and it may find termination of the program politically difficult, if not impossible, because of equity considerations that influence a great many votes.

QUESTIONS TO PONDER

1 If the price of natural gas is held down below its market clearing price, what will happen to the prices of fuel oil and electricity? Explain with the use of supply and demand curves. Will the effective prices of heating homes with gas, oil, and electricity be the same in spite of government regulation? Explain why there might be differences in the prices of different energy sources.

2 In order to operate a taxi in many cities, the owners of a cab must have a medallion that gives them the right to operate the cab. The number of medallions is restricted by government. In spite of the government regulation, which holds the price of cab fares above the market clearing price, cab owners typically complain that they earn only a "competitive rate of return." Drawing on the analysis of this chapter, explain why the rate of return in a taxi industry might approximate the competitive rate of return, that rate which would be received in the absence of government regulation.

3 For decades, the government has controlled the production of tobacco by restricting the total number of acres on which tobacco can be grown and has allotted a limited number of acres to each farmer. What effect will such a program have on the market value of farms with acreage allotments? Who benefits from such a program? Who would benefit and who would lose from the deregulation of the tobacco industry? How can we avoid problems of equity in the deregulation of tobacco?

ADDITIONAL READING

Helms, Robert B. *Natural Gas Regulation: An Evaluation of FPC Price Controls.* Washington, D.C.: American Enterprise Institute for Public Policy Research, 1974.

Phillips, Almarin (ed.). *Promoting Competition in Regulated Markets.* Washington, D.C.: The Brookings Institution, 1975.

Tullock, Gordon. "The Transitionary Gains Trap," *Bell Journal of Economics,* Autumn 1975, pp. 671–678.

CHAPTER 7

Restrictions on Business Mobility: Empirical Issues

CHAPTER PREVIEW

Central Question

What is the case for restrictions on business movements from one part of the country to another and how can that case be evaluated?

Major Objective

To develop and evaluate the case for restrictions on business movements.

Major Points

1 National and state legislation seeks to restrict business movements in several major ways: (a) by requiring firms to give a 2-year notice of intentions to move, (b) by giving the Secretary of Labor the authority to determine whether business moves are "without adequate justification," (c) by taking from firms important tax benefits if they move without giving adequate notice or if they move without government approval, and (d) by requiring firms to make payments to the employees and communities that they leave behind when they move.

2 The populations of all regions of the country have grown over the last several decades, but they have grown at decreasing rates. The population growth rates of the South and West have declined less than the population growth rates of Northern Industrial Tier states. Nonetheless, changes in regional population growth rates are, in only a relatively minor way, related to business movements.

3 Population shifts from the North to the South can be a consequence of economic gains in the North and can further improve the economic positions of Northern states.

4 If restrictions on business mobility are designed to improve the relative economic positions of Northern states, they will have the opposite effect: they will retard the economic development of those states.

5 In spite of claims to the contrary, incomes in the North have continued to rise. However, the incomes of Northern residents have fallen significantly relative to the incomes of residents of Southern states. The improvements in incomes of Southerners, which may have partially resulted from business movements south, have contributed to improvements in the standards of living of Northerners.

6 People in the North tend to pay more to the federal government than they receive in the form of federal government expenditures; the opposite tends to be true in the South. However, the discrepancies in taxes paid by residents in different regions are partially a reflection of regional income differences and the progressive tax system employed by the federal government. Differences in federal tax collections and expenditures by regions may be stimulating some business movements. The problem should, perhaps, be corrected by changes in tax and expenditure policies, but not by additional controls on business movements.

7 The overwhelming majority of job losses in the North are due to deaths and contractions of firms in the North, not business movements.

8 The reasons businesses move south can be summarized as (1) lower wages in the South, (b) the absence of unions in the South, and (c) lower taxes in the South.

Representative William Ford of Michigan, with eighteen cosponsors, has introduced in Congress a little-known bill called the "National Employment Priorities Act of 1977."[1] If enacted, the bill will bring about a dramatic and far-reaching shift in domestic economic policy and will increase substantially supervision of business decisions by the federal government.

[1]U.S. Congress, House, *National Employment Priorities Act of 1977*, H.R. 76.

DESCRIPTION OF THE NATIONAL EMPLOYMENT PRIORITIES ACT OF 1977

The general purpose of the legislation, which has not yet emerged from committee, is to remedy what Representative Ford calls the "runaway plant phenomena."[2] To accomplish this end, the bill proposes to establish within the Department of Labor a "National Employment Relocation Administration." Its purpose will be to "conduct . . . investigations and issue reports on *any* proposed closing or transfer of operations of . . . a business with 50 or more employees" and "to determine the extent of the employment loss on the individuals and communities involved, whether such closing or transfer is *without adequate justification*" (emphasis added).[3] Under the act, the Secretary of Labor, with the assistance of the National Employment Relocation Advisory Council,[4] will be empowered to provide financial and technical assistance (1) to employees who lose their jobs because of business closings and transfers, (2) to communities that suffer because of plant relocation, and (3) to businesses that plan to close or move but may be able to stay in their present locations if assistance is made available.[5]

Furthermore, the National Employment Priorities Act requires that a business give a 2-year notice of its intention to move or close.[6] The bill effectively requires businesses with 50 or more employees to petition the federal government for the *right* to move and hands over to the federal government and the Council members the *right* to define what constitutes "adequate justification" for business movements and closings. Finally, if a business move is deemed "unjustified" by the Secretary of Labor, the business will be denied important tax benefits: the investment tax credit, accelerated depreciation allowances, the foreign tax credit, deferral of tax

[2]U.S. Congress, House, *Congressional Record*, 94th Cong., 1st Sess. (June 10, 1974), p. 18559.

[3]U.S. Congress, House, *National Employment Priorities Act of 1977*, p. 6.

[4]The National Employment Relocation Advisory Council is given the authority to make whatever studies it needs to evaluate proposed business closings and transfers and the effectiveness of the Council's decisions.

[5]Government assistance to employees is expected to take various forms, including cash payments, maintenance of health and pension benefits, relocation allowances, rental and mortgage supplements, retraining assistance, early retirement payments, food stamps, and distribution of surplus commodities. The cash payment for income maintenance must be the lesser of the moderate living standard budget established by the Bureau of Labor Statistics or 85 percent of the employee's prior average weekly wage. Community assistance will be made in the form of federal grants to make up for as much as 85 percent of any loss in tax revenues due to plant closings and relocations and in the form of loans "to the communities or to private enterprises for the purpose of expanding existing job opportunities." The bill proposes that assistance to business be given in the form of technical advice, loans, and loan guarantees, but only "if the Administrator determines that such assistance will prevent or alleviate the potential employment loss from such closing or transfer." U.S. Congress, House, *National Employment Priorities Act of 1977*, pp. 6–7 and 20–23.

[6]Ibid., pp. 14–20.

on income earned outside the United States, and deductions from taxable income of any expenses incurred in the move to the new location.[7]

A bill pending before the 1978 session of the Ohio Legislature goes one step further. It requires businesses that move to pay employees left behind severance pay equal to 1 week's pay for each year of service and to pay the community it leaves an amount equal to 10 percent of the gross annual wages of the affected employees.

The purpose of this and the following chapter is to evaluate the argument for legislation such as the National Employment Priorities Act. In this chapter, the contentions of the supporters of the legislation are set in contrast with data on the magnitudes of recent population and business shifts among regions and magnitudes of recent changes in regional income.

THE ARGUMENT FOR THE LEGISLATION IN BRIEF

In describing the changing regional structure of the United States economy, a leading business magazine has written that "the second war between the states will take the form of political and economic maneuver. But the conflict can nonetheless be bitter and devisive because it will be a struggle for income, jobs, people, and capital."[8] In introducing the National Employment Priorities Act, Representative Ford has given us a reasonably clear indication of the way in which the political battle lines will be drawn, the economic basis for them, and the character of the ensuing debate:

> The legislation is based on the premise that such closings and transfers may cause irreparable harm—both economic and social—to workers, communities, and the Nation. . . . My own congressional district suffered the effects of the runaway plant in 1972 when the Garwood plant in Wayne moved and left 600 unemployed workers behind. . . . Mr. Speaker, the reason these firms are moving away is not economic necessity but economic greed. For instance, the Federal Modgul Co. in Detroit signed a contract in 1971 with the United Auto Workers and 6 months later announced it would be moving to Alabama. A spokesman for the company was quoted as saying they were moving "not because we are not making money in Detroit, but because we can make more money in Alabama."[9]

Mr. Ford goes on to cite several other examples of the economic effects of business relocation decisions, including the "catastrophic problems" Hawaii has experienced because of the "runaway pineapple industry," and

[7]Ibid., pp. 33–34.

[8]"The Second War between the States," *Business Week* (May 17, 1976), p. 92.

[9]U.S. Congress, House, *Congressional Record*, 94th Cong., 1st Sess. (June 10, 1974), p. 18559.

he concludes that "these are the types of problems which can be found in nearly every state in the country.[10]

THE CASE FOR RELOCATION RULES: THE SNOWBELT VERSUS THE SUNBELT

The campaign for the governmental restriction of business mobility has been initiated with all the rhetoric of war. Phrases like "second war between the states," "counterattacks," and "fierce and ruinous state warfare" pepper the popular accounts of changes in the regional structure of the United States economy. The rhetoric is useful to proponents of relocation rules and to news reporters because it grabs the reader's attention, makes economic conditions in regions that are declining in a *relative* sense appear desperate in an absolute sense, and encourages the view that drastic political action is not only desirable but unavoidable. Here, the case for relocation rules is presented on an issue-by-issue basis. The rhetoric of the case will be set in contrast with the facts of regional change.

The following analysis will for the most part employ the regions and subdivisions of the country as described in Figure 7.1. However, because so much of the debate on relocation rules and regional adjustments is couched in terms of the "North" versus the "South" or the "Snowbelt North" versus the "Sunbelt South," the focus of attention will be on the Northern Industrial Tier, made up of the states in the Northeast region and the East North Central regions, and the South, composed of the South Atlantic, East South Central, and West South Central states.

Population Shifts

Advocates of relocation restrictions point to relative population growth rates as barometers of the economic health of different regions, as symptoms of the underlying causes of business migration, and as indicators of the consequences of unrestrained business movements. From news accounts of regional adjustments, one is likely to get the impression that a decline in population *rates* should be construed as a decline in population *levels* and that something is fundamentally wrong with economic and political institutions when population growth rates among regions differ.

In its account of "The Second War between the States," *Business Week* writes: "As long as the migration of industry and population was gradual from what was a relatively rich Northeast to what was a relatively impoverished South and Southwest, it [migration] helped to unify the country. But within the last five years the process has burst beyond the bounds that can be accommodated by existing political institutions."[11] The point is made

[10]Ibid., p. 18560.
[11]"The Second War between the States," *Business Week* (May 17, 1976), p. 92.

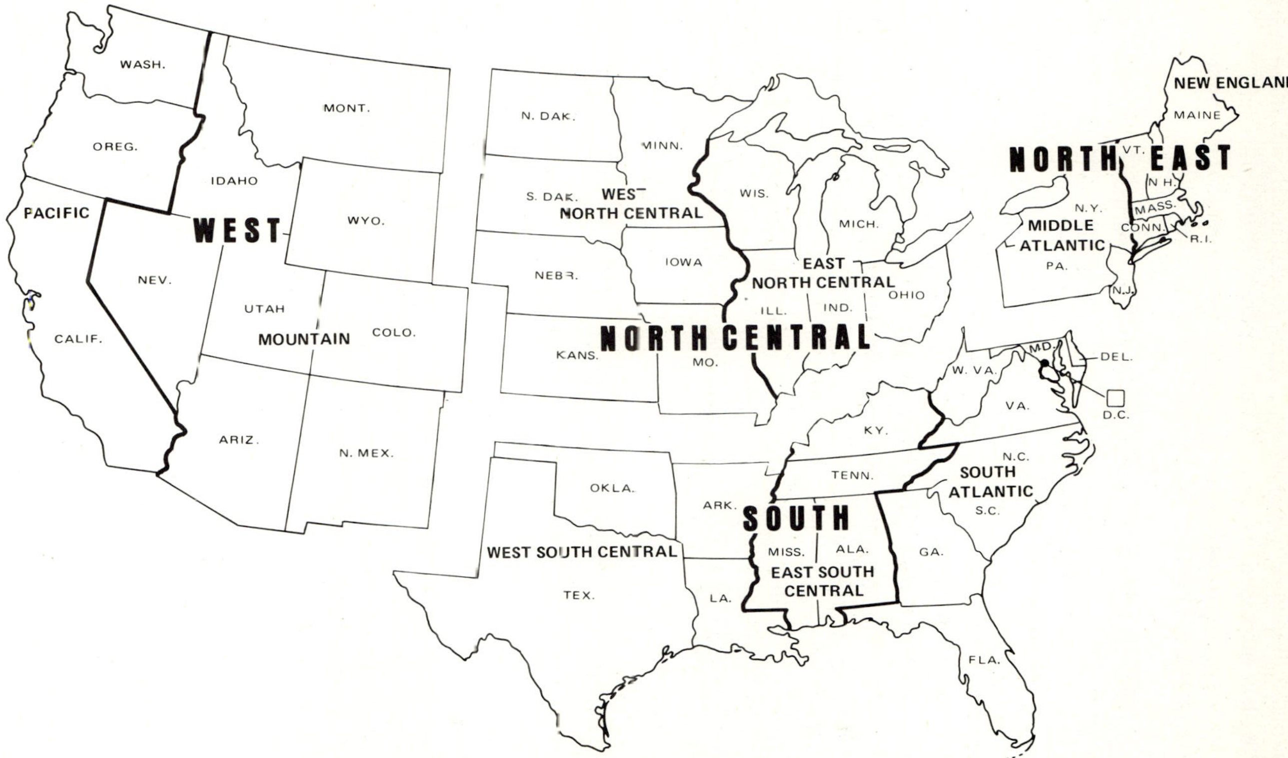

Note: Pacific division includes Alaska and Hawaii.

Figure 7.1 Regions and divisions of the United States.

that New York lost more than 100,000 people when it was expected to gain more than a million and "Pennsylvania, slated to gain nearly 800,000 during the 1970s, has increased its population by barely 30,000 thus far."[12] The publication goes on to suggest that the population growth of the South and Southwest has been "meteoric" because of immigration of people from the Northeast.

In evaluating arguments concerning regional changes in population, we must keep several points in mind. First, the population growth rates of all regions—North, West, and South—declined significantly between the 1950s and 1970s, but the total populations of all regions have increased; some have just increased faster than others. Figure 7.2 reveals this basic fact.[13] Second, the decline in the population growth rate of the North can be only partially explained by migration of people out of the region. According to data, the decrease in the population growth rate of the North has been due as much to natural factors as to migration. Such factors as the increase in contraceptive use and abortions and the trend toward smaller families, reflecting changes in social values, have had as great a role, if not a greater one, in the decrease in Northern population growth.

Second, many migrants from the North are moving out for reasons, such as retirement, that are unrelated to business moves. Third, many people who have moved south have done so to take advantage of job opportunities in new and expanding Southern firms, not firms that have moved south. Fourth, many people who have moved south are returning home from earlier moves north. In short, one must be very cautious in assuming that population growth rate differences have been largely determined by business relocations.

In making the case for the National Employment Priorities Act, the proponents have attempted to garner political support within their region by making the issue one of "us" against "them," much as the case of tariffs is made on the basis of domestic jobs versus foreign jobs. However, one very elementary point must be kept in mind: the division of the country into geographical regions, like those drawn in Figure 7.1, is largely artificial. Such divisions have no economic meaning to a business interested in maximizing profits or to a person who seeks to find the most suitable living place, given his or her preferences. Simply because distance influences the cost of moves and the cost of moves determines how many people move and how far they move, more migration occurs within a region than among regions. This is especially true when accents, relatives, and customs affect the willingness

[12]Ibid.

[13]For more details on all statistical points made in this chapter, see Richard B. McKenzie, *Restrictions on Business Mobility: A Study in Political and Economic Reality* (Washington, D.C.: American Enterprise Institute for Public Policy Research, 1970), chap. 2; and U.S. Bureau of the Census, *Current Population Reports*, ser. P-20, no. 324 (April 1978), "Population Profile of the United States: 1977," table 17.

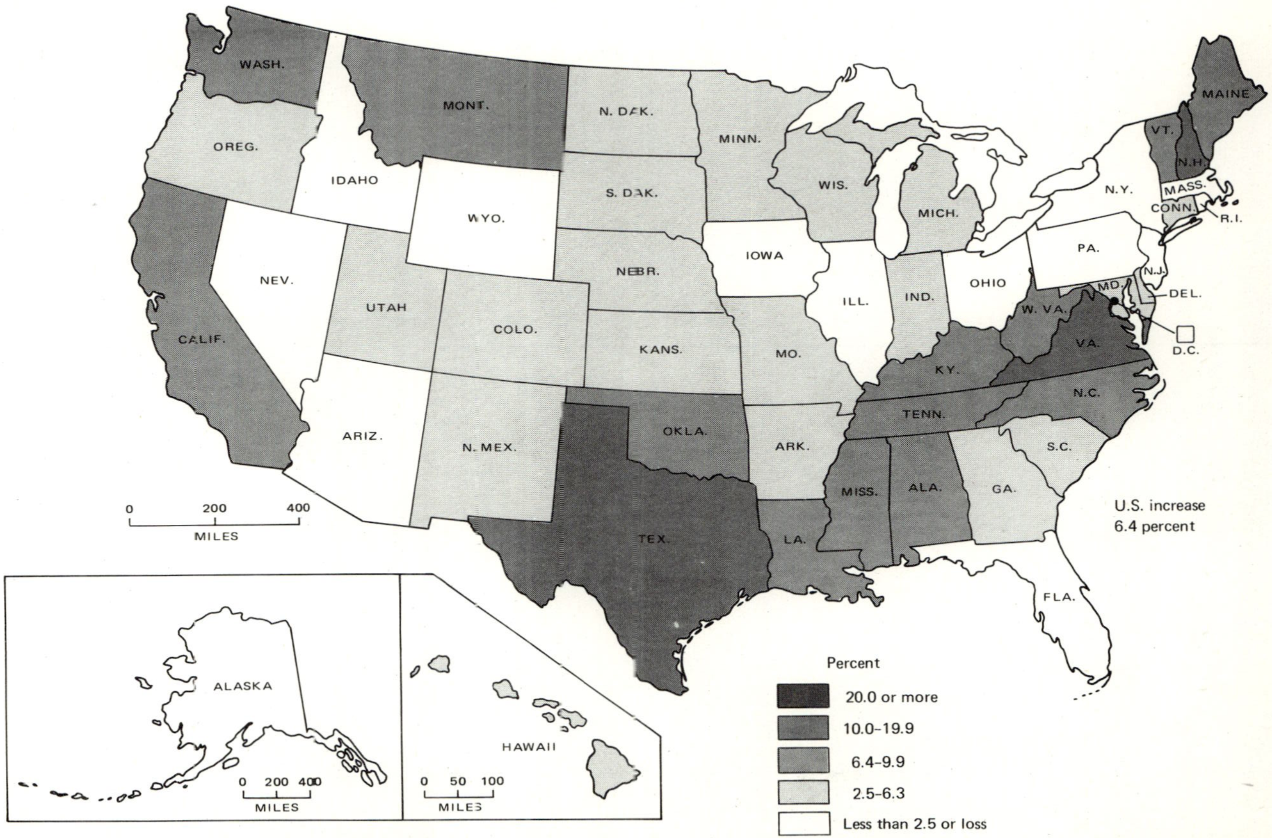

Figure 7.2 Percent change in population by state, 1970 to 1977 [Source: *U.S. Bureau of the Census, Current Population Reports, ser. P-20, no. 234 (April 1978), "Population Profile of the United States: 1977," p. 30 and table 21.*]

Table 7.1 Mobility Status between March 1975 and March 1977 for Persons 2 Years Old and Over, by Region of Residence in 1977
(In thousands)

	Residence in 1977				
	United States	**Northeast**	**North Central**	**South**	**West**
Population 2 years old and over	206,419	47,329	55,611	66,256	37,224
Same house	149,789	37,862	41,262	46,939	23,727
Different house in United States	54,620	9,087	13,927	18,771	12,835
Same county	33,258	5,531	8,797	10,985	7,945
Different county	21,362	3,556	5,131	7,786	4,889
Same state	11,417	2,292	3,014	3,393	2,217
Different state	9,946	1,263	2,117	3,893	2,672
Northeast	1,878	595	249	699	335
North Central	2,479	181	921	762	615
South	3,431	329	581	1,961	560
West	2,157	158	367	471	1,162
Abroad	2,010	380	422	546	662

Source: U.S. Bureau of the Census, *Current Population Reports*, ser. P-20, no. 320, "Geographical Mobility: March 1975 to March 1977," table 2.
Note: Figures may not add up because of rounding.

of people to move. Indeed, Table 7.1 shows that more than 50 percent of the people who moved between 1975 and 1977 stayed within the same county. As for the Northeast, only 36 percent of those who moved to a different county ended up in a different state. Many of these people, no doubt, merely moved a few miles, from one side of a state boundary to the other. Of the nearly 1.3 million Northeasterners who moved to another state between 1975 and 1977, 47 percent stayed in the Northeast. Only 26 percent moved to the South. An even smaller percentage of the Northeasterners who changed states, 12 percent, moved to the West.

As can be seen in Table 7.1, in regions like the North Central, most people who move stay within the region. An important conclusion can be drawn: If business relocation rules are seen as a means of restricting people's migration, they will very likely restrict migration within regions as much as or more than among regions. If business relocation rules are designed to retard the economic development of the South and West by restricting the migration of people and jobs, they will also restrict the economic development of the Northeast and the North Central regions. It is a gross distortion of the facts to develop the case for business relocation rules simply in terms of one region pitted against another.

News accounts of migration between the North and South leave the impression that the Northeast and North Central regions are being adversely affected not only by the number of people who are moving south, but also by the demographic characteristics of the in- and outmigration flows. For example, in one report we are told that "during the 1960's the major movements between the North and South were of middle-class whites to the South and low-income blacks to the North. These flows were almost equal in size, with the South attaining only a small net increase. Since 1970, however, burgeoning economic opportunity—especially in the South and Southwest but also in the Plains states—greatly retarded the outflow and accelerated the inflow."[14] The data, however, do not paint this sort of picture. For instance, the number of unemployed male workers (23,000) who moved from the Northeast to the South were substantially greater than the number of unemployed male workers (14,000) who moved from the South to the Northeast in the 1975–1977 period. Virtually the same thing can be said about the number of unemployed females who moved from the Northeast to the South and from the South to the Northeast. Similarly, the Northeast "exported" more unemployed workers to the West than it "imported" from the West.

Other observations are equally revealing. First, far more people below the poverty line (133,000) migrated from the Northeast to the South than from the South to the Northeast (39,000). Second, while more people with one or more years of college migrated from the Northeast to the South

[14]Ibid.

(151,000) than migrated from the South to the Northeast (102,000), a significantly greater percentage of the Southern migrants to the North had some college education (56.3 percent) than the percentage of the Northern migrants to the South (40.3 percent). Third, although more professional workers moved from the Northeast to the South than from the South to the Northeast, this is true for almost all other categories of workers listed and may be expected when there are simply more people moving out of the Northeast than moving in. On a percentage basis, it is not clear that the South or West is getting from the North a disproportionate number of highly trained people. The South is taking in more highly trained people than it is sending out; but by the same token, it is taking in more unemployed people than it is sending out.[15] Finally, over 50 percent more blacks migrated from the Northeast and North Central regions to the South than went from the South to the Northeast and North Central regions.

In summary, there has been a significant change in the relative population growth rate of the North. However, this relative change has been under way for three decades. There has been a significant change in migration patterns: the relatively modest immigration of people into the North in the 1960s has changed to a relatively modest outmigration of people from the North to other parts of the country. But, as C. L. Jusenius and L. C. Ledebur have commented in a report on the economic myths of Southern growth, "the extent to which it represents a new long-run trend—rather than a cyclical response to the recent severe economic recession—is unclear. Workers, reacting to unemployment in highly industrial areas, may be returning *temporarily* to their place of origin where a network of friends and relatives as well as marginal employment opportunities exist. Such a phenomenon is not without historical precedent: it occurred extensively during the Great Depression."[16] Jusenius and Ledebur conclude that "at this point the evidence is inconclusive. . . . This uncertainty argues for, at least, a reasonable amount of caution in the creation of public policy based on the current migration experience."[17]

Per Capita Income Changes

Reports on industry relocation give the impression that if the North is not now worse off economically than the South and Southwest, it is rapidly approaching the South's lower standing of living because of relocations. Edward Kelly, in his study *Industrial Exodus*, a position paper of the Conference for Alternative State and Local Public Policies that endorses the desirability of relocation restrictions writes, "As the manufacturing base of the [North-

[15]For more details, see McKenzie, *Restrictions on Business Mobility*, chap. 2.

[16]C. L. Jusenius and L. C. Ledebur, *A Myth in the Making: The Southern Economic Challenge and Northern Economic Decline* (Washington, D.C.: Economic Development Administration, Department of Commerce, November 1976), p. 3.

[17]Ibid.

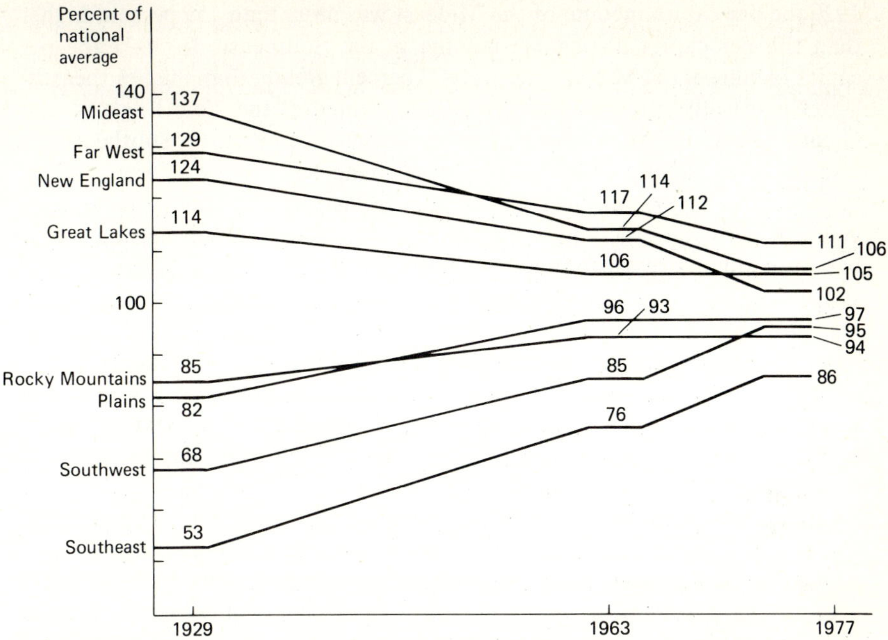

Figure 7.3 Regional per capita disposable income as a percentage of United States average. [*Source: Yale Brozen, Department of Economics, University of Chicago* (*personal calculations*).]

ern] economy declines, so does the tax base. There are fewer taxable industrial locations and fewer people capable of paying taxes."[18]

Contrary to the impression given by these accounts of the relative welfare of residents in the North and South, the per capita income levels of *all* regions of the country rose during the 1970s. This is true even after adjusting for the effects of inflation. Since the populations of all regions grew during the period, it follows that total regional incomes grew. Therefore, although regional tax bases may not have grown as much as desired, the tax bases of all regions grew. (This generality, however, may not hold for individual states and subdivisions of states.)

If there is any basis for concern over the economic health of the North, it must be in terms of the *relative* income levels of Northern states. As clearly shown in Figure 7.3, the per capita personal income of the Mideast (Delaware, the District of Columbia, Maryland, New Jersey, New York, and Pennsylvania) has been on a steady decline *relative* to the Southeast (Alabama, Arkansas, Florida, Georgia, Kentucky, Louisiana, Mississippi, North and South Carolina, Tennessee, Virginia, and West Virginia) since 1929. In

[18]Edward Kelly, *Industrial Exodus: Public Strategies for Control of Runaway Plants* (Washington, D.C.: Conference for Alternative State and Local Public Policies, October 1977), pp. 7–8.

1929 the per capita income of the Mideast was more than 159 percent higher than the per capita disposable income in the Southeast. In 1977 the per capita income of the Mideast was only 23 percent greater than the Southeast's.

Historically, the trend of per capita income of the New England and Great Lake divisions *relative* to the per capita income of the Southeast has also declined steadily. Since the cost of living has generally risen slightly faster in the South than in the Northern Industrial Tier states, the convergence of per capita income of the regions in terms of real purchasing power has been slightly less pronounced than Figure 7.3 suggests. However, it is still clear that Northern industrial states have on average a substantially higher standard of living as measured by income figures. That explains in large measure why more people have not moved south. Furthermore, it is clear from Figure 7.3 that Representative Ford has proposed a solution to a problem—that is, the migration of industry—which, to the extent that it is due to regional income differences, has already been largely resolved through normal market forces.

The movement of industry and people south does not mean that the North is therefore made worse off or that the *growth* in the standard of living in the North has been retarded. Indeed, the converse may be reasonably argued: movements of people and industry have contributed to the growth in the standard of living in the North. By moving south, where production costs are lower, industries are able to provide goods and services to Northern markets at lower prices than they would have been able to provide if they had stayed in the North. The greater production that can result at lower costs contributes to greater national income and, because the prices of goods and services are lower, to an increase in the purchasing power of workers' incomes, including the incomes of workers in the North. Also, incomes in the North have increased because industrial composition has been changed to specialize on those industries in which the North has a comparative advantage. The industries that declined in the North were the low-wage industries, while those that grew were the high-wage industries. Therefore, if industry had not moved south, real incomes in the North would have risen less rapidly than they have.

Granted, when a company pulls up stakes and moves, some people may be left behind without jobs. However, as we will see in a later section of this chapter, the loss in income suffered by persons unemployed due to relocations can be more than compensated for by expanding employment in other, higher-wage areas of the regional economy and by the beneficial effects of reduced production costs and prices of goods and services. The result is some redistribution of income and higher per capita income.

Federal Tax and Expenditure Policies

"Federal tax and spending policies are causing a *massive* flow of wealth from the Northeast and Midwest to the fast growing Southern and Western regions of the nation, according to a *National Journal* survey of financial

Table 7.2 Federal Government Spending and Taxes per Person, by 1975

	Federal government spending per person	Federal government taxes per person
Sunbelt South	$1,356	$1,188
South Atlantic	1,392	1,249
Florida	1,379	1,378
Georgia	1,402	1,217
North Carolina	1,124	1,145
South Carolina	1,240	1,041
Virginia	1,809	1,355
West Virginia	1,318	1,091
East South Central	1,377	1,060
Alabama	1,347	1,026
Kentucky	1,327	1,094
Mississippi	1,599	908
Tennessee	1,296	1,147
West South Central	1,295	1,187
Arkansas	1,202	907
Louisiana	1,236	1,064
Oklahoma	1,443	1,181
Texas	1,296	1,264
Northern Industrial Tier	1,224	1,560
New England	1,510	1,611
Connecticut	1,663	1,800
Massachusetts	1,456	1,535
Rhode Island	1,342	1,457
East North Central	1,064	1,518
Illinois	1,230	1,704
Indiana	1,027	1,441
Michigan	996	1,539
Ohio	1,010	1,441
Wisconsin	966	1,331
Middle Atlantic	1,325	1,594
New Jersey	1,154	1,760
New York	1,449	1,636
Pennsylvania	1,241	1,426
National average	1,412	1,412

Source: "Federal Spending: The North's Loss Is the Sunbelt's Gain," *National Journal* (June 26, 1976), p. 881

relationships between the states and federal government" (emphasis added).[19] That is how the *National Journal* describes the federal government's contribution to the relatively higher growth rate of the South.

Table 7.2 shows that for fiscal year 1975, states in the Northern Industrial Tier on a per capita basis paid more in taxes than they received in the form of government outlays. The opposite was true of the Sunbelt South. On a per capita basis, the Northern states paid approximately 27 percent

[19] "Federal Spending: The North's Loss Is the Sunbelt's Gain," *National Journal* (June 26, 1976), p. 878.

more in taxes ($1,560) than they received in expenditures ($1,224), whereas the per capita taxes of Southern states were only 88 percent of their per person federal receipts. However, as Jusenius and Ledebur explain, "one of the functions of fiscal policy is to redistribute income among groups according to goals determined by society. One of the redistributive goals, however well met, has been to close the gap between 'the rich' and 'the poor.' In part, the federal government has attempted to meet this goal through the federal income tax system: taxpayers with higher income levels also pay relatively higher proportions of their incomes in taxes. On the expenditure side, public policy has been directed toward raising the real income of the lowest socioeconomic groups."[20] As was shown in the previous section, the per capita income in the South is lower than in the North.

In 1975 the Northern states paid, on average, slightly higher tax rates than states in the South. The average tax rate, as a percentage of income, in the Sunbelt South was 23.0 and in the Northern Industrial Tier was 24.9.[21] Since the per capita income in the North was approximately 23 percent higher than in the South, the United States tax rate system is progressive, meaning that tax *rates* rise with income, the slightly higher rate of taxation in the North is to be expected.

The higher marginal tax rates paid by residents in the Northern Industrial Tier very likely may contribute to production inefficiency and increase, albeit slightly, the competitive advantage of poorer Southern states. However, these consequences of redistributive government policies are unavoidable. If the South is not paying its "fair share" of taxes and is receiving an unfair share of all federal benefits, the solution would seem to be a change in the tax laws and a reduction or redistribution of benefits, not the imposition of additional controls such as relocation rules that reduce production efficiency.

Furthermore, if the federal government simply collected taxes and channeled them back to the states in the form of equal outlays, government would not necessarily be acting efficiently. The cost of producing national defense, for example, may be lower in one region of the country than in another. If the federal government were required to allocate defense appropriations in proportion to the taxes collected in each region, defense would be more costly. The higher cost would then require the government either to accept a lower level of defense preparedness or to collect more taxes to develop a given level of defense preparedness. Alternately, if the government attempted to solve the "misallocation" of federal funds via restrictions on business mobility, production inefficiencies, as will be shown, would result in the private economy (as well as the public economy), the aggregate national income level would be lower, and the federal government would

[20] Jusenius and Lebedur, *A Myth in the Making*, p. 28.
[21] For more details, see McKenzie, *Restrictions on Business Mobility*, table 7.

have to raise tax rates to finance any given defense posture. The higher tax rates could spell greater production inefficiencies across regions.

Regional Employment Shifts

In making the case for relocation rules, Edward Kelly points out that the prosperity of the North and Midwest has been dependent upon an established industrial sector.[22] He adds that "the corporate exodus from the industrial states is part of a national problem affecting the entire domestic economy: total manufacturing employment has stagnated, remaining in the range between 18 and 20 million jobs since the 1960's. In 1965 employment was approximately 18 million; now, twelve years later, it is only 18.5 million."[23] Citing additional data in the Kelly study, *Business Week* added emphasis to its continuing report on the regional employment shifts with the mid-page caption, "A loss of 1.4 million jobs in the North since 1966. Work goes south and west."[24]

One point must be remembered when interpreting employment data over a span of years: the picture that is painted of the number of jobs lost or gained in the economy as a whole, in a region, or in an industrial group depends upon the actual years selected for the data comparisons. From 1965 to 1974, total nonagricultural employment in the United States economy grew consistently, although it grew more rapidly in some years than in others. However, there were obvious ups and downs in the level of employment in the major subdivisions of employment. For instance, employment in goods-producing industries went up from 1965 to 1969. It then receded to a low in 1971. Employment in goods industries rose again from 1971 through 1974 and fell temporarily during 1975. Cyclical employment swings in goods industries have been offset in the aggregate employment figures by the strong and steady growth of employment in service-producing industries.[25]

Employment in manufacturing industries is notable because of its strong cyclical movements. In fact, these movements account for almost all the cyclical swings of employment in the overall goods-producing category. A comparison of manufacturing employment in 1970 with manufacturing employment in 1975 suggests that there was a significant downward trend in the number of jobs in that economic sector. Employment in manufacturing during the period decreased by 5 percent in contrast to upward employment trends in other sectors. However, as Kelly suggests, employment in manufacturing over the long run has actually remained fairly level. In short, the number of jobs that are said to be lost in manufacturing—or, for that matter,

[22]Kelly, *Industrial Exodus*, p. 1.

[23]Ibid., p. 2.

[24]"A New Layer of Structural Unemployment," *Business Week* (November 14, 1977), p. 144.

[25]For more details, see McKenzie, *Restrictions on Business Mobility*, table 8.

in any other sector of the economy—can be amplified or dampened by appropriate selection of the base year.

Furthermore, the employment picture of a region can be distorted by narrowing or widening the industrial group or the size of the regions covered. A favorite strategy of proponents of legislation like the National Employment Priorities Act is to focus attention on the area of employment that has had the worst record and not to mention offsetting employment trends in other sectors of the economy.

Table 7.3 contains regional employment data by industry. From that table, it is clear that the North Central region had a marked decline in manufacturing employment from January 1972 to January 1978. Manufacturing employment in the North Central states declined by 11 percent. However, that region was not as depressed as the manufacturing employment figures alone would suggest: there were strong employment gains in the North Central region in mining (65 percent increase), wholesale and retail trade (20 percent increase), and services (30 percent increase). On balance, total employment in the North Central region went up by 18 percent. Furthermore, notice that manufacturing employment rose in the Northeast by 54 percent. On the other hand, manufacturing employment in the South went down by 3 percent between the two dates, but employment in other areas rose significantly. These findings are not what one would expect by listening to advocates of relocation restrictions.[26]

Finally, the loss of employment opportunities in any region can rarely be attributed to one single cause such as the migration of industry. Juxtaposing discussions of industrial migration with data on aggregate employment losses within a region gives a distorted impression of the economic hardship caused by industry movements. The employment patterns of regions change because of relative regional changes: deaths of firms, births of new firms, and expansions and contractions of old firms as well as industry migration. To illustrate, in a study of the employment gains and losses in the Northern Industrial Tier and Sunbelt South states, Peter Allaman and David Birch found that, during the 1968–1972 period, slightly more than 70 percent of the employment gain in the North was due to the expansion of existing firms, and more than 28 percent was the result of the

[26]The dates January 1972 to January 1978 were chosen because the 1978 data provided the latest data and because the two dates appeared to be in approximately the same phases of their respective business cycles. Of course, employment shifts in the Northern Industrial Tier states will appear more drastic if the focus is changed from examining employment in terms of large geographical regions to their smaller subdivisions. Employment shifts also can be dramatized by drawing attention to the economic and personal distress that results when individual companies close down or move. This is what Representative Ford, Edward Kelly, and others have done in making the case for restrictions on business mobility; they have drawn attention to employment swings within small regional subdivisions of states and within one employment sector, manufacturing, and have largely ignored the beneficial and offsetting employment effects of a dynamic economy that is constantly being called on to sway with changes in consumer preferences, income, technologies, labor market conditions, and government policies.

Table 7.3 Regional Employment by Industry, January 1972 and January 1978

	Northeast			North Central			Northeast and North Central combined	South			West			South and West combined
	Jan. 1972 (1,000s)	Jan. 1978 (1,000s)	Percent change	Jan. 1972 (1,000s)	Jan. 1978 (1,000s)	Percent change	Percent change	Jan. 1972 (1,000s)	Jan. 1978 (1,000s)	Percent change	Jan. 1972 (1,000s)	Jan. 1978 (1,000s)	Percent change	Percent change
Total	14,565	16,912	+16	19,262	22,710	+18	+17	25,680	30,082	+17	10,726	12,319	+15	+16
Mining	9	77	+756	102	168	+65	+120	386	336	-13	93	128	+38	-3
Construction	542	419	-23	688	575	-16	-20	1,397	1,819	+30	445	879	+98	+46
Manufacturing	3,542	5,142	+45	4,638	4,144	-11	+14	8,035	7,812	-3	2,066	2,348	+14	+1
Transportation and public utilities	896	605	-33	1,153	840	-17	-29	1,606	2,578	+60	692	579	-16	+37
Wholesale and retail trade	3,067	3,350	+9	4,184	5,047	+20	+16	5,440	6,926	+27	2,432	3,219	+32	+29
Finance, insurance, real estate	995	1,064	+7	904	1,056	+17	+12	1,220	1,552	+27	594	787	+32	+29
Services	2,700	3,163	+17	2,970	3,875	+30	+24	3,942	5,354	+36	1,948	2,748	+41	+38
Government	2,467	2,731	+10	3,382	3,823	+13	+12	5,125	5,194	+21	2,402	2,840	+18	+20

Source: U.S. Department of Labor, Bureau of Labor Statistics, *Employment and Earnings* (May 1973 and May 1978).

establishment of new firms. More importantly for the purpose of this study, only 1.5 percent of the employment losses in the North from 1969 to 1972 was due to the outmigration of business. The overwhelming majority of employment loss, 98.5 percent, was due to the death or contraction of existing firms. Only 1.2 percent of the South's employment gains was the result of the inmigration of businesses.[27]

In short, unless the experience of the last few years is dramatically different from the experience of 1969–1972, proposals designed to remedy regional employment problems by restricting business outmigration will have very little effect in improving overall employment opportunities.

ECONOMIC CAUSES OF INDUSTRY MOVEMENT SOUTH

The reasons for the economic health of the South and West relative to the North cannot be fully dismissed or rationalized away and should be matters of concern for Northern states. These reasons can be discussed under the headings of wages, unions, and taxes.

Wages

In assessing the causes for firms moving out of the North, Donovan Dennis, Vice President of Fantus Corporation, a plant-relocation consulting firm has said: "Labor costs are the big thing, far and away. None out of 10 times you can hang it on labor costs and unionization."[28] In many locations and in terms of many job classifications, Southeastern and Southwestern states have a significant wage advantage over the Northeast and North Central regions in industries not requiring high skill levels.

The total hourly compensation for all United States workers in cotton textiles averaged $3.55 in 1973; for workers in the Northeast it was $5.55; for workers in the South, $3.49. The hourly compensation in the North in that one manufacturing process was on average 59 percent higher than in the South. Although the gap between the synthetic industries in the Northeast and South is much smaller, there was in 1973 a similar pattern of relative compensation: compensation in the Northeast ($4.08) was about 16 percent higher than in the South ($3.53). Furthermore, evidence on the values added per employee suggests that the gap between output per worker-hour in the North and the South has been closing and that textile workers in the South are now only slightly less productive than textile workers in other parts of

[27]Peter M. Allaman and David L. Birch, *Components of Employment Change for States by Industry Groups, 1970–72* (Cambridge, Mass.: Joint Center of Urban Studies on M.I.T. and Harvard University, September 1975).

[28]Donovan Dennis, as originally quoted in *Akron Beacon Journal* (February 19, 1971) and reported in Kelly, *Industrial Exodus*, p. 3.

the country.[29] Slightly lower productivity combined with the significantly lower wage rates spell lower production costs for the final product in the South.

Businesses are concerned with the actual dollar wages they pay, because dollar wages affect directly the dollar cost of producing their products and, therefore, their competitive position. Table 7.4 clearly reveals that, on average, the hourly dollar cost of labor, unadjusted for cost of living, in all subdivisions of the Northeast is higher than in the South. (Of course, it should be recognized that those wage rates are not standardized for differences in the industrial composition of manufacturing and differences in the skill mix.) Although the regional wage gap is not as stark as it is in textiles, many (but by no means all) businesses definitely have a wage incentive to incur relocation costs when the difference in hourly labor cost is greater than the difference in skill. However, the table also reveals that Southern manufacturing workers, after cost-of-living differences are adjusted for, are not *all* worse off than their Northern colleagues. After adjustments are made for the lower cost of living in the South, the real wage rate of manufacturing workers on average throughout the South is higher than the real wage rate of manufacturing workers in the New England area. Still, most real manufacturing wages are higher in most areas of the country than in the South; and Table 7.4 provides rudimentary evidence explaining why some firms and individual workers choose to move from one region to another.

Business movement south is commonly explained, as we have done, in terms of the "wage attraction" of the South. However, it is more illuminating to examine business movement as a consequence of the "wage push" in the North. As is true when one thinks of a "half-full" rather than a "half-empty" glass of water, the change in perspective often changes one's view of social conditions and the economic consequences of industry relocation. From the wage-attraction perspective, one may conclude that "low-paid serfs in the South" are causing economic harm to the North. The wage-push perspective suggests that wages in the North are higher and on the rise for some (economic) reason, such as competition for workers from the developing service sector in the North: manufacturers are forced to pay higher wages or else have their labor forces pulled away by expanding companies in the other sectors. The industry that moves south is "pushed" south, out-competed for the labor resources in the North. From this perspective, industrial movement south, either slight or substantial, is a consequence of gains made by many workers in the North. Seen this way, the case for restriction of business relocation is a case for the retardation of economic growth and development of the North. Restrictions on business mobility will tend to keep resources fixed in place and unavailable for use in expanding, economically

[29]James A Morris and Thomas A. Schaap, *Economic Growth Trends in South Carolina* (Columbia, S.C.: Bureau of Business and Economic Research, University of South Carolina, 1977).

Table 7.4 Comparison of Average Hourly Earnings in Manufacturing Unadjusted and Standardized for Cost of Living Differences—1975

		Northeast		North Central		South			West	
	U.S.	NE	MAT	ENC	WNC	SAT	ESC	WSC	MTN	PAC
Unadjusted earnings	$4.81	$4.42	$4.93	$5.60	$4.92	$3.95	$4.07	$4.45	$4.70	$5.31
Standardized for cost of living	4.81	4.03	4.73	5.54	5.07	4.11	4.47	4.94	4.95	5.09

Source: U.S. Bureau of Labor Statistics, *Handbook of Labor Statistics 1975*, Reference edition, Table 109, as taken from Lynn E. Growne, "How Different Are Regional Wages," *New England Economic Review*, January–February 1978, p. 40.

more beneficial industry.[30] It is an attempt to keep lower-paying jobs and to keep people in lower-productivity work. This will be discussed further in Chapter 8.

Unions

When responding to questions "on the record," businesspersons tend to put wages and unions at the bottom of any list of reasons for moving south.[31] "Off the record," however, the story is different. Then, they often admit that unions or "better labor-management relations" (which is a euphemism for "getting out from under union domination") are a prime reason for their decision to move.

In the North, nonfarm labor unionization varied in 1974 from a high of 38 percent in Michigan to a low of little more than 24 percent in Massachusetts. In the South, Alabama had the highest percentage of its work force belonging to a union, about 19 percent. In contrast, only 6.9 percent of nonfarm workers in North Carolina were members of unions in 1974. In 1974 right-to-work laws were nonexistent in the Northern Industrial Tier states, whereas states in the South and Southwest, aside from Kentucky, Louisiana, and New Mexico, had right-to-work laws in force.

Many businesses understandably want to move away from unions. There is a substantial body of economic research that shows that unions are responsible for wages being anywhere from 5 to 25 percent higher in unionized shops than in nonunionized shops.[32] The average increase found by various studies is about 10 percent. In short, the absence of unions and the cultural bias against them in the South have given Southern states a competitive advantage, however small.

The absence of a highly unionized South has also benefited the nonunion section of the labor force in the North. The threat of businesses moving south in response to union wage demands has kept unions in the North from pushing up wages by as much as they otherwise would have. This, in turn, has kept the prices of goods and services lower than they would have been in the absence of a nonunion South. The nonunion South has, accordingly, contributed to the standard of living of workers in the North, especially nonunion workers.[33]

[30]As we argue in the next chapter, restrictions on business mobility can only slow, not stop, the movement of labor and other resources to the expanding sector.

[31]A. Stanley Austin and Ray C. Roberts, Jr., "The Effects of Wage Levels on Decisions to Locate Manufacturing Facilities in South Carolina," *Business and Economic Review*, University of South Carolina (October 1973), pp. 2–10.

[32]For a brief review of the literature on the effects of unions on wages and employment, see F. Ray Marshall, Allen M. Carter, and Allan G. King, *Labor Economics: Wages, Employment and Trade Unionism* (Homewood, Ill.: Richard D. Irwin, Inc., 1976), chap. 14.

[33]Union success in pushing wage rates above free-market levels in some industries causes a decline in wage rates in other industries as a consequence of the restricted job opportunities in unionized industries, forcing workers to seek jobs in other industries. See Stephen Sobotka, *Profile of Michigan: Economic Trends and Paradoxes* (New York: Macmillan, 1963).

Taxes

State and local taxes in 1975 were one-third higher in the Northeast as a percentage of per capita income than they were in the South. There is substantial variation in both the tax rates of the North and the South, but the general tendency is clear: taxes are higher in the traditional industrial states than in the faster-growing Southern region. New York collected taxes in 1975 that averaged 15.7 percent of per capita personal income; at the other extreme, Alabama collected taxes that averaged 9 percent of per capita personal income. As a consequence, the resident of Alabama had, on average, a state and local tax advantage over New Yorkers of about 75 percent. Conversely, residents of Ohio, a highly industrialized state, paid taxes at an overall lower rate than people in several Southern states.[34]

Higher taxes and tax rates are not necessarily detractions to an industry evaluating a site. Higher taxes can mean greater availability and higher quality of public services. Such services can reduce the cost of doing business. Taxes detract when they are disproportionately levied on business or when the revenue collected is inefficiently used in providing public services. There are several reasons for believing that some tax structures in the North, like unions and wages, are "pushing" industry out of the region. First, many firms can divide their functions in different locations. Production plants can be established in the South where low taxes benefit employees as well as firms themselves, and offices can be located in Northern urban areas, where firms can selectively take advantage of the public benefits offered by states with relatively higher taxes.

Second, a growing volume of literature on the economics of politics reveals a tendency toward diseconomies of scale in government at all levels.[35] With growth in tax collections, the quantity and quality of public services do not rise proportionately. The average cost of services provided tends, therefore, to be disproportionately higher in states with higher tax rates. Many businesses have an incentive to move south, to smaller governmental units with lower tax rates. Alternately, they may move from relatively high tax states to states with relatively low tax rates in the North. New Hampshire is being called the "Northern Sunbelt state" because of the influx of industry that low taxes are causing.[36]

Third, where state and local tax rates are lower and public services are on average provided more efficiently, the supply of labor at any given money wage will be higher, and the wages that must be paid will be lower. The lower tax rates indirectly give businesses a competitive cost advantage over firms in higher tax rate districts.

[34]For more details, see McKenzie, *Restrictions on Business Mobility*, table 17.

[35]See, for example, Thomas E. Borcherding (ed.), *Budgets and Bureaucrats: The Sources of Government Growth* (Durham, N.C.: Duke University Press, 1977).

[36]David Gumpert, "Northern Nirvana: 'New' New Hampshire Finds that Low Taxes Help to Fuel Economy," *Wall Street Journal* (May 25, 1978), p. 1.

CONCLUDING COMMENTS

The case for relocation rules is largely a collection of arguments that carry little force under close scrutiny. The level of business migration has neither been appreciable nor as large as has been claimed. The migration that has occurred has not had the dire employment consequences previously reported. Further, the North is not as economically depressed, relative to the South, as has been suggested or as may be inferred by looking only at the manufacturing sector of the Northern economy. Changes in the Northern service sector have more than compensated for any loss in manufacturing employment and have kept the mean standard of living in the North rising and above the standard of living in the South.

QUESTIONS TO PONDER

1 "Firms in the North are being attracted south by the low wages in the South. The standard of living in the North is being pulled down by the lower standard of living in the South." Evaluate that statement.
2 Explain the reasons Northern state and local governments would be interested in restricting movements of businesses south.
3 Restrictions on business mobility are seen as a way of "keeping jobs in the North." Will they, in the long run, actually keep jobs in the North?
4 Suppose the price of energy for heating goes up. What will be the effect of that change on regional production costs? How can business and people be expected to adjust to the increase in the cost of heating? If government tries to prevent the adjustments you suggest will occur, what will happen to production efficiency in the country? What will happen to the national income? In the long run, can the government actually prevent the adjustments that you predict will occur? Explain.

Additional Reading

Jusenius, C. L., and L. C. Ledebur. *A Myth in the Making: The Southern Economic Challenge and Northern Economic Decline.* Washington, D.C.: Economic Development Administration, Department of Commerce, November 1976.
Kelly, Edward. *Industrial Exodus: Public Strategies for Control of Runaway Plants.* Washington, D.C.: Conference for Alternative State and Local Public Policies, October 1977.

Chapter 8

Restrictions on Business Mobility: Theoretical Issues

CHAPTER PREVIEW

Central Question

From a conceptual point of view, what are the major consequences of imposing restrictions on business mobility?

Major Objective

To employ elementary tools of economic analysis for the purpose of ferreting out the effects that restrictions on business mobility can have on regional economic development, movement of jobs, power of unions, wage rates, wealth transfers, and power of state and local governments.

Major Points

1 Restrictions on business mobility will dampen the economic development of all regions of the country.

2 Relocation restrictions will impede the movement of jobs south but will not stop the movement.

3 Restrictions on business movements will tend to increase the bargaining power of unions and reduce the relative wages of labor in nonunion sectors of the labor market.

4 Relocation restrictions will reduce the rights that business entrepreneurs possess; and they will, in part, cause a wealth transfer from owners of businesses that are restricted from moving to owners of other businesses that can take advantage of the profitable opportunities, and to state and local governments.

Markets enable people to buy and sell what they want at prices they freely choose to accept. They also enable people to adjust to changes in economic and social conditions. Markets are by no means perfect—there are costs involved—but markets achieve the degree of efficiency that they do and yield increasing per capita incomes because they give individuals private incentives to make adjustments to what others want them to do and to changes in available capital and technology. As Adam Smith wrote more than two hundred years ago, market participants, by pursuing their own private interests, are led "to promote an end which was no part of this intention."[1] That end is the expansion of the national product and the satisfaction of consumers.

Competition is the acclaimed benefactor of markets because it forces people to reveal what they are willing to do. At the limit it forces them to reveal the *minimum* prices they are willing to accept for the products or labor services being sold and to reveal the *maximum* prices they are willing to offer for products or labor services they want to buy. Competition, to the extent that it exists in the marketplace, induces people to produce at their limits, given their preference and cost constraints. It is in this sense that competition maximizes national output and income. Government policies that restrict trades or that restrict the ability of markets to adjust to changes in preferences, prices, and profits restrict not only individual choices but also national production and income.

The purpose of this chapter is to explore on a conceptual level the economic consequences of restrictions on business mobility. By discussing in general terms how markets work, we are able to illuminate the economic consequences of relocation rules that are unsuspected and unintended by their advocates. In the following section, the economic effects of business relocation restrictions will be presented. An explanation of the causes of the effect will follow.

[1]Adam Smith, *An Inquiry into the Nature and Causes of the Wealth of Nations* (New York: Random House, Inc., 1937), Modern Library Edition, p. 423: "Consumption is the sole end and purpose of all production; and the interest of the producer ought to be attended to, only so far as it may be necessary for promoting that of the consumer."

THE ECONOMIC CONSEQUENCES OF RESTRICTIONS

Economic Development

Restrictions on business movements will retard the economic development of all regions of the country.

People trade with one another in part because of the comparative advantages they have in production. A person who is relatively more efficient in the production of a good will give up less in producing that good than someone else. Another way of saying the same thing is that a person who has a comparative advantage in production of a good can produce that good more cheaply than others can. Therefore, if people produce those goods in which they have a comparative advantage and trade them for other things they want, production costs will be lower than what they will be if all people try to be self-sufficient. And, since costs are reduced by specialization and exchanges, more output than otherwise can be produced with the resources available to the community.

When evaluating the economic consequences of relocation rules, we must keep two points in mind. First, people in different parts of the country have comparative advantages in different goods, and trade occurs between people in different parts of the country when they find that they can gain from trade. People receive a better deal by trading with others than by trying to produce all the goods they want by themselves. This is the reason that people in the North trade with people in the South. They benefit by the exchanges that they make, and they benefit because specialization results in reduced production costs and expanded output.

Second, the comparative advantages of people in different regions continually change. This is because the conditions of production—that is, the availability of resources, technology, and consumer preferences for work and goods—continually change. Changes in comparative advantage spell changes in relative costs. What was once relatively less costly to produce in the North can—due to, for example, a change in production technology—become less costly to produce in the South. By moving from the North to the South, a firm can keep its costs of production under what they would be if production were not moved.

Regional shifts in comparative advantage may occur because a strategic resource used in making product A becomes relatively more scarce in one region than in another. Therefore, the cost of producing good A in the region rises above the cost of producing it in another region. Additionally, increases in workers' education level or the discovery of more abundant supplies of a given resource may cause a region to experience a reduction in the cost of producing good B, which it formerly was not producing, and to initiate its production of B. Again, a shift in production within the region from A to B can keep the costs of production below what they would otherwise be. The industry that expands due to beneficial cost changes begins to impinge on the resources available to industries that once dominated the region. The costs of producing A in that region go up and, as a consequence, the production of A moves someplace else. Finally, the preferences of people in a region can change. An increase in the demand for services within a particular region, for example, may cause resources like labor to move from the manufacturing sector into the service sector, causing the wages and production costs in the manufacturing sector to rise. One result of the sequence of events may be that some manufacturing plants release their labor to a growing economic sector and move to another location.

Describing the causes of changes in regional economic structures is difficult under the best of circumstances. This is because costs are based on people's subjective evaluation of goods, and those evaluations cannot be *directly* observed in the market process.[2] However, over recent decades the comparative advantages of many sections of the North have changed. Several reasons can be identified. First, the demand for services in the North has increased rapidly, more rapidly than in other parts of the country. Second, the advent of environmental legislation has placed more severe restrictions on production in the congested Northern region than in many other parts of the country and has increased the relative cost of production in the North. The unavailability of "pollution rights" has caused many firms to decide on Southern, less polluted locations. According to one report, a major reason Volkswagen chose Pennsylvania as the site of its first United States plant is that the state of Pennsylvania agreed to reduce pollution from road construction by using a more expensive paving process. The state did that in order that VW might have the pollution rights to start up production.[3]

If the environmental restrictions that affect a region's comparative advantage are ill-conceived, the region's income will be reduced by them and appropriate changes in the environmental laws may be called for. However, if ill-conceived environmental laws cannot be changed, the solution to a region's economic woes is not to restrict business migration. Keeping some businesses from moving out will only cause the cost of production, given the existing environmental legislation, to be higher than they would otherwise be, and the region's income will be restricted.

If the comparative advantage of a region changes, for whatever reason, a restriction on business migration will keep resources tied up in the comparatively inefficient sector of the region. The sector that should be expanding because of its comparative advantage will be restricted from doing so because resources will not be released as quickly from the comparatively inefficient sector. Firms will be forced to retain employees and other re-

[2]James M. Buchanan, *Costs and Choice* (New York: Markham Publishers, Inc., 1969).

[3]T. Bruce Yandle, "The Emerging Market in Air Pollution Rights," *Regulation* (July-Aug. 1978), pp. 21–29. (See also Chapter 11 of this book.)

sources that could be moved to the expanding sector. In summary, governmental rules that impede the movement of manufacturing industry out of the North not only will retard the development of the manufacturing industry in the South but, by the same token, will retard the development of the expanding service sector in the North. Furthermore, restrictions on business mobility will cause production costs to be higher than they would otherwise be and, to that extent, will reduce national production and income.

Job Movement

If existing manufacturing firms in the North are restricted from moving to the South by legislation, the movement of manufacturing jobs to the South will be impeded but not stopped.

Firms are willing to incur the costs of relocation because moving will enable them to protect their competitive positions or to gain competitive advantages over their market rivals. This means that the cost of production is lower in the new location than in the old location. If firms are unable to move to new, more profitable Southern locations, then profitable opportunities are left to be exploited by others. Restrictions on business mobility will cause other firms to spring up in the new Southern locations and existing Southern firms to expand by more than they otherwise would. Because their costs of production are lower, emerging and expanding firms in new locations will be able to undersell firms in old locations. Firms in the old locations will eventually be forced to contract their operations or to go out of business. By way of births of new firms and deaths of old ones, the employment structure of regional economies will shift in the long run in spite of the relocation rules. Such rules will do little to slow the process and, because new firms are required to form, will increase the cost of adjustment.[4]

Power of Unions

Unions are interested in raising wages and fringe benefits for their members. They know, however, that their ability to do this is restricted by the threat of firms moving to new locations. If businesses are prevented from moving, the *immediate* threat of job loss is taken away and, as a conse-

[4]Under the proposed National Employment Priorities Act, the Secretary of Labor, with the advice of the National Employment Relocation Advisory Council, is empowered to keep a firm from relocating if the move is without "adequate justification." Presumably, this means that if a firm is deemed to be making a "fair rate of return on its investment," then it can be prevented from moving. As noted in Chapter 7, Representative Ford seems to be interested in stopping firms that want to move because of "economic greed." However, as indicated, expanded output in new locations will reduce the profitability in old locations. Therefore, even firms in old locations that are not able to provide "adequate justification" for a move at first will eventually be able to present the needed justification. What was once a move for so-called economic greed will become a move for economic necessity. Eventually, the government will find itself subsidizing these firms that it wants to see stay in their old locations.

quence, unions can be expected to increase their demands on employers. The result will be even higher production costs in the old locations; the benefits of relocation rules can be captured in the short-run income stream of union members.

Wages

Wages in many nonunionized labor markets will tend to fall (relative to what they would have been) because of restrictions on business mobility.

The supply of labor in any market is dependent upon a number of pecuniary and nonpecuniary factors: skill and education required, location, climate, risk of injury, and social prestige of the job. Because such factors affect the supply of labor in individual markets, they influence the wage rate. Steeplejacks tend to make more than janitors because the skills required for the job are more difficult to acquire (which restricts the number of people who are *able* to do the job) and because there are risks associated with working on metal beams in high places. Ph.D. accountants teaching in universities tend to make less in money wages than their counterparts in private industry, but they receive the nonpecuniary benefits of flexibility in scheduling their time and tenured employment (which has been described as a one-way, lifetime contract).

The supply of labor in any labor market is also affected by any expectation that the firms in a regional industry will close down altogether or move elsewhere. Generally, the greater the threat that an industry's firms will move, the higher the wage employees with given skills will demand before accepting employment in that industry. Restrictions on business mobility propose to reduce the threat of industrial movement, especially from the North. In the short run, the effect will be to increase the relative attractiveness of employment and, hence, the supply of labor in markets from which firms might otherwise move. To the extent that those markets are competitive, the wage rates will fall. If firms are forced to give severance pay to employees they leave behind, the same thing will happen: in competitive labor markets, the relative attractiveness of employment and the supply of labor will increase, pushing the wage rates down.

Of course, markets are not perfectly competitive and they do not always fully adjust to changes in the economic environment. The general tendency, however, is clear. Wages will tend to be depressed by labor supply responses. Wages may have otherwise gone up; the point of this section is that they will not rise by as much as otherwise. This is because more people will want to work in those areas where the threat of employment loss in the near term is reduced. Workers who were once willing to accept the risk of losing their jobs in order to receive the higher wage will no longer have that opportunity; their real income will be reduced.

In the long run, new labor market equilibriums will be achieved as regional employment structures change to what they would have been in the absence of the relocation rules. On balance, however, the country will be poorer: relocation rules cause resources to be inefficiently allocated among regions, and there will be fewer goods and services produced. The per capita income of the country, in other words, will be restricted; if it grows, it will grow by less than otherwise because of the relocation rules.

Wealth Transfers

Relocation rules will cause wealth transfers and losses.

When people invest in businesses, they are actually buying a bundle of legal rights. The market value of those rights is equal to the present value of the future income stream that can be received from holding those rights. Many people have invested in businesses (either directly through the purchase of plant and equipment or indirectly through the purchase of stocks and bonds) on the assumption that they were purchasing not only the right to operate the business, but also the right to move the business to any location they perceive to be more profitable. Because they thought they had the right to move their business, they paid more for the business (or the stock) than they otherwise would have.

Relocation rules propose to take one of the rights away from business owners, that is, the right of movement; such rules therefore propose to reduce the income stream of the business and the wealth of business owners. Under the National Employment Priorities Act businesses cannot move without effectively having government consent, so the demand for the assets of a firm that would otherwise choose to move will be reduced. The value of those assets also will be reduced. Alternatively, because firms cannot move as readily to seek out profitable opportunities under relocation rules, the demand for and the market price of stock of companies that would otherwise move will be reduced. Consequently, relocation rules will cause a wealth transfer away from owners of businesses. A part of that wealth transfer will go to owners of companies in other places, such as the South, that are able to emerge or expand and to survive more profitably because other businesses have found their movements impeded. A part of the wealth lost by Northern firms with restricted mobility will simply be a deadweight loss because of the subsequent decrease in production efficiency. A part of the wealth transfers will be picked up by government agencies that will be expanded for the purpose of increasing government supervision over business decisions.

Although transferring wealth from one group to another may be a socially desirable goal, relocation rules seem like a particularly clumsy way of achieving such a social objective. Many people who will lose wealth in the transfer process are small investors; many, in fact, are likely to be on retirement plans that are tied to the market prices of various stocks. If the value of these stocks goes down, then the prospective income from retirement programs also will fall. In short, it is doubtful that any analysis has been made to determine who will be harmed by the proposed legislation and by how much each person will be hurt.

Monopoly Power of Governments

Restrictions on business mobility will increase the monopoly power of state and local governments.

As we argue in detail in Chapter 13, the framers of the Constitution attempted to place restraints on government by sharply defining the role of government and by introducing market principles into its organization. In short, the founding fathers believed that the power of government could be constrained in part by *competition among governments*. A government, operating in a world of many governments, would face market constraints similar to those faced by private companies. If a company raises its price or lowers the quality of its product, it can expect to lose customers to competing firms that hold prices down or maintain quality or both. Similarly, a government that raises taxes or reduces the quantity and/or quality of its public services can expect to lose people and its tax base to other (competing) governments. Although the degree of potential competition among governments may be less than it is among private firms, competition can still occur among governments. To the extent that it does, the power of state and local governments to raise taxes and lower the quality of services provided is reduced.

Restrictions on business mobility will hinder response of businesses to tax increases imposed by local governments. To the extent that this occurs, relocation restrictions increase the power of governments to raise taxes and reduce the quality of services that they provide. Consequently, the enactment of relocation rules is likely to lead to higher taxes and lower-quality services in many jurisdictions.

CONCLUDING COMMENTS

Restrictions on business mobility will increase production costs by reducing the efficiency with which resources are allocated on an inter- and intra-regional basis. They will increase the bargaining power of unions. To the extent that they impede business' ability to move into markets where production is more profitable, they will tend to reduce competition among businesses from different regions and foster local monopoly and monopsony power among existing producers. Because businesses will not be able to "vote with their feet" as easily as they would be able to in the absence of relocation rules, the monopoly power of local and state governments will be enhanced, very likely leading to higher tax-prices for local and state government services.

Granted, restrictions on business movement will affect income and wealth transfers, which may be a social objective of restriction proponents. However, relocation rules are a particularly haphazardous way of accomplishing such social objectives, since the resulting transfers will be made in an unpredictable manner. Also, the end result may be the opposite of that which the social engineers planned. After the political rhetoric is peeled away and the emotions of individual employment losses are set aside, restrictions on business mobility have very little to recommend them.

QUESTIONS TO PONDER

1 "Businesses are out to make as many bucks as they can. They have no incentive to give voluntarily reasonable notice to their employees of their intentions to move or close down. Businesses, therefore, must be required to give notice of their intentions." Do you agree or disagree? Explain.

2 What effect will restrictions on business mobility have on imports into the country?

3 "If businesses are restricted from moving, there will be gainers and losers but, on balance, the losses of the losers will exceed the gains of the gainers." List likely groups of losers and gainers. Do you agree with the entire statement?

4 Presently, states and communities often compete for industry by offering firms tax breaks and added services. Is this type of competition economically efficient? Why would state and local governments have an interest in banning together for the purpose of reducing competition for industry? Would such efforts be economically desirable?

ADDITIONAL READING

Lipsey, Richard G., and Peter O. Steiner. *Economics*. New York: Harper & Row, Publishers, 1978, chap. 19.

Spencer, Milton H. *Contemporary Economics*. New York: Worth Publishing Company, Inc., 1977, chap. 5.

For additional readings, see the end of Chapter 7.

Chapter 9

Regulating the Health of Workers: The Case of Cotton Dust Standards

CHAPTER PREVIEW

Central Question

What are the economic consequences of government efforts to regulate the health and safety of workers?

Major Objectives

1 To demonstrate how economics can be used to evaluate governmental efforts to control the health and safety of workers.

2 More specifically, to consider how standards for cotton dust in textile mills affect the wage rates and health of workers, the price and output of domestic textile mills, the use of capital in textile production, and imports of textile products.

3 To consider fines as an alternative to standards in controlling the health of workers.

4 To consider the costs and benefits of increasing the health of workers in textile mills and the trade-offs inherent in regulating the workplace.

Major Points

1 Although the evidence is not incontrovertible, there is some evidence which suggests that byssinosis or brown-lung disease is caused by cotton dust. When a person contracts byssinosis, however, it is not always easy to say whether and to what extent the disease was caused by cotton dust from work in a textile mill.

2 Cotton dust standards for textile mills will tend to reduce textile wage rates, increase the substitution of capital for labor in textile production, decrease textile employment, increase the prices of textile products, increase imports of textiles into the country, and reduce total domestic consumption of textile products.

3 Several counterarguments to standard economic analysis of cotton dust standards are often voiced; however, on close inspection most of the arguments are found to be weak. (Each of the counterarguments is developed briefly in the chapter.)

4 Short of shutting down the entire domestic textile industry, the elimination of all cases of byssinosis in the country is impossible. Since the cost of reducing the prevalence of byssinosis increases as air quality standards for mills are raised, a major question facing policy makers is, "How much cost are we willing to bear to further reduce the prevalence of byssinosis?"

5 At least up to a point, businesses have an economic interest in being concerned about the health and safety of their workers.

6 From an economic perspective, fines on companies where byssinosis is found to be a significant health problem are a better way, in economic terms, of dealing with byssinosis than standards on cotton dust. Standards force firms to be concerned with air quality; fines force firms to be concerned with the health of their workers.

Important New Terms and Concepts

Money wage rate
Real wage rate

In mid-1978, the Occupational Safety and Health Administration (OSHA) issued standards for permissible levels of cotton dust in textile manufacturing processes. The standards require that cotton dust be no higher than 0.2 milligrams per cubic meter of air in opening, picking, carding, spinning, and yarn preparation; 0.75 milligrams per cubic meter of air for slashing and weaving operations; and 0.5 milligrams per cubic meter of air in all other processes where workers are exposed to cotton dust.

Officials of the Carolina Brown Lung Association reacted to the announced standards with restrained enthusiasm: "We are overjoyed that we at least have a cotton dust standard, and while this is cause for celebration, we can be sure that other groups and unions will keep an eye on enforcement. . . . The standard is real now. I wish I had the breath for a small sigh of relief."[1] However, the official stated, "We are most upset that the new standard allows for a 0.75 level in the weave shop. Why these [weaving] people will be subjected to higher risks is a mystery to us."[2] And commenting on the part of the regulation that gives textile manufacturers 4 years to comply with the standards, the association officials noted, "This is simply too long, especially when you realize we are talking about breath and life. Usually these standards take effect immediately, so why four years? What provisions will be made for the workers who contract brown lung over the next four years?"[3]

Representatives of the textile industry, on the other hand, reacted negatively, as might be expected. They appealed immediately to the federal courts to have the standards reviewed. The manufacturers complained that the technology for meeting the standards was currently not available and that the standards "will have overwhelming financial implications for the entire cotton industry, not to mention boosting the price of any product containing cotton."[4] The specific purpose of this chapter is to evaluate the economic consequences of cotton dust standards. More generally, however, the purpose is to show how economic principles can be used to evaluate almost any government attempt to control the health and safety conditions of the workplace.

COTTON DUST AND WORKER HEALTH

The cotton dust standards were promulgated because OSHA had determined that cotton dust presents a "significant health hazard to employees"[5] and that cotton dust causes health problems that "range from an acute reaction manifested by a depression of pulmonary function indicators, or by subjective symptoms such as chest-tightness, shortness of breath, or cough, to a stage characteristic of chronic obstructive pulmonary disease which is often disabling. . . . The chronic stages of cotton dust induced respiratory diseases are . . . similar to chronic bronchitis or emphysema."[6] Byssinosis, characterized by cough, chest-tightness, and shortness of breath, especially felt at the start of the workweek, can be caused by cotton dust in the respiratory passages.

Popularly known as "brown-lung disease," byssinosis is difficult for doctors to identify and to specify the cause of, since textile workers often

[1] "Cotton Dust Standards Reaction Mixed," *Greenville News* (June 20, 1978), p. 1-A.
[2] Ibid.
[3] Ibid.
[4] Ibid., p. 2-A. At the time of this writing, court hearings were being held on the standards.
[5] *Federal Register* (June 23, 1978), p. 27350.
[6] Ibid., p. 27352.

smoke and are exposed to pollutants other than cotton dust that can cause byssinosis. However, according to research reports, the established cotton dust standards are expected to prevent 1,500 cases of brown-lung disease annually.[7] The standards are also expected to prevent innumerable other kinds of respiratory disorders among textile workers.

The evidence on the medical effects of cotton dust is not incontrovertible. On the one hand, OSHA has concluded that "the overwhelming scientific evidence in the record [established at hearings on cotton dust standards] supports the finding that cotton dust produces adverse health effects."[8] Further, OSHA argues that Congress, when it passed the legislation giving it authority to set safety standards in workplaces, did not intend "that the Secretary [of Labor] be paralyzed by debate surrounding diverse medical opinion."[9] Such debate, in terms of the *severity* and *pervasiveness* of adverse health effects of cotton dust, still exists.

On the other hand, the Council on Wage and Price Stability, in its review of the cotton dust standards and the Inflationary Impact Statement developed by OSHA, concluded that "OSHA does not know what the actual substance or substances are that cause the symptoms of byssinosis. Also the toxicity of respirable cotton dust varies depending upon the stage of the manufacturing process, the type of cotton, the blend with synthetics, the ambient dust levels, and the methods of picking and cleaning."[10] In addition, the National Institute on Occupational Safety and Health has found that "by far the most important problem in developing the cotton dust standard is that the identity of the agent responsible for byssinosis and other respiratory ailments of cotton workers is unknown."[11] In short, OSHA has established standards for cleaning up the air quality in textile factories based on inconclusive evidence of the likely effectiveness of the standards. The case of cotton dust standards serves the purpose of raising a fundamental question in public policy issues: How conclusive must the evidence be before government should or can take action?

THE LABOR MARKET EFFECTS OF COTTON DUST STANDARDS

Setting aside for now the issue of the actual effect of cotton dust on the health of textile workers, let us consider the economic consequences of imposed standards in terms of a conventional supply and demand model of labor markets. Objections to this model will be considered later.

[7]"Cotton Dust Standards Reactions Mixed," p. 1-A.

[8]*Federal Register* (June 23, 1978), p. 27352.

[9]Ibid., p. 27351.

[10]Robert W. Crandall et al., *Comments of the Council on Wage and Price Stability: Proposed Standards for Exposure to Cotton Dust*, Occupational Safety and Health Administration, Docket No. H-052 (June 17, 1977), p. 6.

[11]National Institute for Occupational Safety and Health, *Criteria for a Recommended Standard for Exposure to Cotton Dust* (1974), p. 85, as cited in ibid.

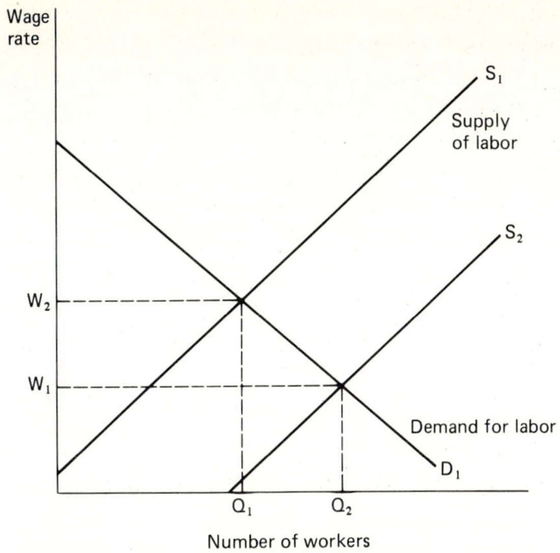

Figure 9.1

Workers are attracted to different jobs for numerous reasons. All these reasons can be summarized in the familiar assertion of economists that rational workers seek employment that maximizes their welfare as they themselves define their welfare. The supply of workers in any particular industry, such as the textile industry, is dependent upon the skill and educational level required, the social acceptability of the jobs, the conditions and attractiveness of the workplace, the relative amount of mental and physical labor required, the geographical area of employment, the availability of alternative employment, the prospect of continued employment, the presence or absence of unions, and so forth. Given the demand for labor, which is dependent upon the productivity of labor and the selling price of the final product,[12] the actual supply of workers going into any employment line will determine the wage rate (which, for our purposes, includes the value of fringe benefits). In competitive labor markets, the greater the supply of labor, the lower the wage rate, and vice versa.

Graphically speaking, if the demand and supply of labor are D_1 and S_1 in Figure 9.1, the wage rate will be W_2. However, if the labor supply is greater, S_2 instead of S_1, the wage rate for the workers will be lower, W_1 as opposed to W_2. The wage rate will be forced downward by the greater supply of workers and also by competition among them: the workers who want a job and who are willing to accept a lower wage will compete for the available jobs by offering to work for a lower wage, inducing all workers in the market to accept a lower wage rate.

[12]For a discussion of how the demand for labor is derived and graphically constructed, see Richard B. McKenzie and Gordon Tullock, *Modern Political Economy: An Introduction to Economics* (New York: McGraw-Hill Book Company, 1978), chap. 14.

These brief introductory comments on the operations of competitive labor markets are useful because they allow us to explore the market effects of cotton dust standards. As noted, the quality of working conditions will contribute to the willingness of people to accept employment in a given industry. Cotton dust, as a condition of work in textile mills, will affect people's willingness to work in the mills and, consequently, will help establish the position of the supply of labor curve in Figure 9.1. If cotton dust adversely affects people's health, then we should expect the supply of labor in the textile labor market to be restricted (S_1 instead of S_2); that is, fewer people will want to work in that industry. Accordingly, the wage rate will be higher than if the cotton dust were not prevalent. Workers breathing cotton dust and running the risk (but not certainty) of contracting respiratory disorders are presumably compensated for the risk they incur by receiving higher wages.

We say "presumably" because the workers have the opportunity of working elsewhere in a free competitive market system. The fact that they choose to work in textiles suggests that they are "better off" (by their own standards) by doing that than by choosing to work in their next-best alternative, a job that may be free of cotton dust but pays less. Furthermore, there are other hazards in other jobs, but that is only an indirect way of admitting a fundamental fact of life: the world, including places of work, is imperfect. Almost everyone has to make trade-offs and to optimize among all the characteristics of employment in such a way as to maximize personal satisfaction from work. Since the value of various employment characteristics must ultimately be individually and subjectively established, we can never be sure that people's welfare will or can be maximized outside of markets that allow people to freely choose where and under what conditions they will work. Any regulation that specifies conditions of work presumes that the people who establish the regulation know what people's subjective values are, a position that requires knowledge not directly observable.

The argument developed here is not meant to suggest that, for example, OSHA employees know nothing about working conditions and what workers do and do not like. Without question, OSHA employs some highly trained experts on the technology of safety. On the other hand, the purpose of these comments is to raise the question of whether or not technical experts know very much about how *different* workers individually *evaluate* working conditions and the relative trade-offs involved and whether or not technical experts know enough to make "better" decisions on working conditions than workers and employers interacting in a market setting.

The establishment of cotton dust standards affects the textile labor markets in two ways. First, it makes employment in textile mills relatively more attractive than it once was and, therefore, increases the supply of labor in the textile market. As a result, the wage rate (or the fringe benefits or some other aspect of working conditions) of textile workers will fall, assuming everything else remains constant.

If the wage rate is not allowed to fall because of minimum wage laws or union contract constraints, unemployment will increase among textile workers. If the wage rate cannot fall, textile firms can force workers to accept higher productivity levels. Workers are caught in the economic bind of either having to accept higher production levels or yielding their jobs to those who are willing and eager, given the absence of cotton dust, to take those jobs. Many workers who prefer to have higher wages and accept the higher employment risks that go with the higher wages, are forced, in order to retain their previous high wage rates, to accept even greater risks in employment areas not regulated to the extent of the textile industry. For example, textile workers who find their real wages falling because of cotton dust standards may choose to accept employment as steeplejacks, which is, perhaps, riskier than textile work.

Second, cotton dust standards have the effect of raising the cost of using human labor in the production of textiles and increasing the relative attractiveness of machinery (capital). As a result, the imposed standards should lead to a reduction in the demand for labor and an increase in the demand for capital equipment that can supplant labor in the mills. Textile firms, in other words, are induced by the cotton dust standards to become more automated in the long run. The result of the reduced labor demand should be a further wage rate reduction; that is, the effects of the increased labor supply should be compounded by the reduced labor demand. In the process, however, the overall cost of producing textiles will be increased, causing an increase in the price of textile products, reduced sales of domestic textile products, and greater textile imports.

As a result of the increase in the supply of labor and the decrease in the demand for labor, the employment opportunities for domestic labor in textiles will be reduced. Graphically, the new equilibrium in the textile labor market can be described as the intersection of the dashed curves in Figure 9.2, with a wage rate of W_1 and employment level of Q_1. Granted, the wage rate is lower in the new equilibrium and the lower wage rate increases domestic employment opportunities *over and above what they would have been.* However, the effect of the lower wage rate is more than offset by the reduced demand for domestic labor, which is caused by the substitution of capital for labor and the substitution of foreign for domestic textiles.

Without question, the greater capital employed in textiles as a consequence of the dust standards can make the labor that is used more productive; in addition, the reduced supply of textile products on the market will cause the price of textile products to rise. The increase in labor productivity and the prices of the textile products may lead one to believe that the demand for labor and employment of labor in textiles will rise. However, this outcome is not predicted, because it is self-contradictory. We know that the cotton dust standards will increase the cost of textile production, increase the prices of the products sold, and reduce the sales of textile products. Since more capital is used, there must be less labor used in order that production

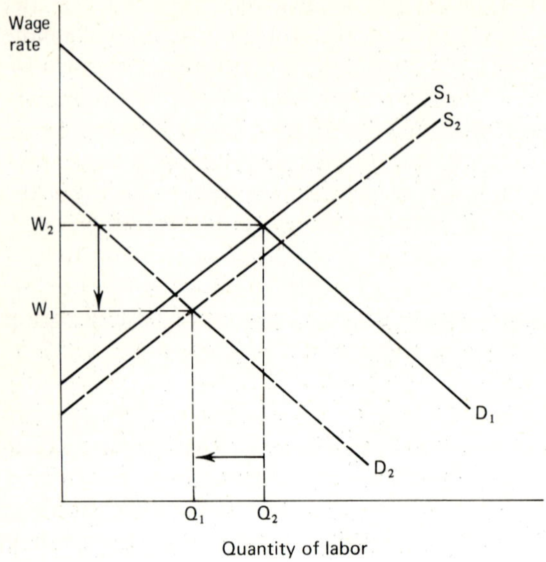

Figure 9.2

will not exceed the lower sales volumes. If more capital *and* more labor are used in textile production, then there must be more textile products produced, which, given the higher cost and price of the textile products, cannot be sold. To avoid the losses implied in excessive production, less labor will be used.

COUNTERARGUMENTS TO MARKET ANALYSIS

Several counterarguments may be suggested by the line of reasoning presented so far. First, some workers in the textile labor market may prefer to have less hazardous working conditions and lower wages; they, on balance, benefit from the imposed standards. However, workers who do not share these preferences will be effectively "taxed" (through lower market wages) for the benefit of these workers. Seen this way, cotton dust standards are a means of redistributing income. To many economists, cotton dust standards may seem like a peculiar device for the federal government to use to achieve its redistributive policies. This is especially true since the taxes and benefits resulting from dust standards are rather haphazardly distributed among workers, with little concern for income levels of various workers.

The second counterargument is that textile labor markets are not competitive; consequently, textile firms may be paying lower wages and providing poorer working conditions than is economically efficient. This argument must be seriously questioned. There are a large number of textile firms in the textile manufacturing areas of the country, like the Southeast, and in many other countries of the world. Because workers can move in and out of these regions, because nontextile firms in these regions can expand if the textile workers are underpaid, and because other firms can move into these regions, the assumption that the textile labor market is not competitive would seem to have little real world support. Admittedly, markets do not always adjust smoothly and quickly to changes in market conditions. However, the connection between cotton dust and health problems is not a particularly new revelation; it has been known by textile workers for years. It is not very difficult for workers to detect a relationship between working in a textile mill and coughing and tightening of the chest on Monday morning. Workers have had years to move to "better" alternative jobs, and many have done so.

In addition, most textile jobs are no more unskilled than the jobs in many other manufacturing processes; and most textile workers are sufficiently intelligent to acquire more education and, if they want, move to higher-skilled, less risky jobs. Many have not moved simply because they have chosen not to bear the costs (financial and time costs) of acquiring the needed education to move to other, less hazardous jobs. In other words, they prefer the combination of employment characteristics that they have to those that they could have.

Third, textile workers, so the counterargument may go, are paid very low wages; their wages cannot go down further. True, textile workers are, on the average, among the lowest-paid industrial workers. But simply because the average wage of textile workers is significantly (about 50 percent) above the legal minimum, the contention would appear to have very little merit. In addition, it should be understood that in inflationary times, such as the 1970s have been and the 1980s are likely to be, the actual *money wage rate—that is, the number of dollars earned per hour*—of textile workers need not fall in order for textile workers to be made worse off financially by the imposed cotton dust standards. So long as the money wage rate rises less rapidly than the rate of inflation, which can be caused by dust standards, the *real wage rate—which is the purchasing power of the money wage rate*—of textile workers will fall.[13]

Fourth, some argue that the cost of cotton dust standards can be passed along to consumers in the form of higher prices for textile products, and sales will not be affected. However, even monopolistic producers face downward-sloping demand curves for their product; that is, they realize that they must give up sales of their final products if they choose to raise their prices. Most economists would agree that textile manufacturers are

[13]Real wages in the textile industry may be on the rise. The main argument is, however, undisturbed. The imposed standards will keep textile wages from rising as rapidly as they would in the absence of textile standards. In this sense, the standards still make the workers worse off; the wages, relative to what they would be, are lowered.

far from monopolists. There are a large number of textile manufacturers in this country, and entry into textile markets is relatively free.

Furthermore, domestic manufacturers face intense competition from abroad. Currently, cotton dust standards are not being imposed in most countries where textiles are manufactured, often at lower prices than in the United States. The threat of foreign competition makes the demand for domestic textile products highly elastic, meaning that if the prices of domestic textile products are raised, a significant, disproportionately higher percentage drop in sales of domestic textiles can be anticipated.

Fifth, the argument is often heard that textile workers do not know what is harmful to them; technical experts, like OSHA officials, do know what is good for workers and should be allowed to make use of their superior knowledge by setting air quality standards in factories. As we have pointed out, OSHA officials may have considerable expertise in many dimensions of working conditions, but there is much knowledge that they are incapable of obtaining. They do not know worker preferences for the assumption of risk in working conditions.

Further, it seems that if workers are ignorant of the risks associated with their work, they can be informed about those risks with appropriate educational programs. Those workers who are unable or unwilling to assume the announced risks can move to other jobs; those who remain and assume the risks will be compensated with higher wages (since the supply of labor will then be lower). If textile workers are as "ignorant" as many (incorrectly) think, then the setting of standards can have unsuspected harmful effects. "Ignorant" workers may not fully understand the limited degree to which the established standards actually reduce the risk associated with their work and protect them from cotton dust. Having faith in the protectors' knowledge, "ignorant" textile workers may be more willing to work in the mills, increasing the supply of labor; and as a consequence, "ignorant" workers can be induced to work for less than if the standards did not exist. Contrary to popular belief, standards that are set for working conditions are based as much on politics as they are on technical knowledge of working conditions and health problems. (More will be said on this below.) If "ignorant" workers cannot be expected to understand the effects of their immediate working conditions on their long-term health, then it is questionable whether or not they will be able to appreciate the connection between politics and established OSHA standards.

THE BENEFITS OF COTTON DUST STANDARDS

OSHA contends that there is "overwhelming" scientific evidence that byssinosis is caused and aggravated by cotton dust. That is essentially correct. However, the evidence does not fully support the contention that the standards that have been set are economically or socially desirable. Respiratory problems have been related to the presence of cotton dust, but it is seriously questionable whether or not the standards that have been mandated for air quality in mills will significantly reduce the incidence of byssinosis among textile workers.[14] Although the new cotton dust standards require textile mills to take cotton dust from the air, the filtering systems that will be used will not take out very small particles of cotton dust. According to several researchers who have evaluated the various studies available, byssinosis is most probably caused by very small cotton dust particles, not by the clumps of dust that will be taken out to meet air quality standards.[15] For all we know, byssinosis incidence will be affected very little by cotton dust standards, suggesting that the costs that will be incurred by manufacturers and textile workers to improve air quality will have few measurable benefits.

Even if future studies show that the incidence of byssinosis is reduced significantly, does it follow that the standards are desirable? The incidence of byssinosis may fall, for example, from 120 per thousand to 119 per thousand of the relevant population. In that case, is the cost of eliminating the cotton dust worth the benefits that are received? Not necessarily. Clearly a person who works for a textile firm may be willing to make a substantial payment to avoid the *certainty* of contracting byssinosis. However, that is not relevant to the position of the prospective individual textile worker who has a probability of much less than 1 of contracting byssinosis. The relevant question to the prospective worker is: "Will the *reduced chance*, which may be quite small, of contracting byssinosis, be worth the cost that I will have to incur?" That is not an easy question to answer. As noted, many people are willing to assume some risks in employment. Most people, beyond some point in the improvement of the air quality, will no longer think an incremental improvement in the air quality is worth the cost that they have to suffer. They will prefer a combination of higher work-related health risks, higher wages, and more goods and services that higher wages permit.

If it is presumed from the start that the "greedy, capitalistic, unfeeling textile firms" do nothing to prevent workers from inhaling cotton dust, then it may be reasonable to conclude that almost any standard, no matter how unscientifically determined, will significantly improve the health of textile workers. As a matter of historical fact, firms do take some care in exposing their workers to cotton and other fiber dust and have been improving their air quality standards over time without government regulation.[16]

[14]OSHA recognizes the problem in the preamble to the cotton dust standards, *Federal Register* (June 23, 1978).

[15]See A. C. Griffin, Jr., J. D. Hatcher, and J. B. Cocke, "Card-Room Dust Levels and Response of Humans to Raw Cotton Cleaned by the Shirley Analyzer," *Textile Research Journal*, vol. 47, no. 2 (February 1977), pp. 129–131; J. D. Hatcher, "Physical Characteristics of Cotton Dust Generated in Different Processing Areas of a Cotton Mill," *Proceedings of the American Conference of Governmental Industrial Hygienists*, Topical Symposium on Cotton Dust (1974), pp. 271–283.

[16]Charles E. Martin and James E. Higgins, "Byssinosis and Other Respiratory Ailments: A Study of 6631 Cotton Textile Mill Workers," *Journal of Occupational Medicine* (July 1976), pp. 455–462.

Furthermore, textile firms have an economic incentive to provide health protection for their workers; the profit motive and compensation of labor give them that incentive. Firms know that working conditions affect the salaries they have to pay. By providing higher air quality and reducing the work-related health costs of employees, employers can reduce the cost of health insurance programs and the salaries paid their employees: capital expenditures for air quality control can effectively be amortized (paid for) through reduced salaries and higher labor productivity.

Finally, it should be noted that workers are not equally susceptible to cotton dust. Some workers are unable to be on mill floors for more than an hour or so without showing symptoms of respiratory problems; others appear to be able to work in high concentrations of cotton dust for long periods of time without exhibiting visible adverse effects. Textile firms have an economic incentive to move allergic personnel to work areas where dust is at low levels. In summary, most of the productive or inexpensive methods of reducing the incidence of dust-related health problems may have been taken. Imposed standards must reduce the incidence of health problems from cotton dust from the level that is determined by sheer economic forces. Therefore, reducing the respiratory problems of workers in cotton mills may be more easily mandated by law than achieved.

THE COSTS OF COTTON DUST STANDARDS

If we accept the fact that cotton dust standards must be mandated, then should we necessarily develop standards so that *all* cases of byssinosis and other respiratory problems of workers caused by dust are eliminated? Not very likely, to say the least. The development of such standards would be the equivalent of shutting down the entire textile industry in the United States, since there is no way that manufacturers could, given current technology, meet those standards. Would such standards be desirable? The answer will depend on who is asked. As we have mentioned, many workers are willing to incur *some* risk in their work in order to be employed and to obtain higher wages.

Then, how should the standards that are mandated be determined? The usual answer of the economist is to weigh the costs of the standard against the benefits. Indeed, the appropriate rule is that the standard should be made more strict until the marginal cost of avoiding another case of byssinosis, for example, is equal to the benefits of avoiding the case. If that point has not been reached, then the standard can be made more stringent; more costs will be incurred to meet the more stringent standard, but the greater benefits achieved through reduced byssinosis will exceed the cost. The net welfare of society will be raised.

As is true in all production processes, the marginal cost of avoiding cases of byssinosis increases as more and more dust is removed from the

Table 9.1 Marginal Cost and Benefits of Ventilation Controls in Yarn Preparation

	Dust concentration (mg/m^3)		
	0.5	0.2	0.1
Total annual cost incremental to next strictest standard (millions)	$36.7	$325.3	$613.8
Additional byssinosis cases avoided per year (all grades)	1,180	569	429
Marginal costs per byssinosis case avoided (thousands)	$31	$572	$1,431

Source: Robert W. Crandall et al., *Comments of the Council on Wage and Price Stability: Proposed Standards for Exposure to Cotton Dust*, Occupational Safety and Health Administration, Docket No. H-052 (June 17, 1977), p. 6.

air of factories, or as the standard is made more stringent. (This is another application of the law of diminishing returns, explained in Chapter 1.) Consider Table 9.1. It contains actual estimates—but only estimates—of the marginal cost and benefits of ventilation controls in one production process, yarn preparation and weaving. As indicated, the *additional* cases of byssinosis avoided go down from 1,180 per year when the dust concentration is 0.5 milligrams per cubic meter of air to 429 per year when the dust concentration is 0.1 milligrams per cubic meter of air. In short, making the air more pure becomes less and less effective in achieving the desired result, reduced incidence of byssinosis. On the other hand, the marginal cost of avoiding an *additional* case of byssinosis has been estimated to be $31,000 when the dust concentration level is set at 0.5 milligrams per cubic meter of air; however, the marginal cost of an additional case avoided is estimated at $1,431,000 when the dust concentration level is set at 0.1 milligrams per cubic meter of air.[17]

Where do we draw the line and set the standard? Although the information in Table 9.1 helps us visualize the problem of equating the marginal cost and benefits of standards, the answer to that question is indeed difficult to develop, especially since the data may not be very accurate. How do we value cases of byssinosis avoided? If a standard is set short of eliminating byssinosis altogether, then monetary values must *implicitly* or *explicitly* be attached to cases avoided in order that those values can be equated with the monetary values for the costs of avoiding cases of byssinosis. Developing the needed monetary values may be more easily talked about than actually done, because byssinosis cases are not "traded" on markets like soap and do not carry a dollar price tag. Whose preferences do we use in making the determination of the value of a case of byssinosis avoiced? Do we defer to the expertise of OSHA officials? People who work for OSHA may have the

[17]Crandall et al., *Comments of the Council on Wage and Price Stability*, tables 1 and 2, pp. 20 and 21.

technical knowledge to compute the number of cases avoided when standards are set at various levels; but, as we have indicated, they are not the ones assuming the risk of contracting byssinosis and it is questionable whether or not their monetary estimate of the value of an additional case of byssinosis avoided is any more reasonable or meaningful than anyone else's. Certainly, it is reasonable to assume that people will differ over how cases of byssinosis avoided are valued. Which valuation do we accept? It is all too easy to conclude that the matter is a public policy issue, to be decided by some kind of collective decision made in Congress. But, we must point out that decisions in Congress are made with votes—"yes" or "no" reactions to proposals put forth—and votes are a rather crude method of reflecting people's preferences, that is, *their subjective values*. Votes do not give a very precise indication of the *intensity* of political positions taken. They are, to that extent, poor indications of the "value" of anything.

Again, how do we equate marginal cost and benefits of avoiding cases of byssinosis? Will the standards selected by collective governmental decision processes be superior to the standards that are worked out in reasonably competitive labor markets? Might we be worse off by making the standards too stringent (in terms of jobs and worker incomes lost) than by having them too lenient? Those are the types of questions that cannot be avoided when decisions are made to regulate the health and safety conditions of workplaces. Those questions do not rule out government action in dealing with cotton, but they clearly reveal the true complexity of the policy issue at stake.

FINES AS AN ALTERNATIVE TO STANDARDS ON COTTON DUST

The Council on Wage and Price Stability notes in its review of the cotton dust standards that "the problem is not that there is too much cotton dust; the problem is that there is too much byssinosis."[18] and the Council proposes that OSHA should concentrate its attention on reducing the incidence of byssinosis and not cotton dust. The Council suggests that, instead of standards, OSHA should impose a fine on firms whose workers come down with byssinosis, or any other respiratory problem, that is shown to be related to cotton dust in workplaces. The penalty can be based on the severity as well as the number of medical problems detected. The reasoning behind the proposal is that the fine will give textile firms the economic incentive they need to take steps to reduce byssinosis. The fine can be raised until firms are induced to reduce the incidence of byssinosis to the acceptable level established by OSHA. (Firms can be expected to react this way to a fine because the marginal cost of reducing the incidence of byssinosis, as

[18]Ibid., p. 6.

pointed out, increases as the prevalence of byssinosis is reduced. Hence, an increase in the fine will entice firms to incur the cost of eliminating the source of the health problem in order to avoid the fine.)

There are several points that can be made in favor of imposing fines on firms rather than imposing standards for cotton dust on firms. First, the policy issue is focused squarely on what is desired, reduced incidence of byssinosis. As opposed to judging the success of the government's policy in terms of reduced cotton dust in the workplace, the policy is judged in terms of the stated objective, reduced incidence of byssinosis.

Second, there are alternative ways by which firms can reduce the incidence of byssinosis. Firms can

- Reduce the amount of cotton dust emitted into the air
- Move the more sensitive workers from areas where cotton dust is prevalent to areas where the air is relatively free of cotton dust
- Develop new fibers that do not have the harmful health effects of cotton
- Require workers to wear respirators or other devices that keep the cotton dust out of the workers' respiratory passages
- Develop new methods of cleaning cotton
- Shift to less toxic grades of cotton

There are probably any number of other ways of reducing the incidence of byssinosis that will become apparent to textile firms when they are confronted with the prospects of paying fines for workers who contract byssinosis. The central point is clear: Reducing the amount of dust from the atmosphere is not the only alternative open to firms for improving the health of workers, and it may not be, and very likely in many production circumstances will not be, the least costly way of reducing the incidence of byssinosis. Indeed, the Council on Wage and Price Stability points out that only the textile firms really know the least costly way of achieving the goal of improving the health of workers. The firms are the ones that have to deal with the cotton dust on a day-to-day basis and know the alternative technology and what will work best (most efficiently) in their individual situations. OSHA can acquire only scant information on the relative effectiveness and efficiency of cotton dust standards from the limited studies that it undertakes or has other people do.

The third point in favor of imposing fines on firms is that the cotton dust standards require firms only to meet the set standards for cotton dust; there is no incentive for them to do any more than meet the set standards. When firms are fined for each case of byssinosis, they have an incentive to search for ways of reducing the incidence of byssinosis down to zero.

As an alternative to standards and fines, firms can be required to carry insurance that will compensate victims for work-related respiratory problems. The greater the incidence of respiratory problems, the greater will be the insurance premiums. As in the case of fines, required insurance gives firms an economic incentive to reduce the incidence of the health problem, not just the incidence of cotton dust. Indeed, required insurance has essentially the same effect as governmentally imposed fines. Both methods make firms legally liable for the work-related health problems of their employees.

We do not mean to suggest here that fines or required insurance is necessarily a desirable policy course. Our earlier discussion raises serious reservations about the efficiency of any government action. The analysis suggests only that if government intervention in the labor market is warranted, then fines and required insurance are more cost-effective than standards. That is, given the cost incurred by firms, fines and required insurance will tend to reduce the incidence of respiratory problems by more than standards will and the objectives of regulation will be accomplished more efficiently.[19]

CONCLUDING COMMENTS

Cotton dust standards have become a part of the burgeoning administrative law in the United States. Without question, the regulation of cotton dust is an effort on the part of many well-intended people to "do good." As we have pointed out, some people benefit from the standards: a portion of the textile labor force, the people who write and research such standards, the manufacturers of automated textile machinery, and foreign producers of textile products.

However, these benefits are achieved at the expense of many workers and consumers, an unfortunate but common outcome of many regulatory efforts. The cotton dust standards will tend to raise the cost of textile production; increase the price of the final products to consumers, lowering the real income of consumers; reduce employment in the domestic textile industry; reduce wages and fringe benefits of domestic textile workers; increase textile imports; and, in general, reduce the efficiency of the allocation of resources in the United States economy.

There are risks involved in the production of textiles, as in the production of many other products. Many of those risks can be reduced by administrative fiat. On the other hand, the rule making that is required raises questions that are unavoidable for the person required to vote on proposals like cotton dust standards: What are the costs of the regulation, and are those costs more than covered by the benefits that are received? If we were to eliminate *all* risks in *all* of our daily lives like those which exist in textile

[19]We say "tend to" because it is conceivable that fines and required insurance will be no more cost-effective than standards. This will be true if the elimination of cotton dust is the most efficient means of reducing the incidence of respiratory problems.

mills, what would our individual real incomes be? Would we be better off? How far do (should) we go in protecting people from the perils of daily existence?

QUESTIONS TO PONDER

1 "Standards for cotton dust in United States mills will cause the problem of cotton dust to be exported to foreign countries." Do you agree or disagree? Explain.
2 Do cotton dust standards improve the political position of textile mills in their quest for higher tariffs on imported textiles? Use supply and demand curves in your answer.
3 What will standards do to the effective wage rate of textile workers who retain their jobs after the standards are imposed? What will standards do to the effective wage rate of textile workers who lose their jobs as a result of the standards? Use supply and demand curves in answering both questions.
4 What economic arguments can be offered in support of cotton dust standards? To what extent can "external costs and/or benefits," "public goods," and "monopoly power" be used to support an economic case for standards? Explain the political support for cotton dust standards.
5 Why might producers of synthetic textiles be in favor of cotton dust standards? Will all markets for textile products be affected by cotton dust standards to the same extent?

ADDITIONAL READING

Crandall, Robert W. et al. *Comments of the Council on Wage and Price Stability: Proposed Standards for Exposure to Cotton Dust*, Occupational Safety and Health Administration, Docket No. H-052 (June 17, 1977), p. 6.

Chapter 10

The Pay System and Departmental Discord: The Games Professors Play

CHAPTER PREVIEW

Central Question

How does the university pay system—involving a fixed fund of wages—encourage faculty to engage in productive and predatory behavior?

Major Objectives

1 To develop an economic explanation for much discord that is observed in some institutional settings.

2 To explain how the wage fund pay system, typically used in universities for making annual salary adjustments, tends to divert faculty effort away from productive behavior and tends to encourage predatory behavior.

3 To suggest institutional changes in universities that may modulate internal strife that exists among some faculty groups.

Major Points

1 Universities typically allocate annual raises to faculty from a fixed fund of wages, called a "wage fund." Under the wage fund pay system, a faculty member's *relative*, not *absolute*, performance level is what generally determines the size of a raise. Faculty members can, therefore, increase their own raises by increasing their own performance level or by reducing the performance level of other faculty members.

2 The existence of predation may reduce overall faculty production; nonetheless, predatory behavior can be in the private interests of individual faculty members who have a *comparative* advantage in predation.

3 Department members can be expected to reach a "predatory equilibrium," which may involve more or less predatory actions on many people's parts.

4 The size of departments in which the wage fund operates will affect the extent of predation: predation will tend to be more common in smaller departments than larger departments. However, for other reasons that are briefly discussed, very large departments may not be economically efficient. Predation may, therefore, be a natural consequence of department sizes that are chosen.

Important New Terms and Concepts

Productive behavior
Predatory behavior

Economists are interested in demonstrating how market characteristics, such as the degree of competitiveness among workers and among producers, determine the wages people are paid. They are, in short, concerned with the institutional framework within which labor markets must operate. This chapter is also concerned with institutional characteristics. However, the chapter has a somewhat unusual purpose: it is to show how institutional characteristics can influence the amount of discord among workers. The analysis focuses on the academic labor market, but the basic principles developed are readily applicable to other labor markets in which the same institutional characteristics are observed.

INTRODUCTION

Departmental discord is not uncommon in colleges and universities. Indeed, many university faculty members look upon departmental dissension as an occupational disease. Richard Mandel, in his irreverent but reasonably accurate treatment of some parts of university life, suggests that departmental strife is an integral if not a principal component of the "games" faculty members play. He writes that some faculty members evaluate candidates for positions in their department on the basis of "whether he will be a possible member of their camp or the enemies'."[1] Later Mandel adds: "A treasured skill in provincial academics is the ability gracefully to intercede and patiently soothe tempers . . . in essentially petty or vicious disputes. . . . The lazy intriguers who dominate half the American campuses will put knives in the back of men and women whose manifested energy exposes their lack of it."[2]

Obviously, Mandel is prone to exaggeration. Many faculties in colleges and universities get along quite well with one another. On the other hand, one does not have to fully agree with Mandel's thesis or, for that matter, anyone else's description of academic life to find an important kernel of truth in the general picture he presents. Although frequently kept from students, backbiting, warring factions within departments, and small-scale political intrigue are present in academic circles. The purpose of this chapter is to explore the *economic* basis for much observed departmental discord. More specifically, the system by which faculty members are usually paid contributes to a climate that breeds departmental strife. The analysis presented here is not intended to preclude other, possibly more cogent, explanations for discord among professors; personality conflict, no doubt, plays a role, as do ideological differences and other factors. Rather, the primary purpose of the chapter is to investigate the effects of an institutional characteristic (i.e., the wage fund pay system) on employee behavior and to suggest institutional changes that can modulate internal strife. As stated in the opening paragraph, the educational bureaucracy provides the basis for an excellent case study and a means of drawing out basic conclusions that can be applied to a wide range of social contexts with similar institutional characteristics. Having said that, we will now consider the way in which faculty members are typically paid and their raises typically determined.

THE WAGE FUND PAY SYSTEM

The increase in a department's salary budget in a state university is not usually dependent upon the productivity of the department; rather, it is overwhelmingly dependent upon the appropriations of the state legislature.[3] A legislated 7 percent increase in the salary of state employees, for example, will generally mean a 7 percent increase in a department's budget. Perhaps the university administration, in the course of distributing the

[1] Richard D. Mandel, *The Professor Game* (Garden City, N.Y.: Doubleday and Company, Inc., 1977), p. 156.

[2] Ibid., p. 160.

[3] I restrict the analysis to state universities because that is by far faculty's dominant educational setting.

total salary adjustment it has been given, will hold back a small portion of the overall increase for special purposes such as adjusting the salaries of women, minority groups, or hard-to-replace faculty members who have received offers from other schools and for giving out teaching and service awards. On the other hand, it is reasonably accurate to characterize the typical university pay system as one in which lump-sum salary increase packages are passed down to departments; "necessary" salary adjustment packages are not usually formulated at the departmental level and passed up through channels to the level of the provost or president. Faculty productivity is considered, generally, only in determining *relative* salary increases among department members, not in determining the overall size of the fund that is given a department.[4]

THE INCENTIVE OF FACULTY

As described, the university operates on a wage fund system of pay. The department is given a fund of wages (or "wage pie") to distribute. The concept of the wage fund and the theory of wage determination spawned by the concept were intrinsic to the writings of economists and social philosophers before and after Adam Smith. The theory was that firms had a fixed fund of wages to distribute to their employees; therefore, if one group of workers got higher wages or if more workers were hired, then other workers received lower wages.

A variation of the wage fund theory underpinned Marx's notion of the class struggle anticipated in a capitalistic system. The problem with Marx's use of the wage fund concept has long been recognized: at least in theory, the wage fund does not apply to market economies. The size of the pie from which workers draw their wages is not constant and, indeed, expands with increases in individual and collective productivity—that is, when more is produced, more is sold, and more is available to distribute to workers. Although conflict will always exist among people for scarce resources in any social system, the intense Marxian struggle between workers and their employers over a constant fund of wages does not exist. The wage fund theory has not been repudiated as a theoretical proposition; only its application to the capitalistic system has been rejected. This has been because of

[4]David Katz describes the salary and promotion system at the University of Illinois in this manner: "Once the budget allocations are made to individual departments, the department chairman, sometimes in consultation with his faculty executive committee, determines the salaries to be achieved by individual faculty members. Although final decisions regarding salaries are almost always made at department levels after receiving their budget allocations, department promotional decisions are subject to much greater scrutiny by higher administrative echelons, especially in the college and all-university committees on promotions." [David A. Katz, "Faculty Salaries, Promotions, and Productivity at a Large University," *American Economic Review*, vol. 63 (June 1973), pp. 469–471.]

the inconsistency between the institutional requirements of the theory and the institutional setting of a capitalistic economy.

However, the modern state university—by design—operates on a pay system that closely approximates the institutional requirements of the wage fund theory. As this chapter shows, the spector of Marxian conflict among workers should be present in precisely the type of social context—a government institution—with which Marx was not inclined or prepared to deal. In applying the wage fund theory to education, the conclusion must be altered slightly. The primary conflict (or struggle) will be *among* workers (i.e., faculty), not *between* workers (faculty) and their employers (administrators), although the latter conflict is seldom absent in the university.

Generally, under a wage fund pay system, the faculty member knows that what he or she does will have little or no effect on the size of the department's wage fund. What the faculty member does will affect only the portion of the department's wage fund (or size of the piece of pie) he or she receives. Granted, the overall reputation of a department may have a slight effect on the department's salary allocation. For instance, the department may get 7.1 percent to distribute to department members rather than 7 percent if the state legislature perceives its unusual productivity and legislates, accordingly, a higher across-the-board increase to state employees. A department's aggregate activity can have an external effect that trickles down and is realized in a larger wage fund for the department.

However, this is not likely to happen. It is very difficult for external funding sources such as state legislatures to judge the productivity of an individual department. This is because legislators know very little about one of the principal activities of faculty, which is publishing articles in scholarly journals. If they make judgments on such easily accessible information as the *number* of articles published by departments or universities, they will, not knowing the value of different journals or different articles, stimulate the production of numbers of articles and quality (whatever that is) will be sacrificed for quantity. There is no basis for assuming that under such a system an increase in state appropriations improves the efficiency of the educational process.

The higher levels of a university's administration make across-the-board salary allocations to departments for similar reasons. They are imperfectly aware of what constitutes productivity in individual departments, and deans and department heads cannot always be counted on for help in the matter. Department heads often view themselves as lobbyists for their departments before their deans, and deans typically consider themselves as lobbyists before higher administrators.

Furthermore, department heads and deans are caught in competitive dilemmas with their counterparts at each level of academic administration. Each department head, for example, has an interest in maximizing his or her department's reputation for productivity. Department heads know that the ease of their job is directly related to the size of the salary package that they are able to bring to the department. (The fact that each head is judged partly on how well he or she is able to "bring home the bacon" indicates the political nature of the job.) In addition, salary and tenure for the head of the department are likely to be related to the total or average salary within the department, as well as the salary structure within the department. (The department head is often elected and evaluated by department members.) Given these conditions, department heads have a positive incentive to distort or, in other ways, overdramatize the importance of what their faculty members are doing. They know also that other department heads have a similar incentive; and, therefore, in order to protect their department's relative standing, they have a negative incentive (i.e., the avoidance of a cost imposed by other heads) to distort the quantity and value of their faculty's productivity. In short, each head is in a classic competitive dilemma. Deans are in a similar situation, except, of course, they deal at a higher level of aggregation on the basis of information that, for reasons given, they may only vaguely understand.[5]

The task force, composed of representatives from across the campus, is of little help in establishing even a rudimentary definition of faculty productivity. The reason is twofold: First, each task force member is likely to have little idea of the value of any article not directly related to his or her research interest, much less his or her discipline. For example, few economists can name three journals in physics, much less assess the relative merits of an article in a physics journal. Second, the type of competition among department heads and deans mentioned above comes into play in the task force. Task force members have an interest in distorting the criteria for faculty productivity in such a way that it maximizes the relative ranking of their department and, especially, their own worth to the university. In short, there is no reason to assume that the criteria that will emerge from the task force will reflect truth on the matter of departmental productivity; rather, it will reflect a political outcome—a compromise or median-vector solution—that is dependent upon the voting rule used as well as the exact composition of the task force.

For these reasons, it is understandable why it took a committee of the College of Business at the University of Georgia 6 months to devise criteria for faculty research. The criteria devised were based on the *number* of articles and the *number* of pages in each article and a cardinal ranking of journals. The ranking of various classifications of research extended over 22 single-spaced pages. After being used for a short period, the criteria were

[5]For more on the political environment of bureaucracy in general, see Gordon Tullock, *The Politics of Bureaucracy* (Washington, D.C.: Public Affairs Press, 1965).

eventually dropped because they had become a dubious means of guiding faculty effort. At a regional university in North Carolina, a task force spent 2 years developing a quasi-mechanical method for allocating faculty positions. The scheme required departments to list for the first time their publications and professional activities of their members. With the unspoken approval of their deans, departments "padded" their reports. For those outside each college, it was very difficult to determine what was and was not padding. The allocation scheme was never used.

PRODUCTION VERSUS PREDATION

The size of the wage pie is determined independently of what departmental members do in the aggregate. This reasonably accurate generalization suggests that each individual faculty member is likely to conclude that his or her work-related activity will not affect the size of the pie. With this presupposition, individual faculty members must then concentrate their efforts on securing the largest possible piece of what is (perceived to be) a given-sized pie. Conceptually, individual professors can accomplish the objective of maximizing the size of their piece of the wage pie in two ways: (1) *by increasing their output* (*productive behavior*), and (2) *by taking actions that will reduce the output of others in the department or by failing to help other faculty members in their work and using the time for their own purposes* (*predatory behavior*). Either way, since *relative* productivity determines pay and salary increment, the individual faculty member can raise his or her *relative* ranking within the department.

Faculty members have different efficiencies in productive and predatory behavior. Some will find that, on the margin, they are comparatively more efficient at production—that is, in increasing such things as the number of research grants obtained and papers published. Others will find that they have a comparative efficiency in predation—that is, in reducing the output of others. The possible modes of predatory behavior are limited only by the imagination of the individual faculty members. Predation may include, for instance, tying up department resources such as graduate students, secretarial help, and computer terminals so that other, relatively more productive faculty members cannot use them. Predation may also involve creating a climate of ill-will that induces faculty members to divert their efforts from productive work to defending themselves against rumors and criticisms. It may also involve voting against tenure for potential department members who may be relatively more productive. More commonly, predation may involve being uncooperative in areas in which cooperation could be useful in raising the relative ranking of others.

Needless to say, professors who engage in predation will divert resources away from production of, say, articles; however, so long as they reduce their colleagues' performance by more than they could have increased their own performance, predation can be rational and will be used. Indeed, fully rational faculty members will allocate their time until they are in what may be termed a "predatory equilibrium." The necessary condition for such an equilibrium is that the marginal return from the last hour of work applied to predation and production are equal. That is, faculty members will tend to allocate their work time until the last hour spent on predation has the same effect on raising their relative ranking as the last hour spent on production. If this were not the case, faculty members could reallocate their time and improve their ranking within the department.

If one faculty member has a comparatively greater efficiency in predation and uses predation to improve his or her relative ranking, the relative marginal return from production and predation to other faculty members will be changed. In this way, the predation of one faculty member will disturb the equilibrium of other faculty members, and they can be expected to alter the allocation of efforts between predation and production. Some will engage in more predation, since that form of behavior for them will have become relatively more valuable in terms of determining their share of the wage fund. The predatory reactions of other faculty members will cause the professor who disturbed the initial equilibrium to adjust his or her own allocation of time, increasing predatory activity. Because of the increasing cost of greater specialization in any activity, the predators, both the initiate and the respondents, can reach an equilibrium of sorts in which neither party has an economic interest in expanding predation further: it simply costs too much to do so. This equilibrium may be characterized as a kind of stable anarchistic process, with assaults, counterassaults, and defense maneuvers.

The outcome can be an *aggregate* welfare loss for all department members. This is because members may expend more time and energy and other resources in predatory and defensive activity than they would have spent on production if no one had engaged in predatory behavior. Furthermore, the result of the assaults and counterassaults can be that the participants end up in exactly the same ranking within the department and with exactly the same salary increments that they would have received in the absence of predation.[6] Clearly, in an academic setting the value of a Lockean-style social contract that forbids predation can be productive.

However, the existence of the wage fund system of pay makes any truce

[6]For modern discussions of the types of Hobbesian anarchy and equilibrium that are briefly described here, see Winston C. Bush, "Individual Welfare in Anarchy," *Explorations in the Theory of Anarchy* (Blacksburg, Va.: Center for the Study of Public Choice, Virginia Polytechnic Institute and State University, 1972). For a more complete analysis of social contracts—their productivity, their rational base, and their tenuous nature—see James Buchanan, *The Limits of Liberty* (Chicago: University of Chicago Press, 1975). See also Richard B. McKenzie and Gordon Tullock, *Modern Political Economy: An Introduction to Economics* (New York: McGraw-Hill Book Company, 1978), chap. 5.

that is achieved tenuous. Once the contract is agreed upon, all participants, especially those with a comparative efficiency in predation, have an incentive to chisel on the agreement and to reengage in predatory exploits. Furthermore, there may very well be faculty members who, in spite of the negative aggregate effects of predation, are better off in a state of academic anarchy than they are in a state in which each person must rely on his or her productive abilities. This is partly because the size of the wage fund is unlikely to be affected by the amount of predatory behavior within a department, unless, of course, it becomes so flagrant, in a relative sense, that the provost or president is aware of the disruption being created. However, most anarchistic equilibriums lie submerged below the level that can be detected by remote administrators who allocate the funds to departments and have little incentive to detect predation.[7]

PREDATION AND ACADEMIC FREEDOM

The potential for conflict and predation among team members exists in most team sports, just as the potential for conflict and predation exists among members in an academic department. On a basketball team, for example, there are only five starting positions: there is a kind of "position fund" that must be allocated on the basis of the *relative* performance of competing team players. Each team member can increase his or her chances of securing one of the starting positions by increasing skills (production) or by, in various ways, reducing the skills of others (predation). Covert elbowing in practice is one obvious predatory measure. A primary function of the coach, however, is to minimize the likelihood that team members will shirk their responsibilities and become involved in predatory behavior. Using continual surveillance, the coach and staff direct player efforts away from predation and toward skill development. The coaching staff is able to guide player behavior by imposing costs on those who engage (or threaten to engage) in predation and by constantly exhorting team members to work toward their common and easily evaluated goal, which is winning games.

For several reasons there is much greater difficulty in guiding the behavior of faculty members. First, the goals of the department are only vaguely specified, and the degree to which those goals are attained is extraordinarily difficult to measure. The problem of measurement is surely more difficult than the problem of measuring the success of a basketball team. Second, the behavior of individual faculty members is shrouded in the cloak

[7]To the extent that the state of the wage fund is influenced by the level of internal strife—predatory and counterpredatory behavior—department members have an incentive to hand over to the department head powers that, although they require all to give up a portion of their academic freedom, will control the predatory actions of all. Beyond some level of internal conflict, the size of the wage fund can be adversely affected by the conflict in the department. This may partially explain why "all-out wars" within departments are very rare.

of academic freedom. (At least, much predatory behavior can be obscured by the guise of academic freedom.) Department heads and deans simply cannot supervise their "players" the way that a coach can supervise basketball players. Additionally, it would be unethical and a breach of academic freedom for the department head to keep tabs on faculty members the way a coach does basketball players. Because they fear being accused of "snooping," many department heads associate little, socially or professionally, with their faculty members.

DEPARTMENT SIZE AND PREDATION

There are, of course, many factors that determine faculty incentive to engage in predation. Not all of these can be dealt with in the space of this chapter. However, one significant factor is the size of the department. Consider the incentive structure of the individual professor in the context of large and small departments. (You will notice that we apply here our analysis of large and small groups developed in earlier chapters, specifically Chapters 1 and 3.)

The Large Department

In a large department, the productive efforts of one faculty member can increase his or her relative ranking and increase his or her share of the wage fund. Any increase one faculty member receives will be taken from a large number of other faculty members. However, the subsequent decrease in the salary increments of other faculty members may be so small that no one of them has an incentive to engage in predatory, counterproductive acts. In a large department, each faculty member may reason that he or she will have to obstruct the production of a significant number or, perhaps, all the other faculty members in order to *materially* affect his or her own salary. The rational, least costly course of action may be to forget what others are doing and to direct attention to one's own production, over which one has direct control. That is, one may behave *as if* predation were not even an alternative.

The perfect competitor, closely approximated by the individual farmer, is the standard market analog to the large-group member envisioned here. Indeed, the large-group nature of perfect competition is one of the reasons economists are able to deduce that that market structure is efficient. Each perfect competitor is induced to compete by changing the price until the price of the good is equal to the cost of production. In addition, each perfect competitor is induced to compete by production, not predation. Individual farmers do not try to improve their own market position by predation—for example, destroying the crops of fellow farmers—because of the magnitude of the task. There are simply too many farmers whose crops must be destroyed before the price of the product will be significantly affected. By the time even a small portion of the total crop is destroyed, one is likely to have diverted all one's resources away from production and will have nothing to sell even if the price is raised. Therefore, farmers can expect to be treated by other farmers *as if* they are not really competitors, *as if* predation is not an alternative mode of behavior.

The Small Department

In a small department, the sanguinity of perfect competition can be largely removed. An increase in the output of any one faculty member can significantly reduce the share of the wage fund that is received by each of the other members, and other faculty members have an incentive to engage in predatory behavior.[8] As in all small oligopolistic markets, the actions of all oligopolists are interdependent.[9] By definition of the market structure, all oligopolists have an incentive to act and react to each other, in a game theoretic manner. Interestingly, it is in the oligopolistic (and/or monopolistically competitive[10]) markets that charges of unfair competitive practices are most frequently made and that the spector of violence most often appears. To turn to an example in a resource market, an individual coal miner, acting independently of other miners, has no reason to destroy the property of another miner or of a coal company. On the other hand, members of a coal mining union, acting collectively as an economic, oligopolistic unit, have an incentive to destroy the equipment of nonunion coal companies and the personal property of nonunion coal miners.[11] In theory, there is no reason why we should not expect the same predatory-type tactics to be used by faculty members in a market (department) setting.

The Optimum-Size Department

The foregoing analysis does not lead to the conclusion that extremely large departments are necessarily efficient from an economic perspective. This is because two economic considerations have thus far been sidestepped: (1)

[8]The production of an individual department member imposes a significantly negative externality on other members. Contrary to the usual example of external costs, however, the external cost resulting from the wage fund pay system results in underproduction, not overproduction.

[9]An oligopoly is a market with a few competitors who produce a similar product (such as is true in the steel industry) or differentiated product (such as is true in the automobile industry).

[10]A monopolistically competitive market is a market made up of a number of producers who sell a differentiated product. An example of monopolistic competition is the market for textbooks.

[11]The actions of members of United Mine Workers during the coal miner's strike of 1978 is testimony to the reasonableness of the analysis.

the cost of forming social contracts among faculty members that preclude predation, and (2) the cost of obtaining information that is useful in ranking the performance of faculty members within the department.

As the size of the department expands, the cost from predation that a department and university must bear goes down. This is the central deduction from the above analysis of large and small departments. Conversely, as the size of the department expands, the cost that department members must incur to form a viable social contract to modulate predation will tend to increase. This is true because, first, there are more people in large departments who must be brought in on any negotiation to establish a social contract. (It is relatively easy for two people to agree to prohibit predation, but very costly, as can be imagined, for fifty or sixty people to reach a similar agreement.) Second, the difficulty of detecting the source of predation increases with an increase in the size of the department; this is because there are a greater number of individual perpetrators and combinations of perpetrators. Third, the social significance of each individual in the context of the social contract is reduced as the department size is expanded; the free-rider problem associated with any social agreement will increase, making negotiations for a social contract and enforcement of it more costly.[12] Furthermore, given one department head and associated overhead costs, as the size of the department increases, gathering reliable information on what department members are doing and the value of individual effort becomes more difficult.

The analysis leads to the conclusion that some intermediate department size, between large and small, is likely to be economically efficient. In a very large department, although the costs that individual members suffer from their own and others' predatory behavior are very slight, it is quite costly for the members to get together (collude) and collectively agree, implicitly or explicitly, to stop their predation. The cost of trying to stop the predation can exceed the cost that must be incurred if there is no collective prohibition against predation. On the other hand, in a very small department, members can easily agree to prohibit predation; but if the department is small enough to stop predation on a collective basis, it is small enough to go one step further and to agree on a collective curtailment of production. The level of production that is collectively agreed upon in small departments can be lower than the level of production that is realized in the presence of predation. This is especially true when department members believe that the total wage fund is unaffected by the aggregate level of production and when department members obtain little or no personal satisfaction directly

[12]For a more thorough discussion of the viability of social contracts and, what amount to the same thing, commonly adopted ethical precepts, see Chapter 3 and James M. Buchanan, "Ethical Rules, Expected Values, and Large Numbers," *Ethics* (October 1965), pp. 1–13.

from productive activity.[13] For the university interested in generating production, the result should be some optimum-size department associated with some optimum amount of predation reflected in dissension or discord among faculty.

PREDATION AND PRIVATE FIRMS

The line of analysis developed thus far suggests that, for a given department size, departments in private, profit-maximizing competitive firms should engage in less predatory behavior than do academic departments in which the wage fund pay system operates. In theory, the employees of private firms are paid according to their marginal contribution to production. In addition, an increase in the marginal contribution of any one employee increases the total output of the firm and increases the firm's revenue and the ability of the firm to compensate the individual employee for additional production. In short, the greater productivity of an individual increases the size of the wage pie. When a more productive employee receives a pay increase for what he or she has done, the potential earnings of other employees do not fall, as is generally the case in academic departments (or wherever a fixed wage fund exists).

Furthermore, because of the profit incentive, employees of private firms are more likely to be paid their market value than are employees of educational institutions. If an employee of a private firm has to deal continually with predation from coworkers that reduces his or her productivity, then the employee can always accept employment elsewhere at a comparable wage. In short, employees of private firms do not have to put up with the predation of others; they can move elsewhere with little or no loss of income. Professors in a university, on the other hand, may very well be overpaid in a market sense simply because their pay raises for a period of years may have had nothing to do with the movement in their market wage rate. If a professor moves in response to predation, he or she can suffer a significant income loss. For reasons implied in this argument, we would expect, everything else being equal, greater levels of predation and departmental discord in those academic disciplines in which there are surpluses of faculty members looking for jobs than in disciplines in which the labor market is in rough equilibrium. For example, more discord will tend to be present in history and English departments than in accounting and finance departments. This is because there are market surpluses of Ph.D.s in history and English and

[13]The analysis here must be tempered to take account of situations in which the wage fund is affected, although modestly, by the aggregate production of department members. To the extent that the wage fund goes down with a decrease in the department's production, collective agreements to decrease production will not hold. The implied functional relationship will affect only the level of production that is agreed upon.

market shortages in accounting and finance. Faculty members in accounting and finance do not have to put up with predatory actions of their colleagues.

The analysis of this section does not suggest that no predatory behavior will be observed in private firms. Personality conflicts, ideological differences, and the wage fund pay system are not completely absent in private firms either. The point is: To the extent that pay is determined by market principles, rather than through some form of a wage fund system of allocation, less predatory behavior will occur, employees will impose fewer predatory costs on one another, and there will be less dissension. Furthermore, the optimum-size department should be smaller in private firms than in universities (or other governmental organizations that operate on a wage fund pay system.) Alternatively, in order for the same level of predatory behavior to occur in an educational bureaucracy as in a private firm, the educational bureaucracy will have to be larger than the private firm producing a comparable level of goods and services. Perhaps the wage fund pay system and the prospects of predatory behavior partially explain the "bloated" and inefficient sizes of government bureaucracies: government bureaucracies need to be large to keep down predation.

CONCLUDING COMMENTS

In one unfortunate respect, the results of our analysis are inconclusive. We cannot say with precision what exactly the optimum department size is. Even if data on various department sizes were statistically evaluated, it is doubtful that much more guidance than has been offered here could be provided. There are so many variables influencing the level of predatory behavior and dissension among departmental members that to disentangle statistically the value of any one variable would be immensely difficult. Furthermore, the value of all of these variables will differ across departments; therefore, the optimum department size for one university is not likely to be the optimum department size for another.

However, the value of conceptually focusing on the issue of the optimum-size department is not lost by full recognition of the empirical deficiencies of the concept. The concept allows us to examine factors that influence the levels of predation versus production within a department and suggests institutional changes that may reduce the relative importance of predation. First, the analysis developed here makes clear the incentive structure that emerges from a wage fund pay system. In order to reduce predation, a university should put less reliance on its usual pay system and more reliance on market principles, to the extent possible. By relying more on market principles of pay, a university forces individual department members to consider all those outside the university as well as people within the department willing to take their positions as competitors. It forces the individual into a large-group mental framework. Since one individual cannot effectively engage in predation against all market competitors, the individual must be resigned (as must all market competitors) to produce as if predation were not a viable means of raising salary.

Ultimately, a university will have to yield to market pay principles. If it persistently underpays some members of its faculty, then it will lose those faculty members to the market and will then have to return to that same market (with higher pay offers) in order to secure the faculty that it needs to staff its program. If the university persistently overpays its faculty, then it will persist in redistributing income from lower-income taxpayers to higher-income faculty members or it will waste its financial resources and fail to accomplish as many of its educational goals as it would like.

If the university cannot dispense with the wage fund pay system, it should devise a pay system that will make the group within which relative rankings and wage shares are determined as large as possible. If the wage fund is presently set for small, say, ten-person departments, the wage fund should be set for a major subdivision of the university, like a college. The administrative advantages of small departments are retained; however, individual department members are forced to compete for pay with a much larger group of people. The members of, say, the economic department, are more likely to be supportive of a member who is unusually productive. They know that any additional increase that members gets will not significantly affect their salaries; it will be spread over, for example, the members of the accounting, finance, and business administration departments.

The analysis and conclusions of this chapter appear to apply as well to questions of tenure and promotion policy as they do to pay policies. If a fund of tenure slots or positions within advanced ranks is fixed at department levels, then members of the department can be expected to compete, through productive and predatory means, to secure them. The size of the department will affect the allocation of individual faculty time between predation and production. If a university feels compelled to set a limit on the number of faculty that can achieve tenure or the rank of associate or full professor, then the limits should be set at the university level or, if that is not likely to be feasible, at the college level. Setting limits for tenure and promotion in small departments can breed unnecessary strife among members.

Our analysis actually applies to a wide range of social settings in which the goal that is sought by competitors is perceived to be fixed and in which allocations are made on the basis of relative ranking. For instance, because there is only one "prize" to be allocated and that prize is given to the candidate with the most votes, predation or "dirty tricks" is to be expected in presidential politics. Students obstruct the test performance of other students when they know that a scholarship or entrance into graduate school is dependent upon relative class ranking and test performance. Many other examples could be enumerated.

QUESTIONS TO PONDER

1 Why do producers in highly competitive markets not engage in predatory behavior?
2 In presidential politics there is only one prize, the presidency. How and to what extent can the analysis of this chapter be applied to presidential politics? Does the analysis suggest an economic explanation for "dirty tricks" in political contests?
3 In this chapter, one economic explanation has been devised for predatory behavior in universities. List other economic and noneconomic explanations for predatory behavior.
4 Does predatory behavior exist among students? Where? Under what circumstances is it most often observed?

Chapter 11

The Emergence of a Market in Pollution Standards

The process by which a previously "free" natural resource enters a market—that is, the process by which scarcity is recognized, rights established, defined and guaranteed, and the market created—is not an easy one. For this reason, any market in air emission rights may be somewhat limited, perhaps for a considerable time, perhaps permanently. But the market for land is also limited. Owners of land may be required to follow performance standards and zoning ordinances. Excavation, mining, sewage, and waste disposal requirements further reduce the number of potential property rights that are subject to free market forces. Moreover, in some places land is owned by the state and leased for controlled uses. Still, there is a functioning market for land in which significant rights are freely traded.[1]

CHAPTER PREVIEW

Central Question

If the government controls pollution by setting standards, why will a market in pollution standards emerge and will such a market contribute to efficiency in the allocation of environmental resources?

[1]Bruce Yandle, "The Emerging Market in Air Pollution Rights," *Regulation* (July-August 1978), p. 29.

Major Objectives

1 To explain the economic basis for pollution.

2 To explore the relative efficiency of pollution standards and the price mechanism as means of controlling pollution.

3 To demonstrate why, if pollution standards are established by government, a market in pollution standards will emerge.

4 To consider the problems inherent in attempts to control markets in pollution standards.

Major Points

1 An economic source of pollution is poorly defined property rights.

2 There are two basic ways of alleviating a pollution problem: (a) establish pollution standards and (b) set up a price mechanism for selling "pollution rights." The price mechanism is the more efficient means of achieving an established pollution level.

3 If standards for pollution are set, firms are effectively *given* rights to pollute, a form of wealth. So long as firms differ in their cost effectiveness in reducing pollution, a market in pollution rights or pollution standards will emerge. Firms that are relatively less efficient in reducing pollution will buy pollution rights from firms that are relatively more efficient in reducing pollution. The result of the trades will be a more economical—less costly—way of achieving an officially established pollution level.

4 Attempts to control an emerging market in pollution standards will simply deny mutually beneficial trades and will increase the effective cost of achieving an officially established pollution level.

Real estate agents provide a valuable economic service. They "make" a market for buyers and sellers for houses, land, and other real property; they in effect bring buyers and sellers together in order that efficient exchanges can be made. Although the agents are paid a commission for their services (which is about 6 to 7 percent of the selling price), the buyers and sellers are presumably better off financially and in other ways by going to a real estate firm than by not going. If the seller were not better off, why would he or she list property with the real estate agent? The seller presumably thinks the agent, with greater marketing ability and appeal to a wider market, can secure a price for the property that at least covers the agent's commission or can save the seller the time and expense of selling the property. Otherwise, the seller would sell the property through word of mouth or ads in the local newspaper. The buyer is presumably better off by going through a real estate firm because he or she can save a considerable amount of time and trouble in searching the market for the type and style of house desired. Any extra price the buyer pays, because of the commission, can be construed as payment for the services provided by the real estate agent.

The services of real estate agents can be said to be economically beneficial simply because they arise voluntarily, as individuals seek to trade and maximize their own economic positions. The agent serves the economic function of reducing the cost of information search to buyers and sellers who happen to be in the market for property at the same time.

At times, the real estate agent may speculate in the market he or she creates. An agent may buy parcels of land, for example, at what he or she considers to be a low price, hold on to the land, and sell the land to someone else at a later date for a higher price. The profit of the real estate agent is the difference between the purchase and sale price (minus the interest that could have been earned had the agent put the money into a perfectly secure savings account and minus the risk cost of holding onto property that has a chance of going down as well as up). The agent still, in this case, provides an economically beneficial service: he or she moves property from someone who values it less (the person who sells in the current time period) to someone who values it more (the person who buys in the future time period). The trade between the buyer and seller is intertemporal, but both parties are still better off, or else the trade would not occur.

Markets are efficient because the trades that are made within the markets are mutually beneficial, because the trades reallocate resources (or more properly, rights to resources) from less valuable to more productive uses. The result of free exchanges made in markets is an expansion of national product and income. Prices are important because they guide or direct resources into their relatively more valuable and productive uses and because they give people—buyers and sellers—the information they need to have in order to determine how and what they will produce and consume.

What does all this have to do with "pollution," a word that is used prominently in the title of this chapter? Through the Clean Air Act of 1970, Congress set national standards for ambient air quality (standards for the quality of air surrounding any given place). In doing that, Congress set standards for the amount of pollution that can be emitted into the atmosphere. It officially recognized air as an economic resource, which has alternative uses—for example, as a source of oxygen for living things, as a garbage disposal system (which is the function the air serves when smoke is emitted), and as a means of clear vision for watching a sunset. By setting the pollution standards, Congress effectively established limited property rights to the atmosphere. Stated somewhat differently, although the intent of the standards was to reduce pollution, a goal that the standards will accomplish, Congress, through the Environmental Protection Agency (EPA), allocated to some producers the rights to emit certain limited amounts of pollutants into the air. It also allocated to the general public the rights to a certain level of air quality for breathing; these latter rights will be protected, presumably, by the EPA's enforcement of the pollution standards.

Land rights were once acquired by conquest and by first-come–first-served homestead programs in the nineteenth century as well as by purchase. Land is now bought and sold in real estate markets because it has alternative uses, and the market is seen as a reasonably efficient means of allocating, on a continuing basis, the land to the more valuable and productive uses. Through the Clean Air Act people have acquired rights to air. Should we not expect a market, similar to the one in land, to emerge to redistribute the rights that have been allocated to the air? Will the market in air rights that emerges contribute to expanding the national product and income in much the same way that the market for land rights does? Should we control any market in air rights that emerges? These are the questions with which this chapter is concerned. Before we can answer them, however, we must consider the initial state in which the air rights are distributed.

THE ECONOMIC BASIS OF POLLUTION

Not all pollution of the atmosphere is necessarily bad. The airways do have some absorptive capacity. They can absorb and/or carry away some pollutants, such as sulfur dioxide, without the surrounding animal and plant life being affected or without the sensibilities of people being disturbed. There is, in other words, some level of pollution that cannot be detected by anyone. Pollution becomes a problem only when there is too much of it and when people prefer to use the atmosphere for some other, more valuable purpose.[2]

In past years, use of the atmosphere for disposal of waste has effectively been free to the user: the firm that dumps sulfur dioxide into the atmosphere has not had to pay for that privilege. It has not had to "buy" the air rights away from someone else. This is because the airways have been considered common (as opposed to private) property to be used by anyone at will. No one has had rights to the airways; therefore, no one has had the right to exclude anyone from use of the airways. At a zero price—which does not reflect the opportunity value of the airways—polluters have used and abused the available resource; they have released in many areas so much sulfur dioxide that some people have, at certain times of the day, experienced eye irritation and have had to pay for medication, and other people have had to incur the cost of repainting their homes and businesses. The people who have wanted to see the sunset have not been able to buy that right, even though they may have been willing to pay the

[2]For additional discussion on the economic source of pollution, see Thomas D. Crocker and A. J. Rogers, III, *Environmental Economics* (Hinsdale, Ill.: The Dryden Press, Inc., 1971), chaps. 1–4; Hugh H. Macaulay and Bruce Yandle, *Environmental Use and the Market* (Lexington, Mass,: Lexington Books, 1977), chaps. 1–6; and Richard B. McKenzie and Gordon Tullock, *Modern Political Economy: An Introduction to Economics* (New York: McGraw-Hill Book Company, 1978), chap. 19.

polluters in total a sum sufficient to entice the polluters away from using the airways as a dumping ground. A market in air rights has not existed because the rights to the air have not been legally defined and, therefore, trades (which, of necessity, are trades in rights) could not occur.

There are probably many industrial and governmental polluters who care very little about society's welfare. They simply do not care if their actions harm or impose costs on others. However, when property is held in common, there are probably many people who pollute but do not perceive that their emissions of pollutants are significantly harming others. They may rightfully reason that the amount of waste *they*, by themselves, dump into the atmosphere is well within the tolerance level of the atmosphere and cannot be detected by other people. If they restrict their pollution, no one will be materially benefited by their actions. The rational course of action: make full use of the atmosphere, which common property rights allow.

If all people within a given region follow the same logic and emit a small amount of pollutants, the result can be overuse of the atmosphere, a real environmental problem. The central problem of dealing with pollution is now evident: it is a problem of finding a way of getting people to curtail *collectively* their use of the airways, to restrict the total amount of pollutants being emitted into the airways in order that the atmosphere can be used for other, more valuable purposes. The task is one of bringing about the optimum level of pollution, which is another way of saying the task is one of achieving the optimum level of production of goods and services that people want. Seen this way, the problem of pollution corresponds to a problem of too few of the goods and services (including cleanliness) people want most.

In the area of environmental quantity, the government confronts two problems. First, there is the problem of determining what the optimum level of pollution is, which is a difficult task at best, given the deficiencies of the political system in determining people's relative values.[3] Second, the government faces the problem of achieving whatever level of pollution is established as the optimum. There are two basic ways by which the optimum level of pollution can be achieved: (1) direct regulation of the amount of pollutants that firms, homes, and governments can emit into the atmosphere, and (2) the distribution of pollution rights by some sort of governmental auctioning (pricing) system. As we will show in the next section, the selling of pollution rights is normally held by economists to be the more efficient means of controlling pollution. As we will see also, that conclusion holds only so long as the government does not allow pollution standards as rights to be sold in

[3]As we pointed out earlier, votes do not indicate the relative *intensities* of people's preferences: they only indicate whether a person is for or against an issue, not how much a person is willing to pay for an additional unit of a good like environmental quality. As we will argue in Chapter 12, people have very little incentive in a political context to understand very much about complex issues like the optimum level of pollution.

markets, which will very likely emerge when government attempts to regulate pollution directly.

EFFICIENCY IN POLLUTION REDUCTION

To evaluate the relative efficiency of the two methods of reducing pollution, consider an example of five firms that are emitting sulfur dioxide into the atmosphere of a given area and causing a pollution problem. Since the reduction of the pollution is an economic good that must be "produced" at a cost, assume that the marginal cost of cutting back on the units of sulfur dioxide emitted for each firm rises as successive units of sulfur dioxide are eliminated. Further, assume that the firms differ in the cost they must incur to curtail their discharge of sulfur dioxide. These assumptions are incorporated into the construction of Table 11.1 for firms A through E. The table shows that for firm A, for example, the cost it must incur to eliminate its discharge of the first unit of sulfur dioxide is $50; the cost of cutting out the next unit of sulfur dioxide is $100. And the marginal cost of reducing pollution for firm A, and all other firms, rises for each successive unit.

Although the table contains a hypothetical example, the structure of the table is reasonably descriptive of the conditions in most real world pollution abatement problems. Real world firms do not operate in exactly the same conditions as each other. They do not use exactly the same resources in production, and they differ in the technology they have available to reduce pollution. Whether firms are faced with the problem of producing actual goods and services for consumption by customers or producing clean air,

Table 11.1 Cost of Reducing Units of Sulfur Dioxide

Cost of eliminating	A	B	C	D	E
First unit	$ 50	$ 100	$100	$ 300	$ 500
Second unit	100	300	200	500	1000
Third unit	200	900	300	700	1500
		Set standard			
Fourth unit	400	2700	400	900	2000
Fifth unit	800	8100	500	1100	2500

Cost of reducing air pollution by set standards		**Cost of reducing air pollution by price mechanism**	
Cost to A of eliminating 3 units	$ 350	Cost to A of eliminating 4 units	$ 750
Cost to B of eliminating 3 units	1,300	Cost to B of eliminating 2 units	400
Cost to C of eliminating 3 units	600	Cost to C of eliminating 5 units	1,500
Cost to D of eliminating 3 units	1,500	Cost to D of eliminating 3 units	1,500
Cost to E of eliminating 3 units	3,000	Cost to E of eliminating 1 unit	500
Total cost	$6,750	Total cost	$4,650

Note: The dashes signify the number of units of pollution eliminated by each firm under the price mechanism.

they confront a technological fact of production processes, which is increasing marginal costs.

Now, suppose the EPA determines that for the area in question the optimum level of pollution is 10 units of sulfur dioxide in the atmosphere. Suppose further that the EPA seeks to achieve the optimum level of pollution by prohibiting any firm from emitting more than 2 units of sulfur dioxide at the marginal costs that are specified. The total costs each firm must incur to achieve the set limit of 2 units of sulfur dioxide emitted are indicated in the lower half of the table. Firm A, for instance, must incur a relatively modest cost of $350 (derived by adding together $50, $100, and $200, the marginal costs of the first 3 units eliminated). The total cost incurred by *all* firms in the cleanup is $6,750 by the set-standard method.

As opposed to setting the standard that must be followed by each firm, the government can elect to control pollution by selling off 10 "rights to pollute." These rights to pollute may be thought of as "tickets," each of which gives the firm the right to dump a unit of waste into the atmosphere; the more tickets the firm purchases, the more sulfur dioxide the firm can emit into the airways and the more cleanup costs the firm can avoid.

Although this proposal may not sound very attractive, remember that the government ultimately has control over how many tickets it sells. It can achieve what it considers to be the optimum level of pollution by appropriately restricting the number of tickets it sells. Under both methods—the set standards and the pricing system—the government keeps the level of pollution down to 10 units. Under the pricing system, however, the firms that want to avoid the cost of cleaning up the environment must bid for the tickets. The price will effectively rise until the quantity of rights or tickets demanded is exactly equal to 10.

The potential market for pollution rights can be illustrated by standard supply and demand curves in Figure 11.1. The supply curve in this case is determined by government policy makers, who establish the desired pollution level for the area. In this example, the supply of pollution rights is assumed to be invariant with the price, meaning that the supply curve in the graph must be a vertical straight line: as the price goes up, the number of pollution rights remains unchanged. The demand for pollution rights, on the other hand, is derived from the costs that firms must incur in order to clean up the pollution they emit. As the price of pollution rights goes down, firms will individually and collectively demand a larger number of pollution rights. This is because the lower price on the pollution rights will mean that it will be cheaper for the firms to buy the pollution rights than to incur the cost of cleanup. The downward-sloping curve in Figure 11.1 fairly accurately describes the market demand curve for pollution rights; it is based on the figures in Table 11.1.

The market clearing price in the figure is $750. (Actually, from the data contained in the table, the price can be anything between $700 and

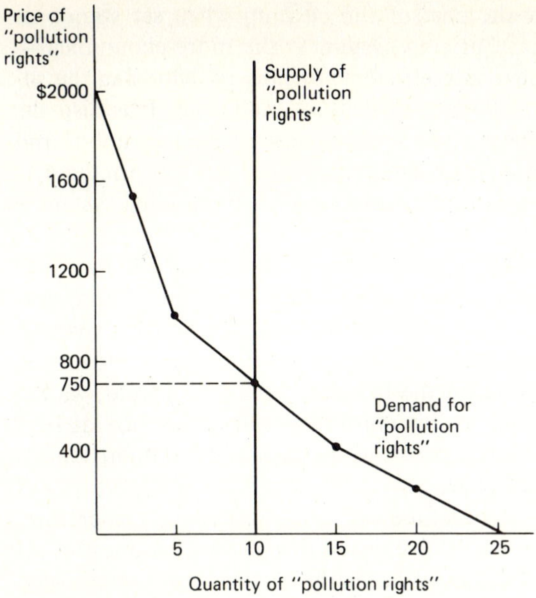

Figure 11.1

$800.) The market clearing price, or equilibrium price, is the price at which the quantity of pollution rights demanded is exactly equal to the number of rights made available for sale by the government. Who will buy those rights, who will clean up the pollution, and what is the cost of cleanup under the pricing system? Those are the questions that can now be addressed.

At a price of $750 per ticket, firm A is willing to buy one and only one ticket. This is because at that price it is cheaper for the firm to incur the cost of cleanup of its first 4 units (cleanup costs of those first 4 are $50, $100, $200, and $400) than to buy the tickets as $750 each. The firm is better off paying $750 for one ticket than incurring the $800 cost of cleaning up the fifth unit of pollution emitted. Through a similar line of reasoning, we can conclude that firm B will buy three tickets (clean up 2 units of pollution), firm C will buy no tickets, firm D will buy two tickets, and firm E will buy four tickets.

The social cost of the cleanup must be measured by the value of the actual resources that go into the cleanup. Those values are approximated by the dollar expenditures of the various firms on the pollution cleanup, not the dollar expenditures on the tickets that give firms the right to pollute. The dollars spent on the tickets do not represent real resources; they represent only a transfer of purchasing power from the firms to the government, which sells the tickets. Accordingly, the economic cost of reducing air pollution to 10 units is $750 for firm A, $400 for B, $1,500 each for C and D, and $500 for E. The total cost of the cleanup is $4,650, which, you may notice, is significantly below the cost of the cleanup when set standards are used ($6,750). In short, the pricing system is the more economical—that is, cost-effective and technically efficient—means of achieving the socially desired (or government established) level of pollution. It is also the more economical way of achieving the socially desired level of goods and services. Indeed, because the cost of cleanup is lower for the pricing system, more goods and services can be produced when the pricing system is used than when the set-standard system is used.

This is the reasoning that leads economists to argue that if pollution is to be reduced, it should be reduced by selling rights to pollute. Again, that method—and the wording used—may not *sound* very attractive; however, remember that when the government sets standards of pollution, it effectively *gives away* rights to pollute. Each of the firms in Table 11.1 is told, via the set standards that are announced, that it must reduce its sulfur dioxide by 3 units. By the same token, each of the firms is *given* the right to dump 2 units of sulfur dioxide into the atmosphere.

Any comparison of the two methods of pollution control, therefore, leads not only to the question of relative costs, but also to the question of whether or not the government should be in the business of giving away, free of charge, rights to the atmosphere, which has many different uses. Why should polluters be *given* those rights? Clearly, rights to pollute may be needed to continue production, but that is not an argument for *giving away* the rights. One can argue that land is needed in many production processes, but that is not an argument for giving away, free of charge, rights to the public land in national forests. Use of the pricing system for distributing the pollution rights allows different potential users to bid for those rights, to express in a market setting the relative values that they place on having the rights to pollute. In this way, the rights can be allocated to the most valuable and productive uses.

THE EMERGENCE OF A MARKET

Suppose the government decides to control pollution by way of set standards. Does it follow that the cost of cleanup will remain at the relatively high level discussed in the preceding section? Not necessarily. *If* the standards that are distributed can be traded among the producers, then not only can mutually beneficial trades be completed among the producers, but the cost of the cleanup can be lowered.

Notice in Table 11.1 that firm E under the set-standard control system must eliminate 3 units of sulfur dioxide. That firm has to incur marginal costs of $500, $1,000, and $1,500 for each successive unit eliminated; and it should be willing to pay something less than those amounts in order to acquire the right to emit units of sulfur dioxide. Further, notice also that firm A, under the set standard, has to incur the cost of cleaning up 3 units of pollution. However, like all the other firms, A can emit—has the *right* to emit—2 units of sulfur dioxide, and it costs A only $400 to eliminate the fourth unit of sulfur dioxide. A mutually beneficial trade can obviously be struck between A and E: E is willing to pay as much as $1,500 for the right to emit one additional unit of pollution, while A is willing to accept anything over $400 for the right that it holds (because of the standards that are set). If the price of a pollution right is set at, say, $750, then E gives up $750 for the emission right (for part of A's standard); but E does not have to incur the $1,500 cost of cleaning up that unit of pollution. E gains to the tune of $750 ($1,500 − $750). A, on the other hand, by giving up one of its rights, has to eliminate an additional unit of pollution; however, it receives $750 from E and has to spend only $400 to eliminate the unit. Moreover, the cost of achieving the officially established optimum pollution level is reduced by $1,100 (which is equal to the $1,500 cost E would have incurred minus the $400 cost that A does incur).

Additional trades can be made. E finds it worthwhile to buy pollution rights from A and/or C. How many rights E buys depends, of course, on their price. Furthermore, B and D are willing to enter the bargaining process for rights that are effectively held by A and C. The competition in the emerging market causes the price to move toward the market clearing price of $750 depicted in Figure 11.1.

The end result of the emerging market is the distribution of rights that would have developed if the government had sold the rights at auction initially; and the total cost of achieving a pollution level of 10 units of sulfur dioxide is $4,650, a reduction of $2,100 from what it would have been if the market transactions had not developed. The only difference between the case in which standards are set and a market emerges and the case in which the government initially sells off the pollution rights is that, under the former system, the government does not receive any of the income transfer that results from the trades. The income transfer is reaped by firms A and C.

REAL WORLD EXAMPLES OF POLLUTION STANDARDS

Bruce Yandle, quoted at the start of this chapter, has provided us with an interesting commentary on the developing market in what we have called "pollution standards."[4] (Actually, as we have tried to stress, the development of standards has been the conceptual equivalent of passing out pollution rights free to the recipients. Therefore, "pollution standards" and "pollution rights" are phrases that can be used interchangeably as is done here.) At this point in time, the market for pollution standards or rights is not a well-oiled, smoothly functioning system. Explicit exchanges of rights for money

[4]Yandle, "The Emerging Market in Air Pollution Rights," pp. 21–29.

have not been made. However, there have been a number of implicit trades made.

Yandle points out that Standard Oil of Ohio has for several years wanted to build a pipeline terminal near Long Beach, California, to unload the oil brought down by tanker from Alaska's North Slope.[5] The unloading of the oil will cause a pollution problem, but the pollution level in the area has already reached the limit set by the California regional air plan. Standard Oil can build its proposed pipeline if it can secure the needed pollution rights now held by others. The company believes it has solved its problem by agreeing to equip three dry cleaners with pollution abatement equipment. Having reduced the pollution in one area, it wants to be able to use the pollution rights that are released to operate its terminal; Standard Oil made a similar arrangement with California Edison. (At the time of this writing, spring 1979, Standard Oil was awaiting approval of its proposed trades.)

In 1978 Volkswagen started producing Rabbits in Pennsylvania. The firm was able to produce the cars in that state because of an implicit trade in air rights between VW and the state of Pennsylvania.[6] Pennsylvania wanted the plant in the state in order to increase the employment opportunities of state residents and the tax revenues of the state. However, the only way that VW could start up production was to acquire pollution rights. To get the firm to come into the state, the state agreed to change the process used for paving roads, reducing its emissions of hydrocarbons and effectively giving emission rights to VW. To obtain the VW plant, state residents are now paying taxes to pay for the higher cost of road paving.

These are not the straightforward *quid pro quo* transactions that we discussed in an earlier section. However, such straightforward transactions may not be far off in the future. Yandle reports that private entrepreneurs are presently looking into the possibility of setting up "real estate firms" in pollution rights, which will make a market for buyers of rights who may want to improve the quality of the air they live in or buyers who may want to expand production, and for sellers who have pollution rights and who may be interested in securing the necessary funds to clean up their emissions of pollutants or who may be interested in contracting their production and investing the funds secured more profitably elsewhere.

CONCLUDING COMMENTS: CONTROL OF THE EMERGING MARKET

Should an emerging market in pollution rights be controlled? To the extent that rights to anything, land or pollution emissions, must be defined and guaranteed, the market for pollution rights must be supervised and con-

[5]Ibid., pp. 26–27.
[6]Ibid., p. 27.

trolled by government. In order to ensure that the officially established level of pollution is achieved on a continuing basis, the government must keep watch on the amount of pollution emitted into the atmosphere. (The government must ensure that the airways do not revert back to de facto common property by its failure to enforce the rights that are distributed.)

Beyond that, however, we have demonstrated that transfers of rights among buyers and sellers are beneficial to the parties and contribute to economic efficiency; the transfers reduce the cost of achieving the goals established by the government. Because fewer resources are involved in reducing pollution, more resources are available for the production of goods and services. Indeed, with exchanges allowed to occur, some of the resources that would have been used to achieve a *given* pollution level can be used to clean up the air further.

Granted, trades in pollution rights mean that the rights distributed free by government will carry a market value. The persons or firms that obtained the rights will experience a wealth increase because of the market that emerges. The distribution of the wealth that occurs may, by some ethical code, be deemed unfair or unjust. The unfairness or injustice of the resulting wealth distribution is a consequence, it should be stressed, of the way in which the pollution rights were initially distributed, not a consequence of market exchanges. As we have pointed out in the chapter, there is no compelling *economic* reason for giving away rights to the air any more than for giving away farming rights to land in national forests. (Also, so long as the rights that are distributed can be resold, there is no compelling reason for not giving them away.) The point of the discussion is that the ethical question of the fairness of the wealth distribution must be dealt with prior to the distribution of the wealth. Given the initial distribution of rights—given its fairness or lack of fairness—economic analysis can show only that resources are saved, that the national income and output levels are raised, by free market exchanges in existing rights. Without question, existing firms that are doing the polluting have an economic reason for favoring set-standards systems of pollution control: they are the ones likely to receive the free pollution rights when they are distributed initially and they are the ones that will then experience a wealth increase when a market in pollution rights emerges.

QUESTIONS TO PONDER

1 People are able to buy land and hold it in an undeveloped state. They effectively "bank" land. Should firms that buy pollution rights be permitted to bank pollution rights? If firms do decide to bank pollution rights, will the banking contribute to economic efficiency?

2 "By allowing firms to trade their pollution rights, less pollution can be acquired at less cost: the officially established pollution level can be 'tightened-up' with

the same cost being imposed on society." Do you agree or disagree with that statement?

3 If businesses are permitted to sell pollution rights, would you expect brokers—that is, real estate agents—in pollution rights to emerge? Why? If they did emerge, would they contribute to the efficiency with which the officially established pollution level is achieved?

4 If pollution rights are traded, should the government impose a price ceiling on the pollution rights? Would such a control system contribute to the efficient allocation of resources?

5 What reasons can you give for expecting the market system to work less well in the allocation of pollution rights than, say, the allocation of cattle?

ADDITIONAL READING

Crocker, Thomas D., and A. J. Roberts, III. *Environmental Economics.* Hinsdale, Ill.: The Dryden Press, Inc., 1971, chaps. 1–4.

Macaulay, Hugh H., and Bruce Yandle. *Environmental Use and the Market.* Lexington, Mass.: Lexington Books, Inc., 1977, chaps. 1–6.

Wonnacott, Paul, and Ronald Wonnacott. *Economics.* New York: McGraw-Hill Book Company, 1979, chap. 23.

Yandle, Bruce. "The Emerging Market in Pollution Rights," *Regulation* (July-August 1978), pp. 21–29.

Chapter 12

Voter Apathy: The Economic Dimensions of a Growing Problem

CHAPTER PREVIEW

Central Question

Why do people not vote, and what may be gained by increasing the voter turnout?

Major Objectives

1 To review data on voter turnout in the United States.

2 To develop sociological and economic explanations for why people do not vote.

3 To explore the possible consequences of increasing the voter turnout.

Major Conclusions

1 Slightly more than a majority of eligible voters actually tend to go to the polls on presidential election days. Less than a majority of eligible voters tend to turn up at the polls on off-year, nonpresidential election days.

2 Voter turnout in the United States has been on the decline for decades and there appears to be no reason to expect a change in the trend in the immediate future.

3 Voter turnout in the United States has been lower than in most European countries.

4 The list of explanations for why people fail to vote developed by political scientists and sociologists is varied and includes sex, race, education, social status, and interparty competitiveness, among others. These explanations, however, have little in the way of a theoretical foundation.

5 An economic explanation of nonvoting suggests that, for many people, voting is not rational: that is, the costs of registering and voting for many people exceed the benefits. An individual's vote has a very small probability of affecting the outcome of the election.

6 There is a tendency for the parties in a two-party political system to take similar positions. The differences in political positions in political systems with three or more parties will tend to be greater than the differences in political positions of the two parties in a two-party political system.

7 Assuming economic considerations affect people's decision to vote, increases in the mobility of the people and in growth of government will tend to lead to a decrease in voter turnout.

8 Because the ease with which people can register and vote can influence politicians' decisions to promote or not to promote various government programs, changes in election laws can be an indirect means of affecting the size and scope of government activity.

By way of the Universal Registration Act of 1977, President Carter proposed to liberalize voter registration procedures. If enacted, the new law will permit individuals who qualify to register and vote on election day and will encourage states, through financial grants, to expand their efforts to register potential voters. In introducing the bill in the Senate, Senator Frank Canon said very simply that "the goal of the Universal Registration Act of 1977 is to increase citizen participation in the electoral process."[1] Senator Edward Kennedy's endorsement of the bill was much less restrained: "Election day registration is a brilliant solution to the chaos, confusion, and irrationality of our archaic voter registration laws. By enabling citizens to register at the polling place on election day, we can eliminate many of the most serious obstacles to voter participation in America, and open up the franchise to millions of our citizens. . . . Election day registration will be a giant step forward in our efforts to increase voter turnout, revitalize our democracy and enhance the right to vote."[2]

The basis for the concern over voter participation voiced by Senators Canon and Kennedy has been widely publicized. For decades, the percentage

[1] U.S. Congress, Senate, *Congressional Record* (April 22, 1977), p. S-4561.
[2] Ibid., pp. S-4566–S-4567.

of the voting-age population in the United States that actually goes to the polls has been on the wane. In 1976, less than 56 percent of eligible United States citizens took the trouble to vote in a presidential contest, which, at the end of the campaign, was described as a "real horse race" and "too close to call." Furthermore, voter turnout in the United States is much lower than that of other Western democracies. In television newscasts and newspaper editorials, the American voter is often characterized as "alienated," "disenfranchised," "unappreciative of his basic rights," and "apathetic." All these commentaries presume that something in our political system is wrong and in need of correction and that increasing the turnout is a laudable objective.

Aside from noting that the vote is a fundamental right and that voter participation is necessary for the continued operation of any democracy, few political analysts explain why it is necessary or desirable to have a voter turnout higher than that which occurs in the United States. How will a change in the voter turnout affect the operation of government? How and in what ways will government be improved if the voter turnout is raised from 56 percent to 70 or 80 percent? In seeking to address these questions, we review data that have been collected over the years on voter turnout and present reasons that citizens themselves give for not voting, and then turn to explanations that social scientists have formulated to explain the low and decreasing United States voter turnout. In this chapter we are able to show how economic analysis can contribute to our understanding of citizens' nonparticipation at the voting booth. An important conclusion drawn is that, for many citizens, participation in elections is simply not rational; everything else held constant, whenever government expands and assumes new social responsibilities, a growing proportion of the population will rationally choose not to vote.

VOTER TURNOUT: THE HISTORICAL RECORD

The extent of citizen participation and nonparticipation in elections is shown in Tables 12.1 through 12.3, and Figure 12.1. Table 12.1 contains the voting record by state of the United States public in the 1976 presidential election. At the time of that election, over 146 million citizens age 18 and over were counted as part of the voting-age population. Of that total, 99 million were registered to vote and 81 million actually voted. This means that approximately 74 percent of the voting-age population was registered and 56 percent voted. Voter turnout was lowest in the District of Columbia, where only about one-third of those eligible to vote actually went to the polls. The state with the lowest turnout was South Carolina, where 42 percent of the voting-age population voted. Turnout was highest in Minnesota, where a little over 72 percent of the people who could vote actually did. The high

Table 12.1 Final Report on Registration and Voting in the Presidential Election of 1976

	Percent VAP registered	Percent VAP voting	Percent registered voting
Alabama	74.77	47.42	63.42
Alaska	91.55	54.42	59.44
Arizona	64.79	49.12	75.81
Arkansas	68.08	51.20	75.20
California	69.43	54.72	78.81
Colorado	76.31	61.95	81.18
Connecticut	77.97	64.52	82.75
Delaware	64.52	59.08	78.34
District of Columbia	51.54	33.10	64.22
Florida	67.65	52.05	76.95
Georgia	64.84	43.67	67.35
Hawaii	66.37	53.25	80.23
Idaho	92.43	61.11	66.12
Illinois	83.48	63.01	75.47
Indiana	81.19	61.45	75.69
Iowa	70.22	63.88	90.95
Kansas	73.07	59.71	81.71
Kentucky	72.32	49.26	68.12
Louisiana	74.14	50.79	68.50
Maine	94.89	65.92	69.46
Maryland	68.97	51.02	73.97
Massachusetts	77.67	62.99	81.09
Michigan	84.35	59.24	70.23
Minnesota	94.84	72.07	75.98
Mississippi	NA	72.07	——
Missouri	76.63	58.64	76.52
Montana	88.33	63.83	72.26
Nebraska	78.27	56.49	72.17
Nevada	60.64	48.76	80.41
New Hampshire	84.48	60.00	71.02
New Jersey	76.78	60.48	78.76
New Mexico	69.43	54.81	78.94
New York	66.76	53.20	79.69
North Carolina	66.64	43.81	65.74
North Dakota	NR	68.93	——
Ohio	NSR	55.61	——
Oklahoma	72.63	56.62	77.95
Oregon	87.01	63.10	72.51
Pennsylvania	68.75	55.25	80.36
Rhode Island	85.58	65.68	76.74
South Carolina	57.86	41.71	72.08
South Dakota	90.92	64.24	70.65
Tennessee	72.90	50.04	68.64
Texas	76.56	49.33	64.43
Utah	90.95	69.83	76.78
Vermont	88.29	57.11	64.68

Table 12.1 (*Continued*)

	Percent VAP registered	Percent VAP voting	Percent registered voting
Virginia	60.37	48.54	80.40
Washington	83.03	62.57	75.31
West Virginia	84.85	58.73	69.21
Wisconsin	NSR	66.00	——
Wyoming	73.71	59.22	80.33
UNITED STATES	73.82	55.63	(2) 75.05

(1) The Iowa voter registration total is as of August 1, 1976; county clerks are not required by law to report totals for general election day.

(2) Excludes Mississippi, North Dakota, Ohio, and Wisconsin.

Notes:

VAP: Voting-age population.

NA: Not available. (Voter registration date for Mississippi is available only from individual county clerks.)

NR: No registration. (In North Dakota, preregistration prior to voting is not a requirement for voting.)

NSR: No statewide registration. (Prior registration is required in some, usually metropolitan, but not all jurisdictions.)

Secondary Source: U.S. Congress, Senate, *Congressional Record* (March 22, 1977), pp. S-4565–S-4566.

Primary Sources:

Voting-age population estimates: U.S. Bureau of Census, *Current Population Reports*, ser. P-25, no. 626, (May 1976), "Projections of the Population of Voting Age for States: November 1976," p. 6.

1976 voter registration totals: Telephone survey of the election boards or offices of Secretary of States of the 50 states.

Turnout in 1976 Presidential election: *Congressional Quarterly* weekly report (December 1976), p. 3333.

Participation percentages were computed by the Congressional Research Service.

percentage turnout in Minnesota has been attributed mainly to the fact that election-day registration was introduced there in 1976. (In the presidential election of 1972, 68 percent of the voting-age population voted.) In Maine, North Dakota, Oregon, and Wisconsin, where registration on election day was permitted, the turnout was noticeably higher than the national average. Wisconsin, which introduced election-day registration in 1976, had a turnout of 66 percent. Maine and Oregon, which have permitted election-day registration for years, had turnouts of 65 and 63 percent, respectively. In North Dakota, where registration is not required at all, a turnout of almost 69 percent occurred.[3] Obviously, election-day registration has had a positive influence on election turnouts in the states where it has been initiated; however, this influence has not been dramatic. More will be said on this later.

The last column of Table 12.1 reveals that in 1976 a little over three-quarters of those citizens who were registered actually voted. The consistently high percentages in that column indicate to the proponents of the Universal Registration Act and other similar measures that the central im-

[3]One explanation for the high percentage of the voting-age population in Iowa that were registered is that Iowa does not close out registration in the state until shortly before the election. Furthermore, in some rural areas of Iowa, registration is not required at all.

Table 12.2 Reported Voting Rates, by Region, Race, and Spanish Origin: November 1964 to 1976
(Numbers in Thousands. Civilian Noninstitutional Population)

Regions, race, and Spanish origin	Presidential elections				Congressional elections		
	1976	1972	1968	1964	1974	1970	1966
United States							
Total, voting age	146,548	136,203	116,353	110,604	141,299	120,701	112,800
Percent reported voted							
Total	59.2	63.0	67.8	69.3	44.7	54.6	55.4
White	60.9	64.5	69.1	70.7	46.3	56.0	57.0
Black	48.7	52.1	57.6	58.5	33.8	43.5	41.7
Spanish origin*	31.8	37.5	NA	NA	22.9	NA	NA
North and West							
Total, voting age	99,403	93,653	81,594	78,174	96,505	83,515	78,355
Percent reported voted							
Total	61.2	66.4	71.0	74.6	48.8	59.0	60.9
White	62.6	67.5	71.8	74.7	50.0	59.8	61.7
Black	52.2	56.7	64.8	72.0†	37.9	51.4	52.1
South							
Total, voting age	47,145	42,550	34,941	32,429	44,794	37,186	34,445
Percent reported voted							
Total	54.9	55.4	60.1	56.7	36.0	44.7	43.0
White	57.1	57.0	61.9	59.5	37.4	46.4	45.1
Black	45.7	47.8	51.6	44.0	30.0	36.8	32.9

NA: Not available.

*Persons of Spanish origin may be of any race.

†Black and other races in 1964.

Note: Includes persons 18 years old and over in Georgia and Kentucky, 19 years old and over in Alaska, 20 years old and over in Hawaii, and 21 years old and over in the remaining states in 1964, 1966, 1968, and 1970. Includes all persons 18 years old and over in 1972, 1974, and 1976.

Source: U.S. Bureau of the Census, "Voter Participation in November 1976 (Advanced Report)," *Population Characteristics*, ser. P-20, no. 304 (December 1976), p. 1.

Table 12.3 Reported Voting for Persons of Voting Age, by Sex and Age: November 1964 to 1976
(Percent of Civilian Noninstitutional Population)

	Presidential elections				Congressional elections		
Sex and age	**1976**	**1972**	**1968**	**1964**	**1974**	**1970**	**1966**
Sex							
Both sexes	59.2	63.0	67.8	69.3	44.7	54.6	55.4
Male	59.6	64.1	69.8	71.9	46.2	56.8	58.2
Female	58.8	62.0	66.0	67.0	43.4	52.7	53.0
Age							
Total, 18 years and over	59.2	63.0	67.8	69.3	44.7	54.6	55.4
18 to 20 years	38.0	48.3	33.6	39.2	20.8	25.6	21.9
21 to 24 years	45.6	50.7	51.1	51.3	26.4	30.4	31.7
25 to 34 years	55.4	59.7	62.5	64.7	37.0	46.2	45.9
35 to 44 years	63.3	66.3	70.8	72.8	49.1	58.1	59.7
45 to 54 years	67.9	70.9	75.1	76.1	55.9	63.8	64.2
55 to 64 years	69.7	70.7	74.7	75.6	58.3	64.7	64.7
65 to 74 years	66.4	68.1	71.5	71.4	55.8	61.2	61.0
75 years and over	54.8	55.6	56.3	56.7	43.7	50.1	46.9
Median (years)	45.1	44.9	46.7	46.2	47.8	48.1	47.8

Note: Includes persons 18 years old and over in Georgia and Kentucky, 19 years old and over in Alaska, 20 years old and over in Hawaii, and 21 years old and over in the remaining states in 1964, 1966, 1968, and 1970. Includes all persons 18 years old and over in 1972, 1974, and 1976.

Source: U.S. Bureau of the Census, "Voter Participation in November 1976 (Advanced Report)," *Population Characteristics*, ser. P-20, no. 304 (December 1976), p. 3.

pediment to expanding citizen participation in elections is the prevalence of "archaic voter registration laws," to use Senator Kennedy's words.

Since 1964, the Bureau of the Census has surveyed the electorate after each presidential and congressional election. The results of its surveys are contained in Table 12.2 and Figure 12.1. Since the percentage figures are computed from a sample survey, they are not fully consistent with the data on actual voter turnouts such as those contained in Table 12.1. The Bureau of the Census has consistently calculated a higher percentage turnout both nationally and regionally than actually occurred. However, the Bureau's surveys are useful to the extent that they indicate *relative* participation over time. Given these qualifications, Table 12.2 shows that the percentage of the voting-age population going to the polls for presidential elections has decreased from a computed level of nearly 69 percent when Barry Goldwater was pitted against Lyndon Johnson in 1964 to 59 percent when Gerald Ford ran against Jimmy Carter in 1976. The voter turnout during off-year congressional elections has always been much lower than it has been in years of presidential elections. Indeed, only 45 percent of the voting-age population voted in the congressional election of 1974. That percentage figure was 10 percentage points lower than in 1966, a significant decrease.

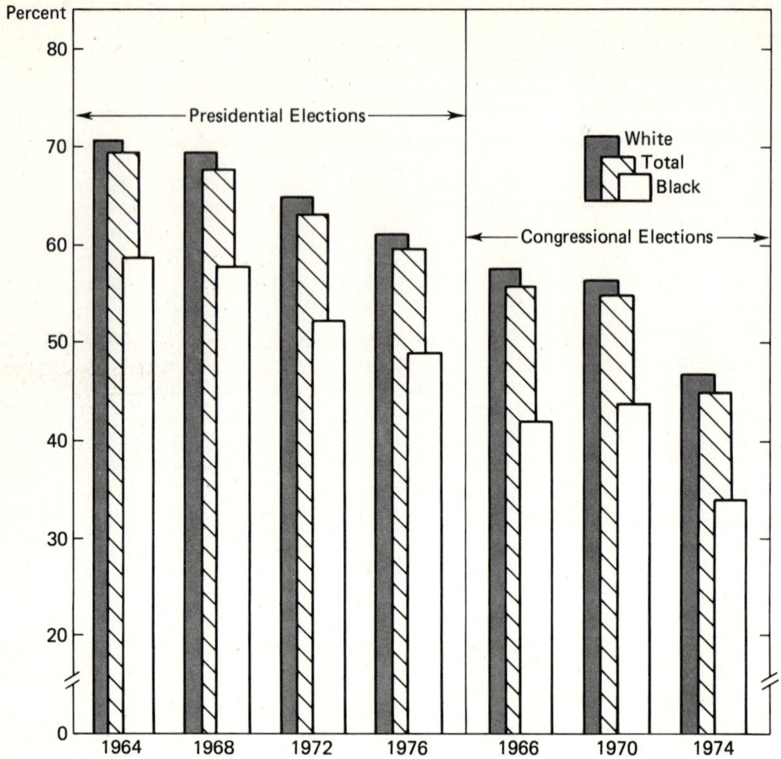

Figure 12.1 Percent voting of persons 18 years old and over, by race: November 1964 to 1976 (reported participation rate by civilian noninstitutional population). [*Source: U.S. Bureau of the Census, "Voter Participation in November 1976 (Advanced Report)," Population Characteristics, ser. P-20, no. 304, (December 1976), front page.*]

Table 12.2 also reveals that a greater proportion of whites go to the polls than blacks, and blacks have significantly higher turnout rates than persons of Spanish origin. People in the North and West have higher turnout rates than people in the South. The drop in the turnout rates for blacks, whites, and the entire population is dramatically portrayed in Figure 12.1. That figure and Table 12.2 show a consistent drop in voter participation. However, between the 1966 and 1970 congressional elections, voter participation for blacks went up slightly. This was due solely to higher participation by blacks in the South, which in turn was due to election-law changes designed to increase the registration of blacks in the South. After this initial success, the black voter turnout returned to its historical downward trend in presidential as well as congressional elections.

The drop in voter turnout is not completely a recent phenomenon. It has been in progress since the last quarter of the nineteenth century. For instance, nearly 82 percent of the electorate turned out at the polls in the

1876 election, and approximately 73 percent turned out in the election of 1900. Voter turnout went up in most areas of the country in the late 1940s and the early 1950s, but it has since continued its long-term downward trend.[4]

Table 12.3 contains additional information on the demographics of voter participation in the 1964 and 1976 elections. While the turnout rates for both men and women have been on the decline, we can observe in the table that men had a slightly higher participation rate than women in the 1976 election; however, the gap in the turnout rates between the sexes has become narrower. The table shows in addition that the lowest turnout rate in the 1972 and 1976 elections belonged to young voters between the ages of 18 and 20. The 55- to 64-year-old group had the highest turnout rate, almost 70 percent.

From earlier study of the 1974 election survey, the Bureau of the Census described the following groups of persons as having high or low percentage turnouts at the polls[5]:

High voting and registration groups	Low voting and registration groups
Persons 45 to 71 years old	Persons 18 to 24 years old
Residents outside of the South	Residents of the South
College graduates	Less than 8 years of school
Annual income of $25,000 and above	Annual income under $5,000
Professional and technical workers	Laborers
Whites	Blacks

REASONS FOR NOT VOTING: WHAT CITIZENS SAY

In the election survey, the Bureau of the Census asks citizens who do not vote why they do not. Table 12.4 provides a list of the reasons given and the estimated distribution of responses. Nearly 24 percent of the estimated 47 million people who did not vote in 1976 were registered. About half this group indicated that, for one reason or another, they were "unable to vote." Illness or emergency was the single most frequently reported reason for registered voters not voting. A little over 3 percent of those not voting were out of town or away from home. Only 1.6 percent of the total group of nonvoters reported that they "couldn't take time off from work." Those who reported that they did not want to vote or were not interested in voting accounted for slightly more than 5 percent of those registered but not voting.

[4]For more on the long-term trend of voter turnout, see Kevin P. Phillips and Paul H. Blackburn, *Electoral Reform and Voter Participation: Federal Registration, A False Remedy for Voter Apathy* (Washington, D.C.: American Enterprise Institute for Public Policy Research, 1975), chap. 2.

[5]U.S. Bureau of the Census, "Voting and Registration in the Election of November 1974," *Population Characteristics*, ser. P-20, no. 293 (April 1976), p. 1.

Table 12.4 Reasons for Not Participating in the November 1976 Election
(Percentages, Civilian Noninstitutional Population)

Did not vote (total estimated number of persons 46,667,000)	100.0
Registered, but did not vote	23.7
Unable to vote	12.6
Had no way to get to polls	0.9
Illness or emergency	4.6
Couldn't take time off from work	1.6
Lines too long, machines not working	0.5
Out of town or away from home	3.3
Other reason	1.5
Did not want to vote or not interested	5.4
Did not prefer any of the candidates	2.7
Politicians are not interested in my problems	0.1
My vote would not make a difference in the election	0.3
Just don't want to get involved in politics	0.3
Not interested in election this year	1.7
Other reason	0.3
Other reason	4.0
Reason not reported	1.8
Not registered[1]	76.3
Unable to register:	
Residence requirement not satisfied	2.3
Recently moved; never got around to it	3.2
Permanent illness or disability	3.0
No transportation, hours, or place of registration inconvenient	3.2
Did not know how or where to register	2.1
Can't read English	0.6
Other reason	3.6
Did not want to register or not interested:	
Did not prefer any of the candidates	5.8
Politicians are not interested in my problems	0.9
My vote would not make a difference in the election	1.6
Just don't want to get involved in politics	5.0
Not interested in election this year	9.1
Other reason	2.1
Other reason	30.1
Reason not reported	3.7

[1]Does not include estimated 13,183,000 people who reported they were not citizens or who did not report on registration in the survey from which this table is developed. These people are included in the percent distribution calculated by the Bureau of the Census. See source.

Source: Bureau of the Census, Department of Commerce, *Population Characteristics*, Series P-20, No. 304, 6.

On the other hand, over three-quarters of those who did not vote in 1976 were not registered. The two reasons most frequently cited by this group for not registering were that they "did not prefer any of the candidates" (5.8 percent), and that they were "not interested in the election this year" (9.1 percent). Thirty percent of those not registered gave various and miscellaneous reasons for their nonparticipation, which the Bureau does not report separately. Only a little over 11 percent of all nonvoters gave reasons for their nonparticipation that were related to registration laws.[6] Of this 11 percent, not everyone can be expected to participate in elections even if registration requirements are fully eliminated. Further, nearly 40 percent (and possibly as many as 80 percent) of the nonvoters gave reasons for nonparticipation that indicate that they simply did not care about the election or politics or that they were unwilling to go to the trouble of registering and voting. In short, as indicated by the Bureau of the Census survey, a substantial portion of the nonvoters are not likely to be affected by any realistic change in the election laws.

REASONS FOR NOT VOTING: WHAT SOCIAL SCIENTISTS SAY

The list of reasons that social scientists gave for explaining the failure of citizens to participate in elections is extensive, including virtually all factors that affect human behavior in general. This list includes sex, race, education, location (rural versus urban), marital status, social status defined in various ways, length of residence, occupation, extent of legal restrictions, interparty competitiveness, and religion, all of which may be construed more as categories of reasons than specific explanations themselves.

The general impression one gets from reading literature on voter turnout, which is summarized in the appendix to this chapter, is that changes in registration requirements are unlikely to have a substantial effect on voter turnout. Certainly, one cannot expect the Universal Registration Act to be the "giant step forward" in increasing voter turnout of which Senator Kennedy has spoken. Kevin Phillips and Paul Blackman, in a study that we have already cited, estimate that countrywide election-day registration will probably increase voter turnout by 5 percentage points, raising voter turnout from 56 percent in 1976 to about 61 percent.[7] They infer this from a study of the change in voter turnout when registration was introduced at the turn of the century and the 5-percentage-point increase in voting that resulted from the introduction of compulsory registration and voting in Australia. From our earlier perusal of data for 1976, their estimate seems reasonable.

THE ECONOMIC THEORY OF RATIONAL NONVOTERS

Many empirical studies of nonvoting have little or no theoretical underpinning. They base their findings primarily on the general proposition of environmental determinism: that virtually anything can affect behavior,

[6] Included in this group are those nonvoters who have the following reasons for not voting: "residence requirement not satisfied" (2.3 percent), "recently moved, never got around to it" (3.2 percent), "no transportation, hours or place of registration inconvenient" (3.2 percent), and "did not know how or where to register" (2.1 percent).

[7] Phillips and Blackman, *Electoral Reform*, p. 53.

in this case, voter behavior. The problem of the empirical researcher is to discover through manipulation of statistics what these factors are, not to verify or refute some conceptually rigorous theory of voter behavior. One of the most powerful theoretical explanations of nonvoting has been developed in the study of the economics of politics. For this reason, we consider in detail here the economic theory of voter and nonvoter *behavior*. A central conclusion of the theory is that for the individual who is interested in maximizing his or her welfare solely through the election of a candidate, it is not rational to vote. This conclusion is based on cost-benefit analysis, which in turn is predicated upon the argument that, contrary to high school civics courses and the exhortations of political figures, each individual vote counts for very, very little in determining the outcome of an election. Therefore, the individual decides not to vote rather than incur the costs of registering and voting. Let us pursue this theory in more detail.[8]

Rational Politicians and Voters in Two-Party Politics

In a two-party political system, candidates for a particular office can generally be expected to take similar but not identical stands on issues and to be "middle-of-the-roaders." Otherwise, they run a considerable risk of being defeated. For example, suppose, as in Figure 12.2, that all potential voters are normally distributed along the political spectrum, which goes all the way from the extreme left (liberal) to the extreme right (conservative). Interpreted freely, this distribution simply means that far more voters take moderate political positions (represented by the hump in the middle) than extreme left or right positions (represented by the two tails). If one candidate, for example, the Republican, takes a political stance at R, the other, the Democrat, can take a political position just to the Republican's left at, say, D. The Republican will receive all the votes in the right tail of the dis-

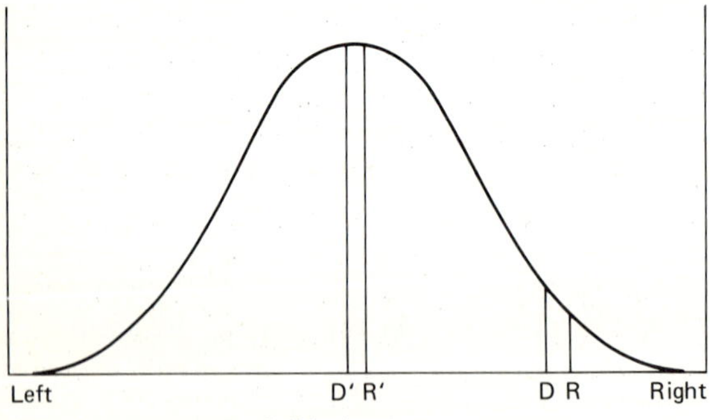

Figure 12.2 Distribution of voters.

[8]This line of analysis was first formalized in Anthony Downs, *An Economic Theory of Democracy* (New York: Harper and Row, Publishers, 1957).

tribution. The two candidates will divide the votes in between their two political positions. However, the Democrat will take all of the votes to his or her left and will, therefore, easily win the election. Indeed, if the Democrat takes a stance at D′, he or she can still win. To avoid losing or to increase the chances of winning, the Republican is forced to follow the Democrat into the center of the distribution and adopt a position at, say, R′. The competitiveness of the political process will ensure that the parties are close but sufficiently far apart that many people will view them as two distinct parties under these circumstances. The recurring concern of many voters is that, to use George Wallace's now famous phrase, "there's not a dime's worth of difference between the two of them."

In a political contest in which the two candidates are exactly identical in all respects, there is no *economic* reason whatsoever for the rational person to vote. One's vote will not affect the stream of benefits one receives from government. In a political contest in which the two candidates are similar, but not identical, there is some reason to vote; however, that reason is restricted to the *perceived difference* in benefits that the person expects to receive from one of the two candidates' winning. However, before it follows that a person can be expected to vote, the perceived difference in benefits must be adjusted downward (or "discounted," to use the technical term) by the probability that the individual's vote will actually determine the outcome of the election. In national and most local elections, this probability is virtually zero, which means that the discounted benefits from voting will be very small, so small that they may not be as great as the costs that are associated with registering and voting.

Consider this example. Suppose that a typical, rational voter believes that the net benefits she will receive from the Republican candidate's winning are $5,000; that is, we assume that the individual believes that over the course of her life she will be $5,000 better off if the Republican wins than if the Democrat wins. Further, suppose that she estimates that the probability of her vote's determining the outcome of the election is 1 in 10 million (0.0000001) and that it will cost her $1 in terms of the value of her time lost to register and vote.[9] These seem to be rather generous estimates of the probability, cost, and benefit figures involved[10]; however,

[9]Gordon Tullock suggests that the net benefits should be further discounted. Politicians have been known to lie and mislead voters; the individual can never be fully confident that the candidate he or she votes for will actually deliver the benefits expected. See Gordon Tullock, *Toward a Mathematics of Politics* (Ann Arbor: University of Michigan Press, 1967), chap. 7.

[10]I suggest that the figures are rather generous, because in most presidential elections most (but not all) citizens would not be willing to pay $5,000 to see their favorite candidate win, since the candidate is not likely to have $5,000 worth of an effect on their lifetime welfare and because the probability of each one's vote determining the outcome of an election is virtually zero. (An aerospace engineer, whose job may hinge on the outcome of the election, will, of course, assess the net benefits of the election outcome as being greater than $5,000.) Furthermore, if a candidate ever wins by one or even a few votes, the election count will be challenged in court and an number of ballots disputed; as it has done in the past, the court can be expected to order a new election.

on the basis of cost-benefit calculation, the individual will not vote. In the jargon of economic theory, the payoff is negative:

$$\text{Discounted benefits} - \text{cost of voting} = \text{payoff from voting}$$

$$(0.0000001)(\$5{,}000) - \$1 = -\$0.9995$$

Contrary to the inference that may be drawn, this theory of voting behavior does not lead to the conclusion that no one will vote. If each person believes no one else will vote, then each person can reason that his or her vote will determine the outcome of the election: each person will become, in a limited way, a de facto dictator. The probability of a person's vote determining who wins will rise to 1.0 and that payoff from voting in the equation above jumps dramatically to $4,999 ($5,000 in net benefits minus the $1 in voting cost). Further, many people may vote because participation in the political process and talking about politics is a hobby; in other words, they vote because of the entertainment value of political participation. Voting is then economically justified. Others may vote out of a sense of civic or moral duty.

The Optimum Voter Turnout

The economic view of voting behavior does suggest that there is some equilibrium (or optimum) turnout sought by voters and politicians over the course of a series of elections. Consider first the equilibrium sought by voters. Given the perceived net benefits and costs of voting for each individual, when the turnout varies, citizens' assessment of the probability of each vote's affecting the outcome changes. Over time, different individuals with different assessments of the costs and net benefits draw different conclusions about whether or not to vote. If, for example, the voter turnout is 60 percent, some voters will calculate that the discounted benefits of voting do not justify the cost of continued voting; they will drop out in the following election and the turnout as a percentage of all voters will fall. The drop in the turnout, on the other hand, will increase the probability that an individual vote will affect the outcome, will increase the discounted benefits, and will create voter resistance to a further fall in turnout. There is, in other words, some percentage figure below which the turnout of rational voters will not fall. This is the equilibrium or optimum turnout. If the turnout rises above this equilibrium level, the discounted benefits will fall and nonvoting, for many, will become a rational choice; the turnout will then fall back down in subsequent elections.

Candidates also seek an equilibrium voter turnout in a two-party system. They know that if they adopt identical political positions in the middle of the voter distribution (see Figure 12.2) and have identical personalities, etc., then no one has any economic incentive to go to the polls and vote. By pulling away from each other politically, they create a net differential in benefits, as perceived and evaluated by voters. This movement induces some voter response. However, as we pointed out before, the competitiveness of two-party politics keeps candidates from pulling very far apart; it therefore restricts the net differential and people's incentive to vote.

On the other hand, because the center of voter distribution has a powerful attraction to political candidates, voters in the wings of the distribution have less incentive to vote. If they are far removed from the mainstream positions of the candidates or if they are "alienated," then the two-party system makes it likely that they will continue not to vote. We note that the more heterogeneous the views of the voters on political issues (the more spread out the distribution), the larger this group will be. In short, many people in the middle of the distribution fail to vote because of the lack of distance between the candidates, which has been rationally determined by the candidates. The voter turnout in the United States may, in some sense, be "bad," but it may also simply be a reflection of how the political system works.

Three-Party Politics

An economic theory of politics predicts that in a multiparty political system there will be greater political distances between the candidates. The economic incentives for people to vote will be greater and alienated voters fewer in number—that is, to the extent that alienation is a function of the distance that exists between a voter's personal political views and the views or programs articulated by the candidates. This is illustrated in Figure 12.3, where we consider the political predicament of three candidates in a two-issue campaign. The issues concern the appropriate budget size for the military (vertical axis) and educational (horizontal axis) bureaucracies. The political positions of all voters are represented by the various points in the square.

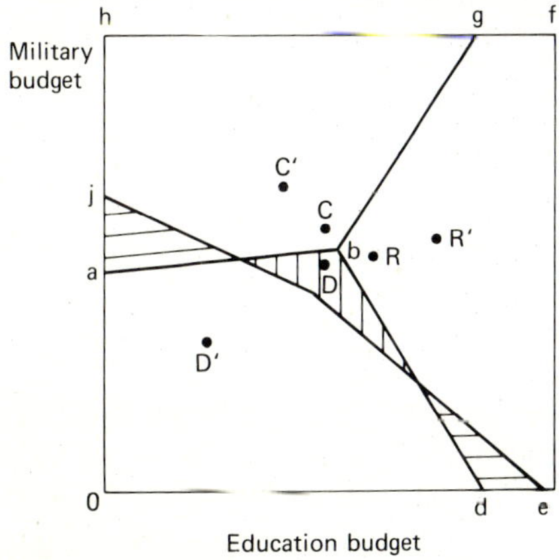

Figure 12.3 Two-issue, three-party model of political behavior.

We assume that voters are evenly distributed in the "political space" represented by the figure.

Suppose that all three candidates are initially located in the center of the distribution at positions D, R, and C and divide the votes among themselves as indicated by the various segments of the regtangle that are marked off. For instance, with a political position in the center (D), the Democratic candidate will get all the votes in the area bounded by abd0; the Republican (at R), the votes in defgb; and the Conservative candidate (at C), the votes in abghj.

However, each candidate has an incentive to move away from the center. If, for example, the Democrat moves to D′, he or she will lose votes in the center of the distribution to the rivals but pick up votes from the rivals in the outer wings of their parts of the distribution. In fact, the Democrat will lose the votes in the vertically striped area but gain all the votes in the horizontally striped areas. If the other candidates do not move, the Democrat will take more than a third of the votes and will win the election. However, in order to pick up votes or to fend off loss of support to political rivals, the other candidates will also move away from the center. They will move to positions like C′ and R′. At these points they may be characterized as representing parties of a particular social class, like the Conservative and Labor parties in Great Britain. Regardless of the terms by which they are described, distinctly different political positions and parties should reduce voter alienation and increase the incentive citizens have to go to the polls. Because of the nature of the political system and not because of some innate quality of the citizenry, voter turnout in multiparty countries like Great Britain or France should be greater than in the United States. Viewed from this perspective, the lower turnout in the United States occurs not because voters here are more apathetic than voters are elsewhere but rather because they are responding to the two-party system, a system that politicians promote, consciously or unconsciously, by their own instinct for survival in a competitive process.

Changes in Institutional Constraints

Over time, political and economic institutions evolve. Such evolution promotes changes in the costs and benefits of voting, which in turn can be expected to result in changes in voter turnout. In this section, we deal briefly with three institutional changes.

Population Mobility An increase in people's mobility can be expected to reduce voter turnout, at least in state and local elections. The more times a person moves (or even an increase in the probability of future moves), the greater the cost a person must incur in becoming and remaining involved in politics. Greater mobility requires that the individual become acquainted with more political candidates and institutions. It also means greater costs in registering and finding out where the polls are, who the candidates are, and where they stand on issues. Granted, these costs *may* not, in absolute terms, be very great. On the other hand, the discounted benefits from voting may be as small as, if not smaller than, the cost of continued political participation. As the cost of participation in elections increases due to increased mobility, we may reasonably expect that more and more people will join the ranks of the nonvoter.

Government Growth Growth in government is also likely to reduce voter turnout. In recent years, government at all levels has tried to solve ever more complex problems and has devised budgets that are ever more difficult for the ordinary citizen to interpret. As candidates are called upon to espouse views on a growing number of issues, it has become more difficult for the individual citizen to determine which candidate is "better" for him or her. The individual who cannot or will not put forth the effort to determine what the differences among candidates are and how these differences will affect him or her can be said to be flipping a coin in the voting booth. An economic theory of politics suggests that the increased cost of political participation in light of government growth means that, over time, fewer and fewer people will vote.

Legal Restrictions Legal restrictions, such as voter registration rules and the number of hours polls are open, add to the cost of political participation and to a reduction in voter turnout. Their elimination tends to reduce the cost of voting and increase the turnout. Although it may not be recognized as such, the supporters of the Universal Registration Act and registration-by-mail proposals must have an economic-type model of voter behavior embedded in their arguments. The central question in the debate on the elimination of registration requirements is not whether or not such proposals will have the expected directional effect on voter turnout but how much the effect will be and whether that extra voter response is worth any extra registration cost and the risk-cost of increased voter fraud.

REASONS FOR EXPANDING THE TURNOUT

Several arguments can be advanced in favor of increasing voter turnout. The purpose of this section is to develop those arguments.

Distorted Representation

One intended purpose of expanding voter turnout is to increase the degree to which the popular vote reflects the will of the entire citizenry, by which is meant the will of the median-voter group or that group of voters in the middle of the eligible voter distribution. We noted earlier that candidates in a two-party race will tend to move toward the center of the distribution of *those persons who are likely to vote*. The actual voter distribution is determined by self-selection of the voters themselves, not by some random drawing process; the group of people who elect to go to the polls under current registration restrictions may not accurately reflect the distribution of all potential voters. The distribution of those who are likely to vote may be skewed to the left or to the right of the distribution of all potential eligible voters. Therefore, in the attempt to be elected (by going to the center of the distribution of those who are actually likely to vote), political aspirants will devise platforms that are to the left or right of the potential median-voter group. Through an increase in voter turnout, a more complete representation of all voters will be realized; and candidates will take, so the argument may be developed, positions more closely approximating the views of those in the center of potential eligible voters. This result is considered desirable by those who feel this is what two-party politics is supposed to accomplish. It also may be argued that a political platform in the center of the distribution minimizes the political distance between what government actually does and what the citizenry as a whole wants it to do. To the extent that the political system accomplishes this end, it lessens political discord between government and the people.

Moral Imperative

The right to vote is considered to be fundamental to the operation of democracy. Any restriction not absolutely necessary on the use of that right disenfranchises citizens and denies to them that to which they are entitled by the social contract as stipulated in the Constitution. If unnecessary impediments to voting exist, then those who have imposed the impediments are failing to live up to the contract to which they have explicitly or implicitly agreed. Viewed this way, it is morally imperative (for the sake of holding to a social contract) that voter turnout be maximized by eliminating as many obstacles to voting as possible. Registration requirements should be eliminated, according to this line of argument, unless an overwhelming case can be made for them; minor potential for fraud in the absence of registration procedures is insufficient justification for the use of those procedures.

Furthermore, although an increase in voter turnout reduces the incentive to vote, Goodin and Roberts contend that increased turnout makes the votes of those who do vote a more accurate reflection of their ethical position.[11] Individuals who go to the polls when voter turnout is high knows that their vote will not materially affect them (or their "egoistic" interest, to use Goodin and Roberts' phraseology). They are, therefore, induced to vote that

[11] R. E. Goodin and K. W. S. Roberts, "The Ethical Voter," *American Political Science Review*, vol. 69 (September 1975), pp. 926–928.

course of action which they consider to be right from a social or ethical perspective. As Goodin and Roberts write, "precisely the same factor that makes it irrational for an egoist to go to the polls makes it rational for a less than thoroughly self-centered man to vote his ethical preferences once there. As one in the multitude, his vote cannot much affect the outcome. Since there is little he can do inside the poll booth to further his egoistic interests, a man is freed to vote his ethical preferences."[12] Goodin and Roberts conclude that "electoral results should be interpreted as reflecting essentially ethical preferences insofar as partisans have structured the debate to allow those to emerge."[13] There is, however, one problem with their argument: voters in the context of the "multitude" have little incentive to thoroughly investigate exactly what constitutes an ethically correct position. From this point of view, election results may be characterized as the "ethical gut reaction" of morally concerned voters.[14]

Special Interest

An increase in voter turnout can (but not necessarily will) make it more difficult for special-interest groups to influence election results. If a special-interest group expects any additional turnout to be divided between two candidates in the same way as all other votes are divided, it will need to marshall more total votes in order to have its favorite candidate win. It will then need to get a higher proportion of the group's membership to the polls, and to accomplish this can be costly. Seeing the difficulties facing special-interest groups, politicians will be less likely to cater to their demands. If the total vote is quite large, the special-interest group may become comparatively insignificant, in which case it will lose its political clout.

Political Advantage

As we have pointed out, nonvoters tend to have relatively lower incomes, to have less than the average amount of education, to be younger, and to be members of the black and Hispanic minorities. A high percentage of the members of these groups tend to vote for Democrats, so the result of an increase in voter turnout may be to increase voter support of Democratic candidates. President Carter himself stands to gain from the Universal Registration Act. By the same token, many Republicans can be expected to be less than enthusiastic about any measure that will increase voter turnout, because it will only make more difficult their task of regaining a majority of the House and Senate or the Presidency.

[12]Ibid., p. 927.

[13]Ibid., p. 982.

[14]We make here the reasonable assumption that the morally correct course of action is not always obvious and may be more obscured than clarified by the rhetoric of political campaigns.

Social Engineering

Some supporters of measures to increase turnout see in such proposals a means of increasing or decreasing the scope and diversity of government activity in the economy. They hope to indirectly realign the public and private sectors and, in that way and to that extent, to engage in social engineering. There are two competing hypotheses about the relationship between government size and voter turnout. On the one hand, an increase in voter turnout may, up to some point, bring into the political process a large number of people who, because of their relatively low education, income level, and social status, are inclined to vote for "more government." On the other hand, an increase in the turnout may result in more people monitoring, through their votes, the activities of government. With their behavior being more closely watched, politicians will have to be more careful about the usefulness and extent of their spending programs.

To assess which of these two competing hypotheses is correct, Robert McCormick and I undertook a cross-sectional empirical study of voter turnout and per capita state government expenditures in 1960.[15] After controlling statistically for differences among states in per capita income, racial composition, population density, and median age, we found, as have others, that voter turnout had a statistically insignificant negative effect on per capita state expenditures. That is, there is no statistical basis for thinking that a negative or even a positive relationship actually exists. However, we then turned to the effect that voting restrictions have on state per capita expenditures and per capita state debt. We found that an *increase* in the degree to which states facilitate registration and voting, everything else equal, will tend to result in a *decrease* in per capita state expenditures and a *reduction* in per capita state debt.[16] In short, facilitated registration and voting procedures make states more fiscally conservative. Although the findings are very preliminary and a great deal of additional work needs to be done, one conclusion seems worth mentioning: control of election procedures may be a way of controlling government expenditures. And passage of legislation like the Universal Registration Act may be partially dependent upon how liberals and conservatives think the act will affect government programs in which they have a political stake.[17]

[15] Robert McCormick and Richard B. McKenzie, "Facilitated Voting Procedures as a Means of Putting the Fiscal Brakes on State Government," *Public Choice* (forthcoming).

[16] Again, we controlled in this statistical test for state per capita income, racial composition, population density, and median age. For our variable that measures the degree to which states facilitate registration and voting, we used an index of "legal facilitation" developed by Jae-On Kim, John R. Petrocik, and Stephen N. Enokson, "Voter Turnout among the American States: Systematic and Individual Components," *American Political Science Review*, vol. 69 (March 1975), pp. 107–123. The study was restricted to the 1960 election because that was the only year for which this index was available. It was also a year in which registration and voting restrictions varied greatly among states.

[17] Our empirical findings can be easily explained. Facilitated registration and voting procedures may not substantially affect voter turnout, as several studies have found; however,

CONCLUDING COMMENTS

Voter turnout in United States congressional and presidential elections is low by European standards and on the decrease. Explanations for nonparticipation in the electoral process run the gamut of social research. Nonvoting can be explained by such factors as income level, culture and race, educational level, and age. Nonvoting also can be caused by legal restrictions on voting and by the competitiveness of the two-party system. For many people, voting is simply not a rational course of behavior; this is because individual votes have little or no influence in determining election outcomes. One conclusion of our analysis is that the two-party political system is designed to produce an optimum voter turnout, which is the same as saying that it is designed to produce an optimum level of nonvoting by citizens. Given the cultural, individual, legal, and political factors that affect voter turnout, the decrease in voter turnout experienced in the United States may be construed as a natural movement of the citizenry toward an optimum output level.

Economic principles cannot possibly explain all people's actions and inactions, but this chapter has tried to demonstrate that economic analysis can be helpful in unraveling the mysteries of a complex process like politics. Economics concentrates on the rational component of people's behavior and is, therefore, a partial view of the world, a partial explanation of why people behave the way they do. However, the analysis still offers insight concerning the consequences of social policies. First, it suggests changes in election laws that facilitate registration and voting will tend to expand directly the voter turnout. Second, it suggests that changes in election laws may be used to affect indirectly the size and scope of government. These secondary, hidden effects must be kept in mind in evaluating the rhetoric that often shrouds proposed changes in election laws.

QUESTIONS TO PONDER

1 Should the voter turnout be affected by the wage rate? What factors must be considered in answering that question?

---

making it easier for citizens to vote increases the *threat* that politicians face when they attempt to expand state programs, budgets, and tax burdens. With facilitated voting procedures (making it easier to vote), citizens can react with greater ease and consequent force to objectionable extensions of government and pork-barrel politics. Our results are consistent with the work of Robert McCormick and Robert Tollison, who found that voter turnout has a monitoring influence on state legislatures: an increase in voter turnout tends to reduce the value of state legislative seats and the degree to which legislators can pass bills to benefit themselves. Robert E. McCormick and Robert E. Tollison, *Wage Pay and Outside Earnings of Politicians*, Working Paper Series (Clemson, S.C.: Department of Economics, Clemson University; and Blacksburg, Va.: Center for the Study of Public Choice, Virginia Polytechnic Institute and State University, 1977). See also Robert E. McCormick and Robert E. Tollison, "Legislatures as Unions," *Journal of Political Economy* (forthcoming).

2 Does the economic analysis of voter behavior lead to the conclusion that no one should vote?
3 Develop an economic explanation for laws against "buying votes."
4 Many high school and college courses are designed to "make students better citizens." What does economics have to say about the incentive that people have to retain knowledge that is designed to make them better citizens?
5 Economics cannot possibly explain all behavior. What noneconomic explanations can you offer for why many people vote?

ADDITIONAL READING

Gwartney, James D. *Economics: Private and Public Choice*. New York: Academic Press, Inc., 1976, chaps. 28–30.

McConnell, Campbell R. *Economics: Principles, Problems, and Policies*, 7th ed. New York: McGraw-Hill Book Company, 1978, chap. 6.

Phillips, Kevin P., and Paul H. Blackburn. *Electoral Reform and Voter Participation: Federal Registration, A False Remedy for Voter Apathy*. Washington, D.C.: American Enterprise Institute for Public Policy Research, 1975.

APPENDIX TO CHAPTER 12: Research on Voting

As noted in the body of the chapter, explanations developed by social scientists, primarily political scientists and sociologists, for low voter turnouts are varied. Some of the more important recent studies are categorized and summarized below.

CULTURAL AND SOCIOECONOMIC FACTORS

Kevin Phillips and Paul Blackman have argued at some length that the heterogeneity of the United States population partially explains low voter turnout in the United States compared to that in Western European countries.[18] They argue that if there are cultural, social, and economic similarities in a population, people will express similar views on political issues. One's own political views tend to be reinforced when similar views are articulated by others. Individuals in the relevant group or class are not subjected to the crosscurrent of views that is usually expressed in populations with a variety of cultural backgrounds and outlooks. Therefore, it is much easier for people in homogeneous population groups to make up their minds than it is for people in heterogeneous population groups. According to Phillips and Blackman, those persons who can make up their minds readily are much more likely to vote in political contests than those who cannot. In support of their argument, they point to the relatively high voter turnouts that have been experienced in France, Germany, Australia, and Finland—countries that are composed of highly homogeneous economic and social classes. Western European countries,

[18] Phillips and Blackman, *Electoral Reform*, especially chap. 4.

unlike the United States, do not have large minorities that have not been fully integrated into the mainstream of society. In the 1976 election, blacks and Hispanic people in the United States accounted for 14.7 percent of the voting-age population; however, they accounted for a little over 20 percent of all eligible citizens who did not vote. In fact, over 51 percent of the black voting-age population did not vote, and over 68 percent of the Hispanic voting-age population did not vote.

Phillips and Blackman write:

> America's low voter-participation rate is consistent with its mixed culture and social mobility. These in turn relate to public concern with political efficacy and "responsiveness," factors having much more voter impact in Anglo-American than in continental European societies. Because Germans and Swedes look for government leadership rather than government responsiveness, "alienation" has little effect on turnout in their countries. More ideological parties would presumably increase the rate of U.S. voter turnout. But the question remains whether a change in election laws, especially of voter registration laws, could by itself greatly spur participation in American elections.[19]

Others have stated similar views.

Duration of residence also affects voter turnout. Generally, the less time a person has spent in an area before an election, the less likely he or she is to register and vote. The Bureau of the Census has concluded that "living in a community for 1 year or more not only increases the proportion of persons who registered [sic]. About 75 percent of registered persons who lived at their current residence 6 years or more voted as compared with about 60 percent for those with less than a year's residence at their current address."[20]

A number of other socioeconomic variables are frequently cited as explanations for nonparticipation in elections. Seymour Lipset summarizes the findings of a number of sociological studies. He writes, "Men vote more than women; the better educated more than the less educated; urban residents, more than rural; those between 35 and 55, more than younger or older voters; married persons, more than unmarried; higher status persons, more than lower; members of organizations, more than non-members."[21] These conclusions, drawn from studies of elections in the 1950s, are applicable to more recent elections.[22] However, the arguments that are typically offered in support of these kinds of conclusions tend to be solely statistical and, thereby, superficial.

INTERPARTY COMPETITION

Social scientists cite the competitiveness of political campaigns as an important determinant of voter turnout. In races in which there is only one unopposed candi-

[19]Ibid., p. 44.

[20]U.S. Bureau of the Census, "Voting and Registration in the Election of November 1974," p. 5.

[21]Seymour Lipset, *Political Man* (Garden City, N.Y.: Doubleday & Company, Inc., 1963), p. 187.

[22]See U.S. Bureau of the Census, "Voter Participation in November 1976 (Advanced Report)," *Population Characteristics*, ser. P-20, no. 304 (December 1976).

date, voters have no reason other than civic duty to go to the polls. Tight races spur more interest because the outcome is uncertain, and candidates in tight election races are likely to spend more time and money trying to attract citizen participation in their campaigns and voter support at the pools on election day. Candidates who anticipate an easy victory do not have the incentive to "get out the vote." Walter Burnham attributes the drop in voter turnout just after the turn of the century to the overwhelming victory of the Republicans in the 1896 election.[23] The relatively low turnout in the South has been attributed to the fact that, until recently, most Southern states were largely one-party states. V. O. Key notes that, although the turnout at the time of the general election in the South is typically lower than it is elsewhere, the turnout in primaries, in which there are opposing candidates most of the time, has approached the turnout levels that exist for the rest of the country in the November election.[24]

Following this line of reasoning, the emergence of the Republican party as a viable political force in the South should have led to a greater turnout. In fact, although the turnout in the South has been on the decrease, just as it has been in the rest of the country, the drop has not been as great as in other parts of the country.[25] A comparison of regional turnouts for the 1964 and 1976 elections does indicate, as expected, that the *relative* turnout in the South has been on the increase. In the 1964 presidential election, the percentage turnout in the North and West was 1.41 times the percentage turnout in the South; however, by 1976, the percentage turnout in the North and West was only 1.11 times the percentage turnout in the South. Furthermore, in the 1966 congressional election, the percentage voter turnout in the North and West was 1.42 times the percentage turnout in the South; by 1974, that ratio had fallen to 1.36.

Political parties in Europe tend to be closely associated with economic and social classes; and political campaigns tend, therefore, to reflect an underlying class struggle for the division of the "public pie." Political parties in the United States are much more broad-based, which is another way of saying that their basic function is less clear cut. Voters in the United States simply have fewer reasons for going to the polls.

LEGAL RESTRICTIONS

Most studies of voter turnout lead one to conclude that election rules, such as required registration, literacy tests (no longer legal), residency requirements, and restrictive voting hours, tend to have the expected effects: that is, restrictive rules, especially as they are applied in the South, tend to decrease voter turnout, and vice versa. However, researchers are not in agreement on *how much* effect state regulations have on voter turnout. For example, in their extensive study of the American

[23] Walter Dean Burnham, "The Changing Shape of the Political Universe," *The American Political Science Review*, vol. 59 (March 1965), pp. 7–28.

[24] V. O. Key, *Southern Politics in State and Nation* (New York: Alfred E. Knopf, Inc., 1951), p. 492.

[25] The drop that has occurred in the South may be partly explained by several of the socioeconomic factors we have already considered, such as increased social mobility.

voter, Campbell, Converse, Miller, and Stokes conclude that "the data . . . indicate that here again we encounter a significant difference between the South and the rest of the nation. In the South the proportion of citizens who have never voted is clearly associated with state-imposed restrictions on voting. Moreover, among those *who have voted* in some previous presidential elections, the residents of the more restrictive states have voted less regularly in those elections for which they were eligible."[26] The authors go on to argue that restrictive voting rules encourage people to be "irregular, in-and-out voters," an effect that is not observed in the North. Later they add:

> A number of major conclusions are suggested by this analysis: (1) it is the informal, extralegal barriers—not state legislation—that account for much of the variability in the turnout of the Southern Negro; (2) greatest regularity in voting among Whites is reported most often in heavily Negro counties and, in particular, in those counties where voters are not greatly hampered by state-imposed limitations on voting; and (3) the institutional pattern relating legal regulations to individual behavior persists in all four major categories formed by combinations of race and racial composition of countries.[27]

Campbell et al. are unable to draw conclusions on the quantitative (as opposed to the directional) effect of state regulations because they do not control for other variables that, in addition to state regulations, may affect voter turnout.

Kim, Petrocik, and Enokson are critical of the statistical techniques that Campbell et al. and other authors use, and they use more sophisticated econometric techniques in their work. They still draw conclusions that are similar to but in some ways different from prior studies.[28] Kim et al. write:

> In general, the effects of legal restrictions . . . are in the expected direction. The states which have rules that are generally supposed to facilitate turnout do, in fact, tend to have higher rates of voter participation than those which do not. There are, however, some noteworthy exceptions. Contrary to our general expectations, states without registration systems show lower turnout than states with such systems, and states that allow precinct registration show lower turnouts than states that do not. In both instances, the correlations are relatively low, indicating great internal variation.[29]

This conclusion is drawn after the authors controlled statistically for what they call "individual" (race and income) and "systematic" (party competitiveness) variables.

[26] Angus Campbell, Phillip E. Converse, Warren E. Miller, and Donald E. Stokes, *The American Voter* (New York: John Wiley & Sons, Inc., 1960), pp. 276–277.

[27] Ibid., p. 281.

[28] Kim et al., "Voter Turnout."

[29] Ibid., p. 119.

Chapter 13

Government Organization: Economies of Scale and Monopoly Power

CHAPTER PREVIEW

Central Question

What are the major arguments for and against movements to consolidate government?

Major Objectives

1 To explain how economies of scale and external benefits contribute to the case for government consolidation.

2 To explain how competition among governments contributes to the control of government.

3 To show how different theoretical perspectives can lead to different evaluations concerning the social desirability of public policies like revenue sharing.

Major Points

1 Significant economies of scale are a technological reality in some industries, private and public. The cost savings that are implied by the existence of economies of scale can be a major reason for consolidation of local governments.

2 Economies of scale vary in the production of public goods and services. Hence, different levels of government are appropriate for the production of different public goods and services.

3 External benefits in the production of public goods and services can lead to underproduction and can be a major argument for the consolidation of local governments.

4 The framers of the Constitution were interested in developing a federal or "compound" republic. They believed that competition among governments would be a means of dispensing power and placing additional control on the governments that exist.

5 Revenue sharing can be evaluated in two ways: (a) as a means of dispersing government spending power and increasing the efficiency of government, and (b) as a means of monopolizing state and local governments.

Important New Terms and Concepts

Economies of scale
Revenue sharing

The United States is governed by one federal government that attracts a great deal of attention because its annual budget exceeds one-half trillion dollars. However, the control of the remainder of the public sector is fragmented among 50 state governments and over 80,000 local governmental units, including more than 3,000 counties, 18,000 municipalities, 17,000 townships, and 21,000 special districts.[1]

In the Los Angeles–Long Beach area alone, there are over 200 local governments, and in the Chicago area, which covers about 7 million people, there are more than 1,000 governmental units.[2] These are the governmental units that are responsible for public provision of such basic services as police and fire protection, sewage and water services, road maintenance, and garbage collection. They are the governments that are "closest to the people," but they are also the governments that, in terms of voter participation, attract the least interest among the citizenry. It is not at all uncommon, as indicated in the previous chapter, for off-year local elections to be decided on the basis of less than 20 percent of the eligible voters going to the polls.

Should there be so many governments? As you will see in this chapter,

[1] Robert L. Bish and Robert J. Kirk, *Economic Principles and Urban Problems* (Englewood Cliffs, N.J.: Prentice-Hall, Inc., 1974), p. 101.

[2] Ibid., p. 102.

there are two basic lines of thought on that question. There is the frequently heard argument that many local governments duplicate the services of each other, that there are *economies of scale* in the provision of many public services—meaning that *the size of government can be increased with a resulting reduction in the average cost of services*. This line of argument leads to the conclusion that local governments in the United States often operate inefficiently and that they should be consolidated to improve the the efficiency of the public sector. In other words, the argument suggests that governmental control should be *centralized* in larger governmental units, not fragmented as is presently true. Indeed, some suggest that many public services presently administered by local governments can be better and more efficiently run by the federal government. There are moves being made at this writing, for example, to have the federal government administer what are now locally run welfare programs.

The second line of thought, one that is voiced less frequently than the above argument, is that the fragmented nature of the "local government market in public services" contributes to the efficiency of all local governments. This is because local governments have to "compete" with each other for their tax bases, which come in the form of people and businesses that choose to live and operate within a given governmental jurisdiction. Following this line of thought, consolidation of local governments into one governmental unit is not necessarily any more desirable than the consolidation of major automobile producers in the country. The consolidation of local governments, according to this point of view, promotes monopoly power in the same way that mergers of businesses within the same industry do.

This chapter cannot attempt to settle the implied controversy, which will continue to be heard in communities long after this book has gone out of print. The issue at stake is largely an empirical one. However, we can in the short space of a chapter explore in greater depth the nature of the arguments that are presented. Further, we can use this topic as a means of reflecting on why the founding fathers, in the writing of the Constitution, sought to construct a "federal republic." As we will see, they may have had some basic economic principles in mind when they set out to establish their new form of government in 1787.

ECONOMIES OF SCALE AND GOVERNMENT SIZE

In some lines of production, a basic principle operates: "the bigger, the better." This means that as the scale of operation expands, the average cost of production falls. There are, in other words, cost savings simply from expanding the size of the firm. There is no logic that supports this often-observed relationship between average cost and scale of operation; the relationship simply exists as a technological fact of life in some industries.

Economies of scale are normally believed to be extensive in the production of national defense and very limited in the production of emergency rescue squads.

In industries with economies of scale, we would not want more than one producer. If there were several producers, each producer, supplying only a fraction of the market, would be operating on a small scale and would, therefore, have an average cost of production that would be higher than the average cost of production that could be achieved by one firm serving the entire market. Indeed, in such an industry, we would expect only one firm to survive a competitive market process. If there were several firms in an industry with extensive economies of scale, then all firms would have a relatively high average cost of production and all firms would have to charge a high price to compensate them for the costs they incur. Because of the economies of scale, one firm could lower its price, expand its output and scale of operation, and lower its average cost; and the lower average cost could justify the lower price that is charged. In such a market, only one firm could minimize the average costs of production and the price that is charged consumers. (Again, this is because average cost falls with expanded output. When one firm serves the entire market, average cost must be at a minimum.)

An important argument for the consolidation of governments is developed along the lines just presented. There are economies of scale, so the argument goes, in the provision of many public goods and services. If several governments divide up the "market," then each will be operating on a relatively small scale and each will be incurring relatively high average costs. By consolidating government, government's scale of operation can be increased and the average cost of producing public goods and services can be reduced. Hence, consolidation of governmental units can benefit citizens through a reduction in tax collections.

To what extent the argument is valid is an empirical question that cannot be answered here. All we can say here is that the economies-of-scale argument does not lead, necessarily, to the conclusion that all public goods and services should be produced on a national level. Granted, for goods like national defense, national production may be quite desirable and economically efficient because of the extensive economies of scale in that production process. For other goods and services, like street cleaning or even police protection, there may be precious few cost savings from expanding the size of the responsible governmental unit. If the governmental unit is expanded very far in these latter areas, provision of the service will become more, not less, costly and taxpayers will be saddled with higher taxes than they would have had to pay if the service were provided on a more local level. Following this line of argument and recognizing different degrees of economies of scale for different goods and services, we might anticipate some goods and services provided by the national government, some by state or regional governments, and some by local governments. The "smorgasbord" of governments, and their restricted domains, reflect *in part* the technology of producing public goods and services.

One additional economic argument is voiced in almost any movement to consolidate local governments. It is argued that any one local government, especially the government that represents the urban core of a metropolitan area, produces goods and services which have benefits that "spill over" into surrounding governmental units. For example, a central city may provide police protection for businesses and entertainment centers that provide employment and amusement for people who live in the urban fringe and suburban areas.

There are, in other words, external benefits from production. People in surrounding governmental units receive benefits, but in the absence of a consolidated metropolitan government, they do not have to pay for publicly provided goods and services. As we pointed out in Chapter 1, when external benefits exist, a market will tend to underproduce a good. The same can be the case under government provision of a good or service. For purposes of illustration, Figure 13.1 contains a supply and demand curve for police protection, which is assumed, for purposes of argument, to have external benefits received by people outside the government that provides the protection. Supply curve S_1 represents the marginal cost of producing police protection, and demand curve D_1 represents collective marginal benefits from police protection received by people within the central city. With those supply and demand curves constraining production, Q_1 units of police protection will be provided. However, as we have assumed, people outside the

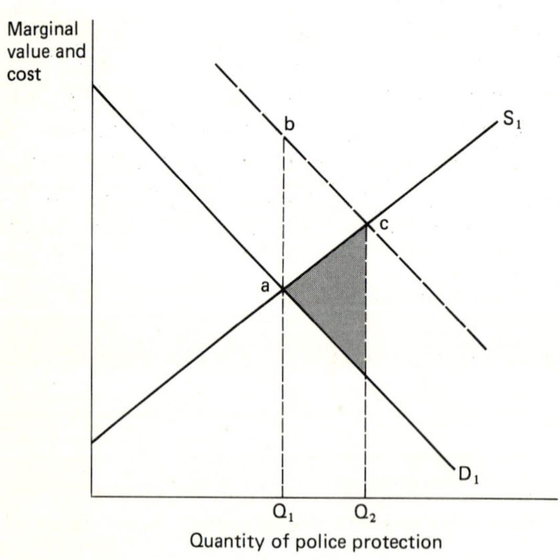

Figure 13.1

central city benefit from the police protection provided by the central city. If their demand were added to the demand of residents in the central city, the demand curve would be higher, D_2 instead of D_1; and if the demand were D_2, then the central city could charge higher tax-prices and receive greater revenues to provide a greater quantity of police protection, Q_2 instead of Q_1. However, given the jurisdiction of the central city government, it is restrained in raising its tax-prices because some people would be induced to move outside the central city into the urban fringe or the suburban areas. The central city would loose its tax base and, possibily, tax revenues.

The conclusion drawn is that government should be consolidated in order that the people in outlying governments can be taxed for the benefits they receive. Again, the argument suggests that consolidation can lead to greater efficiency in the allocation of resources; police protection can be expanded from Q_1 to Q_2. For each of those units, the marginal collective value of all area residents, as indicated by demand curve D_2, is greater than the marginal cost of their production, which is revealed in supply curve S_2. The gain in economic efficiency in moving from Q_1 to Q_2 is the triangular shaded area abc. The total additional benefits of the Q_2-Q_1 units is the area under the demand curve D_2 and bounded by Q_1bcQ_2; the total cost of the Q_2-Q_1 units is the area under the supply curve and bounded by Q_1acQ_2. The net difference between the additional total benefits and the total costs is, therefore, the shaded triangular area. That area in the figure is the increase in citizen welfare due to the greater production of police protection.

THE FEDERAL REPUBLIC AS A COMPOUND REPUBLIC

The framers of the Constitution had reasons other than technology in mind when they devised the *federal republic*. They were obviously intent upon checking the power of government. They sought to control government, particularly the central government, by sharply delineating the legitimate areas of government intervention into the private affairs of citizens. History books have emphasized our three branches of government as a system of "checks and balances" and as a "political obstacle" course through which legislation must pass. That it was meant to be. However, our founding fathers also sought to incorporate into our federal system of government a feature that is as important as, and perhaps more important than, the division of power between the executive, legislative, and judiciary branches. This feature is the notion of a system of *competing* governments, and it reflects attempts to introduce market principles into the organization of government. In the framers' minds, competition among governments, as in the private market, would prevent a "centre" of power and would reduce the ill effects of a monopoly organization, private or public. James Madison, in *The Federalist Papers*, made a sharp distinction between a single republic and a compound republic:

> *First*. In a single republic, all the power surrendered by the people is submitted to the administration of a single government; and the usurpations are guarded against by a division of the government into distinct and separate departments. In the *compound* republic of America, the power surrendered by the people is first divided between two distinct governments, and then the portion alloted to each subdivided among distinct and separate departments. Hence a double security arises to the rights of the people. The different governments will control each other, at the same time each will be controlled by itself. [Emphasis added.]
>
> *Second*. It is of great importance in a republic, not only to guard the society against the oppression of its rulers; but to guard one part of society against the injustice of the other part. . . . [By way of the federal republic] the society itself will be broken into so many parts, interests, and classes of citizens, that the rights of individuals, or of the minority, will be in little danger from interested combinations of the majority. In a free government, the security of civil rights must be the same as that for religious rights. It consists in the one case in the multiplicity of interests, and in the other, in the multiplicity of sects.[3]

Clearly, the democratic system established was intended to be a mechanism for the social control of government; its purpose was to permit maximum attainment of individual freedom by controlling government. And, so long as each governmental unit remained relatively small, the framers believed the democratic system could be a reasonably effective control on government. The citizenry and their representatives could comprehend the limited issues with which government would be concerned. The founding fathers were, without much question, willing to concede some cost saving in the production of public goods and services, if it existed, in order to restrict the power and influence of government. They were very concerned that growth in government would lead to a breakdown in the controlling power of citizens as special-interest groups vied for political favors. Whether or not and to what extent they were right is a question that has been and still is subject to much debate.

COMPETITIVE GOVERNMENTS

Governments can be controlled—made to produce efficiently—in many ways. Democracy is one control mechanism. By voting, people register their feelings and exert control over government in a limited way. In attempting to be elected or reelected, politicians are induced to reflect, to a limited

[3]James Madison, "The Social Foundation of Political Freedom," *The Federalist Papers*, No. 51 (New York: Washington Square Press, 1964), pp. 122–123.

extent, the wishes of their constituencies. However, control over government can be developed by the way in which government is organized. For example, a compound republic gives people alternative sources of public services and forces governments to compete with one another in much the same way as firms have to compete with one another in markets, but to a more limited extent. Consider the way taxes are determined in a system of competing state governments. If one state (or local government) acts independently of all other states (or local governments) and increases its tax rates without compensating increases in the quality of the services that it offers, or increases expenditures that are not desired, then individuals and firms may find it advantageous to move to another state or locality that offers a more favorable tax-expenditure package. That is, individuals can "vote with their feet."[4]

In a system of competing governments, it should be no surprise that state tax schedules on personal income or corporation profits are considerably lower than federal tax schedules. Granted, states do exercise *limited* monopoly power because moving is costly and because it is difficult, if not impossible, for new governments to form and enter the "geographical markets" of existing state governments. Still, states do face limited competition from other state governments, and the fiscal plight of New York City and Great Britain illustrates the financial difficulties that governments can get in when they ignore their competition, as limited as it may be.

In a system of competing governments, individual states that hold down taxes can gain if others around them raise taxes. A state with low tax rates can attract a larger number of people and businesses and thereby develop a larger tax base from which it can draw its tax collections. Because of lower revenues that may result when tax rates are raised, and vice versa, state and local governments are often induced, through competition, to reflect the interests of a minority who are not willing to accept the rule of the majority and are willing to move elsewhere.

As an aside, our analysis here suggests a plausible *economic* reason for relatively low voter turnouts in local elections. Citizens may be able to express more effectively and decisively their views of what is happening in their local government by moving than by participating in local elections. Furthermore, political leaders at the local level are, perhaps, more aware of what their constituencies can do "with their feet." Therefore, there is less need for the local citizenry to go to the polls to get their views across.[5] It is more difficult for voters to move at the state level and, therefore, one

[4]The analysis in this section is based on a model of government developed by Charles M. Tiebout, "A Pure Theory of Local Expenditure," *Journal of Political Economy* (October 1956), pp. 416–424.

[5]Clearly, most people who own stock in companies never vote in corporate elections simply because they know that if they do not like what the officers of the corporation are doing, they can sell out.

would expect people to be more concerned about voting at the state level than at the local level. The analysis leads to the conclusion that, for economic reasons, the voter turnout should be greater at the state level than at the local level and the turnout should be even greater at the federal level than at the state level. This is precisely what we tend to observe in election statistics of voter behavior.

THE INCENTIVE TO CONSOLIDATE

As suggested in our discussion of economies of scale in government, consolidation of governmental units may be desirable in some circumstances. On the other hand, government officials may use the economies-of-scale argument in their pursuit of their own private interests, not the public interest. Therefore, their arguments must be scrutinized carefully before they are accepted. Consider the following line of analysis, which employs principles and tools of analysis developed in earlier chapters.

Governments do not make profits in the same sense that businesses do. However, this does not mean, necessarily, that local government officials do not have an incentive to acquire monopoly power. First, monopoly power gives to the person or persons holding that power the latitude to determine the nature and type of services that will be produced and provided to customers. Monopoly power in government can give the political leaders and their employees considerable latitude to produce the goods that *they*, as opposed to the constituency, want. In short, monopoly power gives the holders of that power the capacity to restrict the quality or quantity of the good produced and to raise the price that is charged.

A government may not be able to earn "profits," but the political leaders and employees of the government can benefit through increased salaries and wages and perquisites of office. The costs of government can be raised, resulting in reduced welfare for the constituency but greater benefits for the political leaders and employees who acquire the monopoly power.

Consolidation can lead to the monopolization of local government, reduced quantity of output of the publicly provided goods and services, and higher tax-prices for the goods and services. To see why, consider an individual who lives initially in local government A, which is surrounded by many other local governmental units. See Figure 13.2, which contains circles representing local governments. If government A decides to raise its tax-price and/or reduce the quantity or quality of the public good provided, the individual can move with relative ease to any one of the surrounding governmental jurisdictions. This is the message of the foregoing analysis; this is how people "vote with their feet." However, suppose that the local governments in the area consolidate, forming one government that sets one

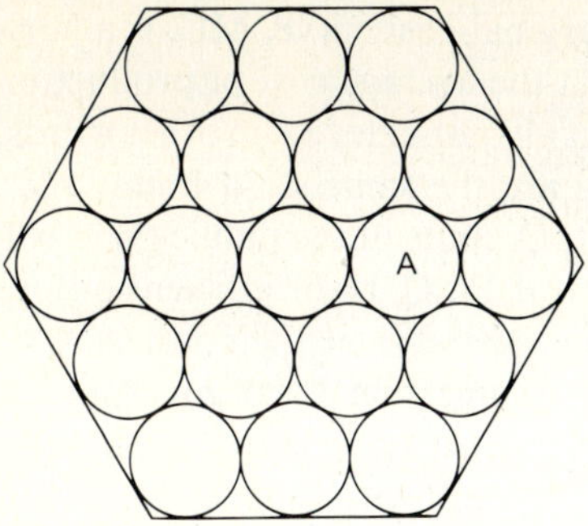

Figure 13.2

tax-price for the goods and services that are provided in what used to be a number of local governmental units. The individual in A must now move further, and incur greater moving costs, to escape the standardized tax-price. The individual should therefore be prepared to accept a higher increase in the tax-price in the consolidated government than he or she would have accepted when living in one small government that set its tax-price in competition with all the surrounding governments.

To see this basic point with greater precision, consider Figure 13.3, which contains the whole area's demand for a given public good, labeled D, and the corresponding marginal revenue curve, labeled MR.[6] For purposes of simplification only, assume that the marginal cost of producing the public

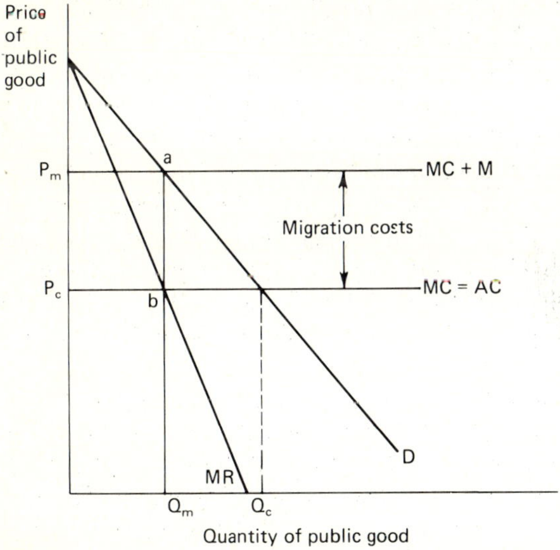

Figure 13.3

[6]For a review of how the marginal revenue curve is constructed and the monopoly model is developed, see the Appendix to Chapter 5.

good is constant, which means that the marginal cost curve, MC, is a horizontal line. This assumption also means that the average cost of production is equal to the marginal cost of production at all output levels: in other words, the marginal cost and average cost curves are the same. In a highly (i.e., perfectly) competitive governmental market, Q_c units of the public good will tend to be produced and sold at a tax-price of P_c. Q_c is the efficient output level.

However, we must not automatically assume that local governments will seek to produce the efficient output level. Local governments can have an economic interest in forming a cartel of governments—that is, a government with monopoly power—through formal consolidation of existing and competing governmental units. As we indicated above, a government with monopoly power can restrict output and raise the tax-price for the quantity of public goods and services provided. Some people may leave the area because of the higher tax-price, but the consolidated government (not its constituency) can still be better off by reducing output toward Q_m and raising the tax-price toward P_m. This is because the marginal revenue (which, as you may recall, is the additional revenue from selling an additional unit) of each unit between Q_c and Q_m is less than the marginal cost of producing each of those units. By reducing output from Q_c toward Q_m, the consolidated government reduces its total revenues by less than it reduces its total cost. "Profit," therefore, rises by moving from Q_c toward Q_m. At Q_m marginal revenue is equal to marginal cost, which is the condition for profit maximization. (See the appendix to Chapter 5 for a review of this point.) The profits of the consolidated government at Q_m are equal to the total revenue ($P_m \times Q_m$) minus total cost [P_c (which equals the average cost of production) $\times Q_m$]. Profits are represented by the area bounded by P_cP_mab. An important question, to which we will return, is whether or not (or to what extent) the democratic political system will keep governments from seeking to "maximize profits."

Even if a consolidated government acts like a monopoly, the political leaders and government employees who run the government cannot generally absorb the profits as "dividends" directly. They can, however, possibly increase their salaries to levels over and above what they would have been if the governments individually had to produce a tax-price of P_c, and they can possibly increase the perquisites of their offices and jobs. In doing these things, political leaders and government employees can raise the cost of production to the point that the perceived marginal and average cost of the public good provided equals P_m. In this case, the government may give the public the impression that it is "breaking even" and is producing efficiently.

The government is, in our model, able to raise the tax-price it charges by consolidating—by acting like a monopoly. It can do this because consolidation increases the "migration costs" to residents. So long as the migration cost is at least as great as the distance between the MC curve and the MC + M curves, the residents will be better off by staying where they are, incurring the higher tax-price. They may be better off by having competitive governments, but that is an option that is precluded by the consolidation movement. If the residents move, they will be even worse off because of the extensive migration costs they will incur.[7]

The conclusions to be drawn from the analysis to this point are very clear: To the extent that the democratic system fails to control political leaders and/or their employees and to the extent that political leaders and their employees are interested in maximizing their own welfare through the tax-prices they charge and the services they provide, we should expect them (like we would expect private entrepreneurs) to make use of the monopoly power they have or can garner. Therefore, our analysis suggests that consolidation of local governments may very well lead to higher, not lower, costs of public goods and services. Further, when laws are passed preventing or seriously restricting the formation of new local governments (i.e., new competitors), as has been done in California, we should not be amazed if existing local governments make use of the newly acquired monopoly power. Our analysis suggests that the restrictions on entry into the "local government market" should, again, lead to an increase in the cost of public goods and services. These tentative predictions have been borne out, sometimes dramatically, in empirical studies that have been done.[8]

REVENUE SHARING

Revenue sharing is the budgetary process by which grants are made by the federal government to state and local governments with very few restrictions on how the funds can be spent. Revenue sharing illustrates how a government program can be evaluated from the two opposing perspectives on government size that have been developed in preceding sections. On the one hand, the State and Local Assistance Act of 1972, which gave birth to revenue sharing, has been heralded as a movement toward the "dimunition

[7]Actually, by the very geographical nature of governments, there are always some migration costs to moving to another governmental unit. Therefore, even when competing with other governmental units, the individual governments do not have to charge the full competitive price of P_c; they can charge that price plus some premium that is less than the cost of the migration expense. So long as the tax-price charged is lower than P_c plus the migration expense, people will not move. From this perspective, the purpose of consolidation of local government can be to *increase* the migration expense of residents and, thereby, increase the tax-price that can be charged residents.

[8]Several of these studies were cited in Chapter 1. See, in particular, Thomas E. Borcherding (ed.), *Budgets and Bureaucrats: The Sources of Government Growth* (Durham, N.C.: Duke University Press, 1977). In reference to the California experience, see Delores Tremenan Martin and Richard E. Wagner, "The Institutional Framework for Municipal Incorporation: An Economic Analysis of Local Agency Formation Commissions in California," *Journal of Law and Economics*, vol. 21 (October 1978), pp. 409–425.

of the power of the federal government" and as "first aid to sick governments."[9] An argument frequently heard in support of revenue sharing is that the federal government cannot possibly do everything efficiently, and it must "share the wealth" that it has with state and local governments, which know what people want and which can operate on an efficient scale of production. From this perspective, revenue sharing is seen as a positive-sum game: the federal government collects taxes and, instead of spending them itself, channels the funds to state and local governments, which can produce a given level of goods and services more cheaply or can produce more goods and services with the same level of funding. From this perspective, the federal government merely serves as a conduit through which taxes flow; and the political support that revenue sharing enjoys is a reflection of the increased efficiency in the production of public goods and services.

Another possible explanation for the political support of revenue sharing may be developed by reflection on a few facts relating to state and local government finances and on the analysis of competing governments. Today, most states have extensively tapped or even exhausted the traditional bases of taxation. For example, in 1950, 16 out of the 48 states did *not* have a state income tax. In 1974 all but 5 out of 48 had income taxation. In 1950 there were 15 states that did *not* have a corporate income tax, while only 4 states did not tax corporate income in 1974. In 1950 there were 19 states that did *not* have a general sales tax; by 1974 this number decreased to 5 states.[10]

As the argument may be developed, the exhaustion of previously untapped tax sources has increased the comprehensiveness of the tax base and has probably left many state and local governments in a kind of competitive equilibrium, in which individual governments fear that further *independent* increases in their tax rates will lead to a loss of their tax base to such an extent that their tax revenues will fall. It is, therefore, understandable that mayors, governors, state legislators, and local and state bureaucrats, interested in pursuing their own programs, have strongly supported revenue sharing. Revenue sharing represents a potential source of tax revenue that is not subject to *competitive pressures* since the collection of these revenues is through one national (monopoly) government. A well-worn dictive may be applied here: what cannot be accomplished independently can be accomplished by *collective* action. Seen from the perspective of the analysis of foregoing sections, revenue sharing may be viewed by mayors and governors as a way by which state and local governments can increase their revenues and avoid the competitive pressures they face when they act independently.

Proponents of revenue sharing argue that revenue sharing is an efficient way to collect taxes because there are economies of scale in the

[9]For a fairly comprehensive review of revenue sharing, see Charles J. Goetz, *What Is Revenue Sharing?* (Washington, D.C.: The Urban Institute, 1972).

[10]*Facts and Figures on Government Finance* (New York: Tax Foundation, Inc., 1975).

federal tax collection system. Opponents may contend that if this were the sole reason for instituting revenue sharing, then there should be no penalties involved if local and state governments reduce their taxes by the amount of revenue-sharing funds they receive. However, the formula for the allocation of revenue-sharing funds has a "tax-effort factor" that penalizes local and state governments that attempt to substitute revenue-sharing funds for local tax collections. Because of Proposition 13, which drastically reduced local property taxes, for example, California was slated in 1978 to lose several hundred million dollars in revenue-sharing funds. Because of the tax-effort factor, there is an inducement for local and state governments to increase tax rates and there are penalties when they decrease tax rates. For every dollar in local taxes collected, the local government can spend more than a dollar due to increases in revenue-sharing funds.

Opponents of revenue sharing also point out that revenue sharing discriminates against governments that levy user charges for services (like explicit prices for garbage collection and for entry into city parks) because these charges are not considered as part of the tax effort. Therefore, localities that rely on such fiscal devices are discriminated against by receiving a lower share of revenue sharing than they would receive if taxes were collected in a manner independent of discriminatory public provision of goods and services.

User charges have long been advocated as a means of increasing the efficiency of government. The reason given is that user charges make the cost of government more readily recognized by the users of government services. Taxes collected independently of the provision of goods and services create a "fiscal illusion" by obscuring the *real* tax-price paid. For example, how does an individual calculate the real price he or she pays for public services when the taxes paid are channeled through the federal government and back to the states and localities via the complicated revenue-sharing formula, which is based on such factors as tax effort, population, and income? The information problem of revenue sharing for the consumer-taxpayer is similar to the one that would be created if a person's grocery bill were largely calculated independently of the groceries bought. To the extent that the costs of local government goods and services are obscured, the public's control of government can be lessened, or so it may be argued.

One simple calculation can be made to show how revenue sharing (or any other form of government grant to local and state governments) can increase tax collections of government. Assume that a person is in a 25 percent federal tax bracket. This means that the person's tax obligation goes down by 25 percent of any deduction from taxable income that can be made. If, for example, the person is able to deduct $100 from his or her taxable income, the tax obligation will fall by $25; this is because the person would have had to pay 25 percent of the $100 in taxable income if there had been no deduction. State and local taxes are deductible from taxable income:

for every dollar of state and local taxes paid, federal tax obligation goes down by $0.25. Consequently, if state and local expenditures are financed through federal tax collections—not state and local tax collections—the taxable income and taxes paid to the federal government go up. Indeed, in our example, $1 of revenue-sharing funds that are collected by the federal government and dispensed by the state and local governments costs the individual, effectively, $1.25 in taxes. Furthermore, opponents of revenue sharing point out that the increase in taxes is accomplished without an increase in explicit tax rates.

CONCLUDING COMMENTS

An economic theory tends to yield unambiguous predictions. However, individual theories are based upon assumptions concerning, for instance, demand and cost relationships. Different assumptions regarding those relationships can produce different predictions. In this chapter we have attempted to apply economic principles to the controversial area of government consolidation. More importantly, however, we have attempted to demonstrate how "reasonable persons" can disagree. We have shown in this chapter how different assumptions about the nature of cost relationships can lead to different conclusions about the social desirability of government consolidation. We have also shown how difference in assumptions about the motives of political leaders and their employees can lead to different conclusions about the social consequences of consolidation efforts. The chapter is not intended to settle any issue—theory is rarely able, by itself, to do that—but it serves the purpose of demonstrating how different theoretical positions can lead to different hypotheses concerning government actions. Those hypotheses can be subjected to real world, empirical tests; and those tests can help, in a limited way, to resolve the controversy. That is a small but important contribution of economic science.

QUESTIONS TO PONDER

1 Explain in economic terms the simultaneous existence of (a) local police forces, (b) state highway patrol systems, and (c) the FBI.
2 The chapter discussed the external benefits that emanate from the central city and are received by residents in surrounding governmental units. Do external benefits always flow in that direction? Does the direction of the flow change the case for consolidation of area governments? Suppose that external benefits flow in both directions at the same time. Do opposing flows change the case for consolidation?
3 Many states have consolidated university systems. Discuss the possible case for and case against such consolidated systems.

4 If people can "vote with their feet," does it follow that all government decisions are made on the basis of majority rule?

5 Should there be laws allowing local governmental units within larger governments to form and to secede from the larger government?

ADDITIONAL READING

Bish, Robert L., and Robert J. Kirk. *Economic Principles and Urban Problems.* Englewood Cliffs, N.J.: Prentice-Hall, Inc., 1974, chaps. 2, 4, 6, and 8–10.

Madison, James. *The Federalist Papers*, Nos. 10 and 51. New York: Washington Square Press, 1964.

Chapter 14

The Social Desirability of Tax Avoidance: A Question of Perspective

CHAPTER PREVIEW

Central Question

Should tax avoidance, which may be accomplished through taking advantage of tax loopholes, be permitted?

Major Objectives

1 To contrast the economic effect of a discriminatory tax with a perfectly general tax on *all* sources of income and in that way to evaluate the welfare implications of tax avoidance.

2 To argue that one's assessment of the social desirability of tax avoidance depends upon the perceived goals of government and the perceived effectiveness of democratic controls on government.

Major Points

1 A tax on money income reduces a person's spendable income, increases the relative price of goods and services, and reduces the relative price of leisure. A tax on money income will cause leisure to be substituted for goods and services in consumption.

2 By substituting a general for a discriminatory tax, a government can collect the same tax revenue but the taxpayer can be on a higher level of utility. Therefore, a general tax on all sources of income can, in this limited respect, be economically superior to a discriminatory tax on money income.

3 If the tax base is broadened by the elimination of means of tax avoidance, government acquires considerable monopoly power. If government is perceived as an instrument for serving the public interest and is adequately controlled by democratic procedures, then a perfectly general tax may be socially desirable. However, if government is perceived as a means by which people pursue private interests and is only partially controlled by democratic procedures, then a general tax can lead to increases in tax collections and a reduction in people's welfare.

4 People who take advantage of means of avoiding taxes can be a force holding down tax rates for the rest of the population.

Important New Terms and Concepts

Discriminatory tax
Transformation curve
General tax

Each year newspapers carry reports on several hundred millionaires who manage to escape paying federal income taxes altogether. The reports also reveal that many other very high income earners pay very small percentages of their income in federal taxes. Without question, these revelations irritate many people who, with much lower incomes, pay into the federal government a significant percentage of their weekly or monthly wages. Without question, these revelations form the basis for many calls by politicians for tax reform, for "closing up all the tax loopholes" that presumably high-income earners are exploiting to their own advantage.

Clearly, there is some truth to the claims that many people have been able to weasel their way around the tax code and to pay very few taxes; there is some justification for the concern that the tax code is being manipulated by tax accountants and lawyers who can charge very high fees because of the substantial tax savings they can provide their clients. The tax regulations do produce some taxpayer responses that were not completely intended by Congress. For example, the regulations encourage people not to work—to take their "income" in the form of leisure, which is not subject to taxation. They also encourage sellers of services, like television and furnace repairs, to take payment in the form of cash, which is not traceable and, therefore, not taxable. According to reports, service repair people in this country, Britain, and Italy, as well as in many other countries, frequently offer their customers discounts for cash payments. So long as the discount is less than the taxes that would have been paid if payment had been received by check, the repair person who gives the discount gains in spendable income. In general, tax regulations increase the rate of return on illegal activities, which are not subject to taxation, relative to the rate of return on legal activities, which are subject to taxation.

The tax regulations also encourage people, especially highly paid executives, to take a substantial portion of their incomes in the form of stock options and fringe benefits, like chauffeured limousines, health and life insurance policies, nice offices, parking spaces, memberships in country clubs, and business trips (which may have little to do with business) with all expenses of the husband or wife paid by the company. The Internal Revenue Code also allows people to buy into businesses that are incurring losses and to use those losses for the purpose of reducing the buyer's taxable income and tax liability.

On the other hand, the tax regulations direct people's private expenditures into areas thought by Congress to be socially desirable. For instance, charitable contributions are deductible from taxable income. Many high-income earners (as well as low- and middle-income earners) are able to reduce their taxable income by giving away a significant portion of what they earn. These taxpayers may pay little in the way of taxes, but their spendable income is reduced because of what they have to do to avoid tax payments.

Many people are able to avoid taxes by buying state and local government bonds, the interest on which is not subject to taxation. The persons who buy tax-exempt bonds may pay no taxes on their interest income, but they also forego the greater interest income that could have been had on the bonds of private corporations. Because of the tax-exempt status of state and local bonds, the interest rates on those bonds are driven down below the interest rates of comparable private corporate bonds. The buyers of tax-exempt bonds may have more spendable income because of their purchases, but state and local governments also are able to borrow funds at a lower interest cost.

The purpose of this chapter is not to explore the appropriateness or efficiency of specific tax regulations. Rather, its purpose is to consider a broad issue in tax policy: Are tax loopholes—or, in general, ways of avoiding taxes—socially desirable? Are they beneficial to taxpayers other than the persons who take advantage of them directly? Stated differently, these questions reduce to one of whether or not the loopholes should be closed, or whether or not the tax base should be broadened. We will not be able to fully answer those questions here within the next few pages, but we will be able to consider some of the economic consequences of expanding the tax base.[1]

[1]The analysis of this chapter is based largely on the work of Geoffrey Brennen and James M. Buchanan, "A Tax Constitution for Leviathan," *Journal of Public Economics* (December 1977), pp. 255–273; and "Tax Instruments as Constraints on the Disposition of Public Revenues," *Journal of Public Economics* (June 1978), pp. 301–318.

A DISCRIMINATORY INCOME TAX

Conventional discussions of tax policy in economics suggest that a tax that is levied only against money income is a *discriminatory tax*, and *a discriminatory tax is a tax that tends to favor leisure at the expense of earnings.* In short, a discriminatory tax can induce people to work less and to take more of their real income in the form of leisure-time activities, which are not subject to taxation. In general, a money income tax causes distortions in the allocation of resources and reduces people's welfare from what it could have been if the tax had been applied to all activities, not just activities that result in money income.

To see this point more clearly, consider the hypothetical case of a woman who has at maximum 40 hours of leisure time available each week, which she can use for activities like golf, fishing, and watching television or for work that results in money income. Assuming our person can earn \$10 an hour, she can choose to use all her leisure time in work and earn \$400 in money income per week (\$10 × 40 hours) or she can choose to spend less than all her time working and can spend some time at leisure-time activities. She can, for example, work 20 hours a week, earn \$200, and have 20 hours of leisure. In summary, our individual can "consume" any of a number of combinations of leisure-time activities and money income (i.e., the goods that money can buy). All the possible combinations open to our individual are represented in Figure 14.1 as M_5L_5. This curve is called a *transformation curve: it is a locus of points that represents alternative combinations that can be chosen by an individual.* (It is a curve that represents the ability of the individual to "transform" leisure into money income.) In our illustration, our hypothetical person can choose any point on M_5L_5. If the individual chooses combination a, we must assume that it is the preferred combination, that a maximizes her utility.

As stated, combination a is the income-leisure combination the individual will take in the absence of a tax on *money* income. If the government imposes a 50 percent tax on all money income earned, then the individual's transformation curve will pivot on L_5 and move down to M_3L_5. If the individual wants, she can still choose to spend all 40 hours on leisure activities, L_5. However, if the individual now spends all 40 hours working for money, she will have a spendable, after-tax income of \$200 and will pay \$200 in income taxes. The money income tax effectively increases the relative prices of goods and services that can be purchased with money income; it effectively reduces the relative prices of leisure and leisure-time activities. This is because the individual must now give up more leisure to acquire any given level of purchasing power.

Aside from the effect of reduced income stemming from the tax system, the relative price change in leisure causes a substitution in favor of more leisure time being taken by the individual taxpayer. The taxpayer in our example, being constrained in her choices by M_3L_5, can choose combina-

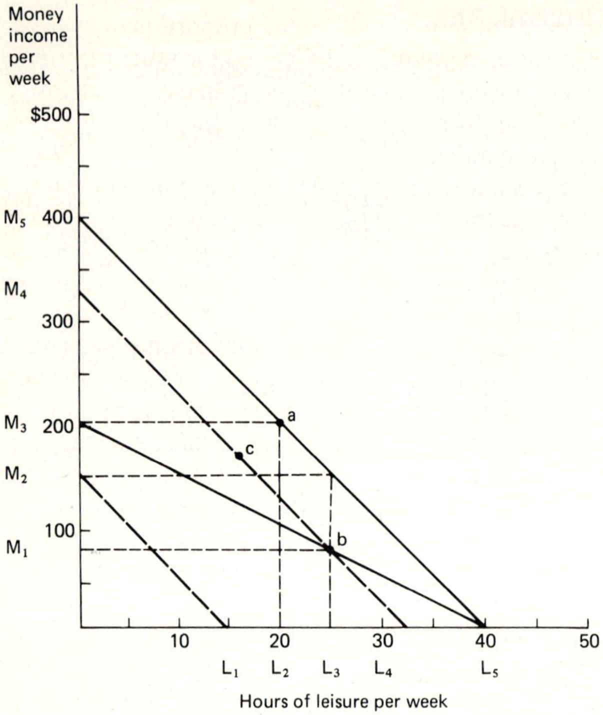

Figure 14.1

tion b, representing more leisure and less money income than would have been chosen in the absence of the money tax system. Other combinations of leisure and money income are, of course, possible; but the central point is clear: because of the tax system alone, the individual taxpayer is placed on a lower utility level; combination a is no longer within the taxpayer's relevant choice domain.[2] If b is chosen, our taxpayer will pay \$75 in taxes ($M_2 - M_1$). She will earn \$150, 50 percent of which must be paid to the government.

A GENERAL TAX

A general tax is a levy that is applied to all sources of income proportionally. Instead of taxing just money income, suppose that the government decides to make the tax base completely "general." That is, suppose that the govern-

[2]The money income tax system can cause the individual to work longer hours, that is, take less leisure. However, our purpose here is to concentrate on the substitution effect of the tax system. That is the only reason a point like b is highlighted. The basic conclusions of the analysis are unaffected by the point we have selected. There will always be a substitution effect in a money income tax system.

ment decides to tax the value of money and leisure proportionately, meaning it taxes the value of leisure, measured in dollars, to the same percentage extent that it taxes money income. Instead of the taxpayer's transformation curve pivoting on L_5 as it does in the above example, the transformation curve will move inward parallel to M_5L_5.

Is the taxpayer better off under this more general tax system than under the discriminatory money income tax system? The answer of economists has typically been that taxpayer welfare is higher under the general tax system than under the discriminatory money income tax system. Using our two-dimensional money income and leisure model, the reasoning is as follows. The government can apply a tax to both money income and leisure, shifting our taxpayer's transformation curve inward until it intersects M_3L_5 at b, and can collect the same amount of taxes, \$75 ($M_2 - M_1$). The relevant transformation curve is then M_4L_4, along which the taxpayer can choose any combination of leisure and spendable money income. Since the individual can still choose combination b (which is still on the individual's transformation curve M_4L_4), she *cannot* be worse off under the general tax system than under the discriminatory money income tax system.

Since the shift in the transformation curve from M_3L_5 to M_4L_4 effectively lowers the price of money income in terms of the number of hours that must be given up for a given amount of money income,[3] the individual can be expected (because of the law of demand) to move up the transformation curve M_4L_4 from b, substituting in the process money income for leisure or leisure-time activities. She can be expected to choose some combination like (but not necessarily) c. Whatever combination she does choose upward and to the left of b must be preferred to b, or else it would not be chosen. Consequently, we can conclude that a general tax system, which imposes a proportional tax on all things, not just money income, is preferred by taxpayers to a discriminatory money income tax system. Under the general tax system the government—at least theoretically—can collect the same total tax revenues, but as we have shown, taxpayers can be better off in the sense that they reach higher utility levels than they otherwise would.

THE TAX SYSTEM FOR "LEVIATHAN"

The foregoing analysis is correct as far as it goes. An assumption implicitly undergirding the analysis is that government is some kind of "nice guy" or "benevolent despot" who seeks to collect a given level of revenues (\$75 in the example) to finance public goods and services that are determined to be

[3]The slope of the transformation curve is the ratio of change in money income to change in leisure time ($\Delta M/\Delta L$). As the transformation curve is moved from M_3L_5 to M_4L_4, the slope of the curve ($\Delta M/\Delta L$) is increased, meaning that more money income is acquired for each hour of leisure time given up.

socially desirable by the political system. The analysis does not presume that the government will use its taxing authority to maximize the size and scope of its activities or the economic well-being of the politicians and bureaucrats. With these assumptions stated or unstated, it is reasonable to favor a general tax system, if such a system could be made operational in the sense that taxes could actually be collected on the basis of the value of leisure-time activities.

However, suppose that government is not the "nice guy" that the above analysis assumes. Suppose the government is some kind of "Leviathan," to use a term made popular by Thomas Hobbes in the eighteenth century, out to use the powers that it has to benefit those who run government. Using this view of government, would a general tax system be preferred to a discriminatory tax system? Geoffrey Brennen and James Buchanan contend that if government is viewed as some kind of Leviathan, then the discriminatory tax system would be preferred to a general tax system.[4] Under the completely general tax system, all human activities are taxable. There is no way that the individual can escape the taxing authority of government. There is no way that individuals can reduce their tax burden by altering their activities.

This is one of the reasons general taxation is desirable, but Brennen and Buchanan contend that making all human activities subject to taxation is equivalent to giving the government virtually complete monopoly power to extract resources from the public and to expand its own domain. Under such a system, we cannot assume, according to Brennen and Buchanan, that the government will be "nice" and move the transformation curve inward only so far as M_4L_4. With monopoly power in hand, government may raise its tax collections as far as the political constraints of democracy will allow. It is conceivable that the government might move the taxpayer's transformation curve all the way to, for instance, M_2L_1, in which case the taxpayer would be worse off than under a discriminatory tax system.

The Brennen-Buchanan message is clear: The social desirability of restricting the tax base of the government (by having tax loopholes, deductions, and nontaxable activities) depends upon one's view of government. If one perceives government as being effectively constrained by democratic processes to achieve socially desirable, collectively established goals, then one may conclude that expanding the tax base—eliminating ways of avoiding taxes—is socially beneficial. At least, no harm will be done.

On the other hand, if the government is perceived as being less than effectively controlled by democratic processes, then restricting the tax base of government—maintaining and expanding tax loopholes, deductions, and nontaxable activities—can be socially beneficial. Those persons who

[4]Brennen and Buchanan, "A Tax Constitution for Leviathan."

take advantage of the loopholes and deductions put pressure on government to restrict its overall tax rates. Because people can make use of loopholes and nontaxable activities when tax rates are raised, the government, by raising tax rates, has to fear that its tax collections (as opposed to rates) will fall. The tax rates may rise, but the income subject to taxation (because of the adjustments that people make) may fall to such an extent that the tax collections of government actually fall. Fearing a fall in total tax collections, government can be restrained in raising its tax rates. Following this line of argument, those persons who are prone to take advantage of tax loopholes may be doing those who do not take advantage of those loopholes a favor; they are causing tax rates for everyone to be lower than they otherwise would be. This, at least, is the line of argument that has been developed by Brennen and Buchanan and cannot be summarily dismissed.

CONCLUDING COMMENTS ON CONTROLLING GOVERNMENT

The overriding purpose of government is to provide goods and services that benefit the people whom the government is supposed to serve. However, historical experience has shown that government often does not serve its general purpose. Frequently, the government has been used by special-interest groups to promote special purposes and not the general welfare. Frequently, the government has served the purpose of improving the welfare of the people who run the government. As a consequence, many citizens have concluded at times that there is much waste in government or that the cost of many government programs exceeds the social benefits of the programs.

In the private market sector of society, people are naturally concerned with controlling the market power of individual firms. There is a presumption that private entrepreneurs will use whatever power they have at their disposal to further their own interests. Accordingly, there is a social interest in controlling the market behavior of entrepreneurs and in guiding their behavior in socially desirable directions. People's private market behavior is controlled and directed by government enforcement of legally defined property rights. It also is controlled and directed by competitive forces. Through competition, entrepreneurs are induced to produce efficiently and to maximize the national product (see Chapter 1).

People within a society are similarly interested, for essentially the same reasons, in controlling government. There is the fear that, unless they are properly constrained, public entrepreneurs with the power of government behind them will fail to pursue public goals and produce public goods and services efficiently. There are several ways of controlling government. Democratic elections are one way of controlling political entrepreneurs. Politicians can be thrown out of office when they abuse their powers. However, as we have pointed out in Chapter 12, democratic procedures are a far from perfect means of controlling government. People have very little incentive in elections to become politically intelligent on the particular issues and candidates and to become politically active. In addition, "yes" or "no," "for" or "against" votes are a poor means of registering the preferences of people. Establishing competing governments within a given geographical region, a subject discussed in Chapter 13, is another means of controlling government. If an individual local government attempts to raise taxes or reduce the quality of services provided, people can move to other competing governments. In this way, governments are constrained in the tax-prices they charge and the quality of goods and services they provide. However, as we have pointed out, it is expensive for people to move among governments, especially at the state and federal levels. Because of the migration costs—or the costs of "voting with one's feet"—governments retain some monopoly powers.

A purpose of this chapter has been to consider an additional means of controlling government, which is restrictions on the tax base. By restricting the tax base and allowing tax avoidance, people retain some latitude in individual actions. They can escape government taxes by directing their resources into areas that generate benefits and are not subject to taxation. With a restricted tax base, the government's ability to raise tax rates is also constrained. The government has to fear that an increase in tax rates will lead to a reduction in total tax collections. This can be due to a reduction in total income that is subject to taxation.

With all these means of social control of government, people may still perceive the government as too large or growing too fast. To further control government, people have in recent years become interested in fixing the size of government by amendment to the state or federal constitution. Already, California has, as we have mentioned, restricted property taxes to 1 percent of the assessed value of property and restricted the ability of local government officials to raise the assessed value of property. Voters in Tennessee have restricted the size of state government to a set percentage of the income of state residents; that is, the budget of the state government can, according to an amendment to the Tennessee constitution, be no greater than a certain percentage of the aggregate income of all people in the state. A similar means of control is currently being proposed for the federal government.

These means of control may seem inflexible; they may make government response to changing social conditions sluggish. Some may argue that constitutional restrictions on government contribute to inefficiency in the social system. However, the proponents of constitutional restrictions on government see the measures as a means of keeping government "within bounds" and contributing, in that way, to the efficiency of government. Clearly, constitutional means of controlling government will remain for some time an important issue in social politics.

QUESTIONS TO PONDER

1 If a discriminatory tax is applied to money income (and not to leisure income), will taxpayers tend to reduce always the amount of time spent working?
2 In Great Britain service repair people often give 25 percent discounts to customers who pay in cash. Why do they do that? If tax rates go up, what will tend to happen to the cash discounts given?
3 What are the practical problems in developing a general tax applied to *all* sources of income?
4 List the ways by which private entrepreneurs are controlled in markets and the way by which public entrepreneurs are in democracies. Why are controls necessary? Should we always seek to control perfectly the behavior of people? Is perfect control of behavior possible in a democracy or even consistent with the dictates of a democracy?

ADDITIONAL READING

Pogue, Thomas F., and L. G. Sgontz. *Government and Economic Choice: An Introduction to Public Finance*. Boston: Houghton Mifflin Company, 1978, chaps. 10 and 11.

Student Self-Tests

The following true-false questions will help you to determine how well you understand the material presented in the chapters. These quick tests are designed to examine your understanding of some but not all concepts and arguments presented in the chapters. Do not try to use these tests as a substitute for concentrated study. Answers to the questions are presented at the end of this section.

CHAPTER 1 THE ECONOMIST'S PARADIGM

1 ______ Economics deals only with subjects involving money.
2 ______ A person who works very little is necessarily irrational.
3 ______ When the price of a product falls, consumers will buy more of the product, assuming everything else remains constant.
4 ______ When a person makes a profit from trades, then someone else must be worse off.
5 ______ Everything else held constant, an increase in the price of a product will lead to a reduction in demand.
6 ______ In a competitive market, the price will move toward the intersection of supply and demand.
7 ______ An increase in the demand for a product in a competitive market will lead to an increase in the price and a reduction in the quantity sold.

8 ______ A monopolist will tend to produce less and sell at a higher price than would be the case in a competitive market.

CHAPTER 2 THE COMMON SENSE OF ECONOMICS: THE PRICING OF A PRODUCT

1 ______ A pricing scheme that incorporates lower prices on additional units purchased necessarily means that the marginal cost of production falls with greater output.
2 ______ A $100 charitable contribution to a university's athletic program means that the doner loses $100 in purchasing power.
3 ______ A price support system for milk maintained by the government will lead to a market surplus.
4 ______ If the price of milk is deregulated, the price consumers will pay for milk will rise.
5 ______ If the price of gasoline is higher than the price of water, then we know that for consumers who buy both the marginal utility of the last gallon of gasoline purchased is less than the marginal utility of the last gallon of water purchased.

CHAPTER 3 REGULATION AND PRIVATE PROPERTY RIGHTS: THE CASE OF THE GYMNASIUM LOCKER ROOM

1 ______ Government regulation of a product does not affect property rights that are held.
2 ______ Users of locker rooms will always want to have the government require universities to compensate people for stolen property.
3 ______ Required social security payments have not affected people's saving plans.
4 ______ If consumers are unprotected by government, then they will be left totally unprotected from business firms that attempt to maximize profits.
5 ______ Government-required health insurance will tend to increase the number of doctor visits.

CHAPTER 4 THE ECONOMIC DIMENSIONS OF ETHICAL BEHAVIOR

1 ______ From an economic perspective, the viability of ethical precepts is unaffected by the size of the relevant group.
2 ______ From an economic perspective, it can be said that people who have some interest in common can be expected to pursue their interest regardless of the group size.
3 ______ Producers in a competitive market do not have a common interest in restricting their total market production.

4 ______ From an economic perspective, an increase in the mobility of the population will tend to reduce the viability of ethical precepts.

5 ______ People in a small group may be able to cohere and pursue their common interest in a way that people in a large group cannot.

CHAPTER 5 COMPETITION FOR MONOPOLY PROFITS: THE SOCIAL WASTE FROM RESTRICTIONS ON MARKET ENTRY

1 ______ Economic profit is equal to the total revenues a firm receives.

2 ______ A monopolist will tend to produce an output level at which the price is equal to average cost.

3 ______ When firms can compete for a monopoly position in a market, then the monopoly profits represent a form of transfer payments and do not represent a part of the social waste of monopoly power.

4 ______ Consumer surplus is that area under the demand curve and above the price line.

5 ______ A profit-maximizing monopolist will produce the output level at which marginal cost is equal to marginal revenue. (See the appendix to Chapter 5.)

CHAPTER 6 THE EFFICIENCY-EQUITY DILEMMA OF DEREGULATION: THE CASE OF NATURAL GAS

1 ______ Price controls on natural gas have created a shortage of natural gas.

2 ______ When the meter price of natural gas is controlled, the effective price of natural gas is above the market clearing price.

3 ______ If the meter price of natural gas is decontrolled, the effective price of natural gas will rise.

4 ______ When the meter price of natural gas is decontrolled, the wealth of homeowners with natural gas connections will be reduced.

5 ______ Decontrol of natural gas prices will reduce the aggregate income in the country.

CHAPTER 7 RESTRICTIONS ON BUSINESS MOBILITY: EMPIRICAL ISSUES

1 ______ Most of the changes in regional population growth rates are due to the migration of business.

2 ______ The incomes of Northerners have been rising in recent years in absolute terms but falling relative to incomes in the South.

3 ______ Business movements south have necessarily reduced the real income of people in the North.

4 ______ Business movements south have necessarily caused employment opportunities in the North to fall.

5 ______ The real wages of all worker categories are lower in the South than in the North.

CHAPTER 8 RESTRICTIONS ON BUSINESS MOBILITY: THEORETICAL ISSUES

1 ______ Restrictions on business mobility will retard the economic development of the South and enhance the economic development of the North.

2 ______ Restrictions on business movements will stop the flow of jobs south.

3 ______ Restrictions on business mobility will increase the economic power of unions and local government.

4 ______ Owners of business will lose property rights by passage of restrictions on business mobility.

5 ______ Wages in nonunion sectors of the economy will necessarily rise as a result of restrictions on business movements.

CHAPTER 9 REGULATING THE HEALTH OF WORKERS: THE CASE OF COTTON DUST STANDARDS

1 ______ Cotton dust standards will tend to raise wages in the textile industry.

2 ______ Cotton dust standards will tend to reduce employment opportunities in the textile industry.

3 ______ Cotton dust standards will cause a shift from labor to capital in the production of textiles.

4 ______ Cotton dust standards will increase the imports of foreign textile products.

5 ______ The marginal cost of reducing cotton dust in textile mills goes down as the dust level goes down.

CHAPTER 10 THE PAY SYSTEM AND DEPARTMENTAL DISCORD: THE GAMES PROFESSORS PLAY

1 ______ Typically speaking, as a faculty member's production goes up, total wages paid university faculty rise.

2 ______ Predation can be expected in highly competitive markets like farming.

3 ______ As the size of a department goes up, the incentive that each individual faculty member has to engage in predation rises.

4 ______ Predation can be useful to people operating under a wage fund pay system because the important determinate of individual raises is *relative* performance, not absolute performance.

CHAPTER 11 THE EMERGENCE OF A MARKET IN POLLUTION STANDARDS

1 ______ An economic cause of pollution is ill-defined property rights.
2 ______ Pollution standards are a more efficient means of reducing pollution than "selling rights to pollute."
3 ______ If pollution standards are set and people trade the standards that they have been given, the cost of achieving the desired pollution level will be reduced.
4 ______ If people trade pollution standards and they all profit from the trades, then the pollution problem is made worse.
5 ______ If people are allowed to trade pollution standards freely and if real estate agents operate in markets for pollution standards, then we know that the real estate agents contribute to the efficiency of reducing pollution.

CHAPTER 12 VOTER APATHY: THE ECONOMIC DIMENSIONS OF A GROWING PROBLEM

1 ______ Over the decades voter turnout in the United States as a percentage of eligible voters has been on the rise.
2 ______ According to the economics of politics, the parties in a two-party political system should have divergent views on issues.
3 ______ In terms of the value of the vote determining an election outcome, voting has a positive payoff.
4 ______ From an economic analysis of politics, the parties in a three-party political system are expected to have more divergent views than parties in a two-party political system.
5 ______ By adjusting their relative positions on a political issue spectrum, politicians affect the voter turnout.

CHAPTER 13 GOVERNMENT ORGANIZATION: ECONOMIES OF SCALE AND MONOPOLY POWER

1 ______ Benefits from public provision of goods and services that "spill over" from one government jurisdiction to another result in underproduction of goods and services by local governments.
2 ______ Economies of scale are not legitimate economic arguments for consolidation of government.
3 ______ According to the founding fathers, competition among governments can be beneficial in terms of efficient production of public goods and services.
4 ______ Local government bureaucrats cannot make a profit and, therefore, do not have an incentive to consolidate local governments.
5 ______ Revenue sharing necessarily reduces total tax collections of all governments.

CHAPTER 14 THE SOCIAL DESIRABILITY OF TAX AVOIDANCE: A QUESTION OF PERSPECTIVE

1 ______ A tax on money income does not affect the allocation of people's resources.

2 ______ A tax on money income reduces the relative price of leisure.

3 ______ By levying a proportional tax on all sources of income, including leisure, government can collect the same tax as under a money income tax system and can make the taxpayer better off.

4 ______ A general income tax gives governments more monopoly power than it would have under a discriminatory money income tax.

5 ______ Those people who take advantage of tax loopholes always increase the tax payments of people who do not take advantage of the tax loopholes.

ANSWERS TO SELF-TESTS

Chapter 1 **1.** False **2.** False **3.** True **4.** False **5.** False **6.** True **7.** False **8.** True

Chapter 2 **1.** False **2.** False **3.** True **4.** False **5.** False

Chapter 3 **1.** False **2.** False **3.** False **4.** False **5.** True

Chapter 4 **1.** False **2.** False **3.** False **4.** True **5.** True

Chapter 5 **1.** False **2.** False **3.** False **4.** True **5.** True

Chapter 6 **1.** True **2.** True **3.** False **4.** True **5.** False

Chapter 7 **1.** False **2.** True **3.** False **4.** False **5.** False

Chapter 8 **1.** False **2.** False **3.** True **4.** True **5.** False

Chapter 9 **1.** False **2.** True **3.** True **4.** True **5.** False

Chapter 10 **1.** False **2.** False **3.** False **4.** True

Chapter 11 **1.** True **2.** False **3.** True **4.** False **5.** True

Chapter 12 **1.** False **2.** False **3.** False **4.** True **5.** True

Chapter 13 **1.** True **2.** False **3.** True **4.** False **5.** False

Chapter 14 **1.** False **2.** True **3.** True **4.** True **5.** False

Glossary

The definitions provided in this section are not meant to be complete. For full discussions of the terms or concepts, look them up in any of the standard textbooks on principles of economics.

Absolute advantage The greater efficiency that one person (or country) has in the production of a commodity.

Administered prices Prices set by internal decisions of firms, not by the external forces of market competition.

Appreciation of the dollar An increase in the value of a dollar; in international exchange, a reduction in the dollar price of another national currency. Example: a change in the exchange rate from £1 = \$1.80 to £1 = \$1.50.

Average cost The total cost divided by the quantity produced.

Balance-of-payments deficit The difference between the payments and receipts of one country to all other countries when payments exceed receipts; conceptually, the shortage that exists between the quantity of foreign currencies demanded and supplied when the exchange rate is held down *below* the equilibrium rate.

Balance-of-payments surplus The difference between the payments and receipts of one country to all other countries when receipts exceed payments; conceptually, the surplus that exists between the quantity of foreign currencies demanded and supplies when the exchange rate is *above* the equilibrium rate.

Balance of trade The difference between a country's exports and imports.

Barter system Transactions involving the exchange of goods.

Black market Transactions involving exchanges of goods at some price or in some quantity differing from that set by law.

Budgetary deficit The amount by which government expenditures exceed government revenue.

Business cycle The irregular up and down movement around the growth trend of the economy; that portion of economic movement composed of a recession, trough, recovery, and boom.

Capitalization The process by which anticipated future benefits are captured in the price of an asset that is owned and can be traded.

Cartel An organization of producers whose economic purpose is to restrict the supply, divide the market, and raise the price.

Caveat emptor "Let the buyer beware." Legal rule which means that the consumer bears full responsibility for his or her purchases.

Caveat venditor "Let the seller beware." Legal rule which means that the seller bears full responsibility for what he or she sells.

Choice A selection from among alternatives when not all alternatives can be taken.

Civilian labor force The total number of people classified as employed and unemployed.

Communal property right A condition in which everyone has the right to use a resource, good, or service with no one having the right to exclude anyone else.

Comparative advantage The relatively greater efficiency that a person (or country) has in the production of a commodity.

Competition The regulating force that keeps profit to a minimum and pushes production toward the lowest possible cost level. The process by which market rivals attempt in various ways to outdo or avoid being outdone by other market rivals.

Competitor One producer among many who sell essentially the same good or a closely related good. Example: producer of hand calculators.

Complementary goods Goods which, when one of the goods is used, the other is also. Example: cream and coffee.

Consumer equilibrium Used to describe the consumer in a stable state in which the ratios of marginal utilities to their prices of various goods are equal: $MU_a/P_a = MU_b/P_b \ldots MU_n/P_n$.

Consumer price index The ratio of the cost of a defined market basket of goods sold in retail markets in any year to the cost of the same market basket in some base year.

Consumer surplus Total benefits to consumers minus the total expenditures on a given quantity of a good. Graphically, the area under the demand curve and above the price of the good.

Cost The value placed on the most favored alternative not taken when a choice is made.

Cyclical unemployment Unemployment as a result of an economic downturn.

Decision costs Costs incurred in the process of making choices among alternative proposals. Example: time involved in convincing all persons of the correctness of a proposal.

Deflation A decline in the price level.

Demand (law of demand) The assumed inverse relationship between the price and quantity of a good people are willing to buy, everything else held constant.

Demand curve A locus of points that are downward-sloping to the right, demonstrating the inverse relation between price and quantity demanded of a good, everything else constant.

Demand for labor The assumed inverse relation between the wage rate and the quantity of labor employers will hire, everything else equal.

Depreciation of the dollar Reduction in the value of the dollar; in international finance, an increase in the dollar price of another national currency. Example: a change in the exchange rate from £1 = $1.80 to £1 = $2.00.

Discount rate The interest rate that the Federal Reserve charges on its loans to commercial banks.

Discriminatory tax A government levy against some sources of income, like money income, and not against other sources of income, like leisure. A levy that tends to alter an individual's allocation of resources.

Disposable income The money people actually have to spend after taxes.

Economic profit The part of a firm's revenues in excess of *all* costs, including risk costs and costs that reflect the value of the owner's time used in some other line of production. That part of a firm's revenues that is above the minimum revenue required to keep the firm in the same line of business.

Economics A discipline that can be described as a way of studying human behavior in the context of social interaction.

Economies of scale The characteristics of being able to reduce costs at higher levels of output by increasing all resource inputs.

Effective price The explicit purchase price plus the implicit charges that must be paid in order to buy and/or use a product or service.

Elastic demand An increase in price that results in a decrease in total consumer expenditures, and vice versa; $E_d = \%\Delta Q / \%\Delta P > 1$.

Elasticity coefficient The ratio of the percentage change in quantity demanded to the percentage change in the price, or $E_d = \%\Delta Q / \%\Delta P$.

Equilibrium A market state in which quantity supplied equals quantity demanded; a state of balance between the forces of supply and demand.

Equilibrium price The price at which quantity supplied equals quantity demanded. In a competitive market, the price at the intersection of the market demand and supply curves; in a monopolistic market, the price on the demand curve above the point at which marginal cost equals marginal benefit.

Equilibrium wage rate The wage rate at which quantity demanded of labor equals quantity of labor supplied.

Expected benefit The increase in satisfaction that the individual anticipates for a given choice; the raw benefits discounted by the probability of the benefits actually being received.

Expected cost The cost that the individual anticipates for a given choice; the raw costs discounted by the probability of the costs being incurred.

Expected values The raw costs or benefits discounted by the probability of their being realized.

Explicit cost An out-of-the-pocket expenditure. Example: expenditure on this book.

Explicit logrolling A clearly defined trade of votes between two politicians. Example: one representative agrees to vote for a dam in another representative's district in return for a vote on a sewer system in the first representative's district.

External benefit The economic gain some third party acquires from a transaction between two other parties.

External cost The loss some third party endures as a by-product of a transaction between two other parties.

Externalities The positive or negative effects that exchanges have on people not participating in a transaction.

Federal Reserve System The central bank in the United States created by Congress in 1913 for the purpose of controlling the money stock and regulating banks.

Final goods Goods that have reached their finished market form.

Fiscal policy The tax and expenditure actions of the government to achieve the goals of full employment, price stability, and economic growth.

Fixed exchange rate system System under which the international exchange rate between currencies is set by government.

Floating exchange rate system System under which the international exchange rate is determined by the free movement of supply and demand for foreign currencies.

Free ride The attempt of an individual to gain benefits with no personal cost.

Free trade Exchanges unencumbered by government restrictions.

Frictional unemployment Short-term unemployment due to shifts in market demand. Example: unemployment due to a temporary decrease in the demand for bicycles.

General income tax A government levy that is applied proportionately to all money and nonmoney income sources. A levy that affects overall disposable income but not a person's allocation decisions.

Gross national product The current market value of all final goods and services produced in the economy during the calendar year.

Human capital Those skills and knowledge an individual acquires. Example: college education.

Implicit cost Hidden cost; not an out-of-the-pocket expenditure; typically, the value of an opportunity forgone. Example: the income forgone when one goes to college.

Income A measure of people's contributions to the production of goods and services.

Inelastic demand An increase in the price that results in an increase in total consumer expenditures, and vice versa; $E_d = \%\Delta Q / \%\Delta P < 1$.

Inferior good A good for which demand decreases as income rises. Example: beans or potatoes in low-income neighborhoods.

Inflation A rise in the overall level of prices over a period of time.

In-kind transfers Aid to the poor that is tied to specific commodities. Example: food stamps.

Intermediate goods Goods used in the production of other goods.

Internalizing externalities The process of inducing the one who generates social costs to consider them in his or her actions, or the one who gains from external benefits to pay for benefits received.

International exchange rate The price of a national currency in terms of another national currency. Example: £1 = $1.80.

Investment The purchase of capital goods.

Law of demand Everything else held constant, the assumed inverse relationship between the price of a good and the quantity of the good consumers are willing and able to buy. (People will buy more at lower prices than at higher prices.)

Law of diminishing returns An observed technological relationship in production of any good: as successive units of a resource are added to a fixed quantity of another resource, there is some point beyond which the additional resource will add progressively less to total output.

Logrolling Vote trading.

Luxury goods Goods for which demand increases at a rate greater than the increase in incomes. Example: yachts.

Macroeconomics That portion of economics dealing with large subdivisions of economic activity or with the entire economy.

Marginal benefit Value of an additional unit of a good consumed (same as marginal utility).

Marginal cost The additional cost incurred from producing one additional unit of a good, activity, or service.

Marginal cost of labor The additional cost of an additional unit of labor.

Marginal product (of labor) The additional output acquired from an additional unit of input (labor).

Marginal propensity to consume The percentage of any increase in income that is spent.

Marginal propensity to save The percentage of any increase in income that is saved.

Marginal revenue The increase in total revenue acquired from selling one additional unit of output.

Marginal utility The additional satisfaction received from one additional unit of a good consumed.

Market Any arrangement by which people exchange goods and services. Example: farmer's market.

Market demand The horizontal summation of individual demands for a private good.

Market shortage The condition in which quantity demanded exceeds quantity supplied; exists only when price is below the equilibrium price.

Market supply The horizontal summation of individual supplies for a private good.

Market surplus The market condition in which quantity demanded is less than quantity supplied; exists only when price is above the equilibrium price.

Median-voter group The people who represent the center of the distribution of political viewpoints.

Medium of exchange Money; anything that can be used to carry out transactions and can avoid the use of barter goods (goods traded for goods).

Microeconomics That portion of economics dealing with the economic behavior of individuals, firms, and specific markets.

Minimum wage rate The wage rate below which employers may not legally hire employees.

Monetary policy Government measures aimed at increasing or decreasing the money stock (M_1 or M_2) for the purpose of affecting employment, interest rates, or the rate of inflation in the country.

Money A readily acceptable means of making payment (or medium of exchange) and a financial asset—a form of saving—that represents a store of readily usable purchasing power.

Money cost What is paid in money for some good or service.

Money stock Total quantity of money in circulation measured as M_1 and M_2. M_1 = currency + demand deposits; $M_2 = M_1$ + savings account balances at commercial banks and small certificates of deposit.

Money wage rate The number of dollars earned per unit of time.

Monopolistic competition A market structure in which there are a number of producers who sell similar but differentiated products.

Monopoly (pure) A market in which there is only one producer of a good, there are no close substitutes for that good, and there are barriers to entry into the market.

Monopsony (pure) The sole *buyer* of some good or service or resource like labor.

National income The total payments in the country made to owners of productive resources.

Natural monopoly A firm whose average and marginal costs decline within the range of the market demand for the product.

Normal good A good for which market demand increases when consumer income rises. Example: clothes.

Oligopoly A market structure in which there are few major competitors selling an identical or differentiated product.

Opportunity cost The most highly valued alternative forgone when choice is made. Example: the value of some activity that you would have undertaken in lieu of reading this book.

Opportunity set Range of alternatives open to choice.

Perfect competition A market structure in which there are numerous producers no one of which produces a significant proportion of the total market output and in which there is complete freedom of entry into and exit from the market.

Personal income That part of national income which is paid to individuals.

Positive economics The objective, scientific aspect of economics; the portion that deals with "what is."

Poverty income level The amount of income below which the government judges one to be poor.

Predatory behavior Actions that lead to a reduction in the total output of another person and of the production unit, such as a department.

Present value The value of future costs or benefits in today's terms.

Price What a person gives up for each unit of goods or services purchased.

Price discrimination The practice of setting different prices for different units of a good in a single market or in different markets.

Price elasticity of demand The responsiveness of consumers to a change in price: $E_d = \%\Delta Q / \%\Delta P$.

Private good (pure) A good whose benefits are exclusively received by the person who has possession of it. Example: an ice cream cone.

Private property rights The rights of individuals to possess resources or goods and to exclude others from their use.

Productive behavior Actions that lead to an increase in the total output of an individual and of a production unit, such as a department.

Progressive tax system Tax structure under which the tax rate varies directly with income. Example: federal income tax system.

Proportional tax system Tax structure under which the tax rate remains constant over all income levels.

Public good A good whose benefits are shared by the relevant group if the good is provided or consumed by any one person; the receipt of benefits by one person does not deny those benefits to anyone else. Example: national defense, police protection, environmental quality.

Pure monopoly A single seller in a market protected from competition by technological and legal barriers to entry into the market.

Quota A quantitative restriction on imports or exports.

Rational behavior Actions that are logical and in one's best interests. Basic assumptions: a person (1) knows what he or she wants, (2) is able to order his or her wants, and (3) is able to act consistently upon the wants that are ordered.

Real wage rate The ratio of the money wage to the price index; the purchasing power of the money wage rate.

Recession A downward movement in economic activity.

Regressive tax system Tax structure under which the tax rate varies inversely with income. Example: sales tax.

Revenue sharing Taxes collected by the federal government and passed back to state and local governments as largely unrestricted grants.

Saving That portion of income which is not spent.

Social contract An agreed-on compact that stipulates limits of individual behavior; a set of behavioral rules.

Social cost The costs imposed on others not a party to a transaction; often called "third-party" or "spillover" effects of a transaction.

Spillover A by-product of one individual's behavior that affects others.

Structural unemployment Long-term unemployment due to basic institutional conditions in the economy. Example: unemployment due to unions and minimum wage laws.

Substitute products Goods that may be used in place of each other. Example: coffee and tea, or Coke and Pepsi.

Sunk costs Those costs incurred because of past choices.

Supply The assumed direct relationship between the price and quantity producers are willing to offer on the market.

Supply curve The locus of points indicating the units of a good that will be produced at each price; generally, the assumed direct relation between the price and the quantity of a good producers are willing to offer on the market, everything else held constant.

Supply of labor The assumed direct relation between the wage rate and the quantity of labor workers will offer, everything else constant.

Tariff A tax on imported goods.

Transformation curve A locus of points on a graph that represents the alternative combinations that can be chosen by an individual.

Unitary elastic demand When a price change results in no change in total expenditures or when $E_d = \%\Delta Q / \%\Delta P = 1.0$.

User charge A price firms must pay per unit of each resource used on pollution emitted.

Usury laws Laws designed to restrict interest rates that may be charged on loaned money.

Util The economist's name of a unit of satisfaction.

Utility Satisfaction derived from consumption of goods and services.

Voting rule The degree of agreement necessary for a legislative proposal to pass. Example: simple majority.

White market The legal exchange of goods. Example: proposed legal sale of coupons distributed to ration gasoline.

Wholesale price index The ratio of the cost of a defined set of commodities sold in large quantities in nonretail markets in any year to the cost of the same commodities in some base year.

Index